FabJ

# Become a Business Consultant

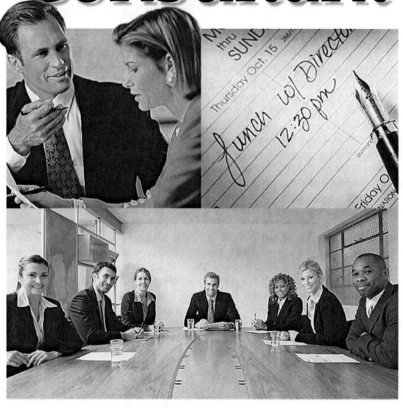

Craig Coolahan, Tag Goulet
and Marg Archibald

**FABJOB® GUIDE TO BECOME A BUSINESS CONSULTANT**
**by Craig Coolahan, Tag Goulet and Marg Archibald**

ISBN: 978-1-897286-93-7



Library and Archives Canada Cataloguing in Publication

Coolahan, Craig
FabJob guide to become a business consultant /
by Craig Coolahan, Tag Goulet and Marg Archibald.

Accompanied by CD-ROM.
Includes bibliographical references.
ISBN 978-1-897286-93-7

1. Business consultants--Vocational guidance. 2. Job hunting. 3. New business enterprises. I. Goulet, Tag, 1959- II. Archibald, Marg, 1946- III. FabJob IV. Title. V. Title: Become a business consultant.

HD69.C6C66 2012 658.4'6 C2012-905426-7

**Important Disclaimer:** Although every effort has been made to ensure this guide is free from errors, this publication is sold with the understanding that the authors, editors, and publisher are not responsible for the results of any action taken on the basis of information in this work, nor for any errors or omissions. The publishers, and the authors and editors, expressly disclaim all and any liability to any person, whether a purchaser of this publication or not, in respect of anything and of the consequences of anything done or omitted to be done by any such person in reliance, whether whole or partial, upon the whole or any part of the contents of this publication. If expert advice is required, services of a competent professional person should be sought.

**About the Websites Mentioned in this Guide:** Although we aim to provide the information you need within the guide, we have also included a number of websites because readers have told us they appreciate knowing about sources of additional information. (**TIP:** Don't include a period at the end of a web address when you type it into your browser.) Due to the constant development of the Internet, websites can change. Any websites mentioned in this guide are included for the convenience of readers only. We are not responsible for the content of any sites except FabJob.com.

FabJob Inc.
19 Horizon View Court
Calgary, Alberta, Canada T3Z 3M5

FabJob Inc.
4616 25th Avenue NE, #224
Seattle, Washington, USA 98105

To order books in bulk, phone 403-949-2039
To arrange a media interview, phone 403-949-4980

**www.FabJob.com**
THE DREAM CAREER EXPERTS

# Contents


**1. Introduction ........ 1**

1.1 Welcome to Business Consulting ........ 1

1.1.1 What is a Business Consultant? ........ 1

1.1.2 A Growth Industry ........ 2

1.1.3 Business Consulting as a Profession ........ 4

1.1.4 Benefits of the Profession ........ 5

1.2 Inside this Guide ........ 8

**2. What a Business Consultant Does ........ 11**

2.1 Business Consulting Specializations ........ 11

2.1.1 Types of Specializations ........ 11

2.1.2 Popular Specializations ........ 12

2.2 Steps in a Consulting Project ........ 23

2.2.1 Conduct a Needs Analysis ........ 24

2.2.2 Determine Project Specifics ........ 27

2.2.3 Gather Information ........ 30

2.2.4 Do a Gap Analysis ........ 30

2.2.5 Identify Possible Solutions ........ 32

2.2.6 Present Your Recommendations ........ 32

2.2.7 Implementation ........ 36

2.2.8 Post-Project Review ........ 38

2.3 Information Gathering Techniques ........ 41

2.3.1 Observation ........ 43

2.3.2 Case Studies ........ 44

2.3.3 Interviews ........ 45

2.3.4 Surveys ........ 47

2.3.5 Focus Groups ........ 51

**3. Developing Your Skills ........ 55**

3.1 Skills Assessment ........ 55

3.2 Problem-Solving Skills ........ 57

3.2.1 Critical Thinking ........ 58

3.2.2 Problem-Solving Techniques ........ 60

3.3 Communication Skills ... 65
3.3.1 Basics of Communication ... 66
3.3.2 Verbal and Vocal Communication ... 66
3.3.3 Non-Verbal Communication ... 68
3.3.4 Listening ... 69
3.3.5 Presentation Skills ... 70
3.3.6 Business Writing ... 73
3.3.7 Second Languages ... 74
3.4 Management Skills ... 75
3.4.1 Project Management ... 75
3.4.2 Organization ... 80
3.4.3 Time Management ... 82
3.4.4 Leadership ... 85
3.5 Business Ethics ... 89

**4. Ways to Learn Business Consulting ... 93**
4.1 Degree Programs ... 95
4.1.1 Undergraduate Programs ... 95
4.1.2 MBA Programs ... 96
4.2 Business Courses and Seminars ... 103
4.2.1 Colleges and Universities ... 103
4.2.2 Seminar Companies ... 104
4.2.3 Other Learning Opportunities ... 105
4.3 Learning By Reading ... 106
4.3.1 Books ... 106
4.3.2 Periodicals ... 108
4.3.3 Websites ... 113
4.4 Learning by Doing ... 114
4.4.1 Volunteer Experience ... 115
4.4.2 Information Interviews ... 118
4.4.3 Internships ... 121
4.4.4 Work Experience ... 125

**5. Getting Hired as a Consultant ... 127**
5.1 Jobs at Consulting Firms ... 128
5.1.1 Career Paths at Consulting Firms ... 129
5.1.2 Top Firms ... 130

5.1.3 Large Firms That Consult to Small and Medium-Sized Businesses ..... 132
5.1.4 Small Firms ..... 134
5.2 Corporate Jobs ..... 136
5.2.1 Internal Consulting ..... 136
5.2.2 Types of Corporate Employers ..... 137
5.3 How to Find Job Openings ..... 139
5.3.1 On-Campus Recruitment ..... 139
5.3.2 Advertised Positions ..... 140
5.3.3 Unadvertised Positions ..... 146
5.3.4 Create a New Job ..... 149
5.4 Job-Hunting Materials ..... 152
5.4.1 How to Prepare a Resume ..... 152
5.4.2 How to Prepare a Cover Letter ..... 162
5.5 Job Interviews ..... 164
5.5.1 How to Prepare for an Interview ..... 167
5.5.2 Interview Questions ..... 173
5.5.3 Case Interviews ..... 175
5.5.4 Following Up ..... 180
5.6 The Job Offer ..... 182
5.6.1 Negotiating Salary ..... 182
5.6.2 Deciding Whether to Take the Job ..... 183

**6. Starting Your Own Consulting Business ..... 185**
6.1 Getting Started ..... 189
6.1.1 Creating a Business Plan ..... 189
6.1.2 Choosing a Business Legal Structure ..... 197
6.1.3 Choosing a Business Name ..... 203
6.1.4 Choosing Your Location ..... 205
6.2 Financial Matters ..... 207
6.2.1 Start-up and Operating Expenses ..... 207
6.2.2 Start-up Financing ..... 213
6.2.3 Taxes ..... 215
6.2.4 Insurance ..... 216
6.2.5 Setting Your Fees ..... 218
6.2.6 Charging for Expenses ..... 229
6.2.7 Getting Paid ..... 232

6.3 Client Contracts .......... 239
6.4 Working With Other People .......... 244
6.4.1 Strategic Partners .......... 244
6.4.2 Support Staff .......... 248
6.4.3 Tips for Working with Contractors .......... 251

**7. Getting Clients .......... 253**
7.1 Choose Your Target Markets .......... 253
7.1.1 Small Businesses .......... 254
7.1.2 Large Corporations .......... 256
7.1.3 Public Sector (Government) .......... 257
7.1.4 Nonprofit Organizations .......... 258
7.2 Marketing Tools .......... 262
7.2.1 Printed Materials .......... 262
7.2.2 Your Website .......... 266
7.2.3 Your Elevator Pitch .......... 268
7.3 Marketing Techniques .......... 272
7.3.1 Advertising .......... 272
7.3.2 Cold Calling .......... 274
7.3.3 Mail Campaigns .......... 278
7.3.4 Networking .......... 281
7.4 Creating Proposals .......... 286
7.4.1 Requests for Proposal (RFP) .......... 286
7.4.2 Responding to RFPs .......... 289
7.4.3 Why Organizations Ask for Proposals .......... 290
7.4.4 Creating a Winning Proposal .......... 292
7.4.5 Sample Letter of Proposal .......... 293
7.5 Your Sales Presentation .......... 299

**8. Succeeding as a Consultant .......... 303**
8.1 Ensuring Client Satisfaction .......... 303
8.2 Advice from the Experts .......... 308
8.3 Professional Associations .......... 311

# About the Authors

**Craig Coolahan** is a freelance writer and editor with degrees in journalism and English. A former newspaper reporter and instructor of job search skills for a business training institute, he has written hundreds of articles for a variety of publications including the *Times Higher Education Supplement*. While working with one of North America's largest customer relationship management companies, he gained a wealth of experience in writing and editorial management of business proposals, case studies, and other documents for clients such as General Motors.

**Tag Goulet** is a leading career expert who has consulted for multi-national corporations and conducted business training programs for organizations such as American Management Association International. Her career advice appears online at AOL, CareerBuilder, CBS MarketWatch, CNN, Fast Company, and Microsoft's MSN, among others, and she has been featured in media from ABC and Oprah.com to *Entrepreneur* and *The Wall Street Journal* online. Tag is a contributor to more than a dozen books including *USA Today* and Amazon.com bestsellers, and has spoken before hundreds of thousands of people in dozens of cities over the past 15 years. Currently, she is co-CEO of FabJob Inc., an award-winning publishing company named "the #1 place to get published online" by *Writer's Digest*. She is also a part-time university instructor of management courses.

**Marg Archibald** started her own consulting business three decades ago and soon after began coaching others how to start consulting businesses and manage them for growth. In her years of consulting to professionals, associations, government, industry and outplacement coaching, Marg has a reputation for enthusiasm, integrity and results-oriented work. A former director of corporate communications for an airline, she has taught university courses on business consulting and presented courses nationally and internationally about the pitfalls to avoid, the systems to establish, the contacts to nurture and the self-discipline to foster. She has traveled the world, alone on her bicycle, and is the author of *Cycling into Your Soul* and three cycling guide books.

**Brenna Pearce** and **Jeff Hagedorn** also contributed to writing this guide.

## Acknowledgements

Thank you to the following experts (listed alphabetically) for generously sharing advice through personal interviews or consenting to reproduction of written material in this FabJob guide. Opinions expressed in this guide are those of the respective authors and not necessarily those of experts interviewed for the guide.

- *John Baldoni*
  Baldoni Consulting, LLC
  Author of *How Great Leaders Get Great Results*
  **www.johnbaldoni.com**
- *Michael Boschitsch, CGA*
  Misam Canada Consulting Ltd.
  North Vancouver, BC
  **www.misamcanada.com**
- *Scott Braucht, MBA*
  President and Founder
  Scott Braucht & Associates
  Verona, WI
- *Andréa Coutu, MBA*
  Marketing Consultant
  Vancouver, BC
  **www.andreacoutu.com**
  **www.ConsultantJournal.com**
- *Pat Curley*
  Founder and President
  St. Lawrence Business Consultants Ltd.
  Buffalo, NY
- *Laura deJonge*
  Corporate integrity expert
- *ArLyne Diamond, Ph.D.*
  Diamond Associates
  Santa Clara, CA
  Author of *Training Your Board of Directors*
  **www.DiamondAssociates.net**
- *James Ege*
  CM Consulting
  Phoenix, AZ
  **www.cmconsultingonline.com**
- *Marty M. Fahncke*
  President
  FawnKey & Associates
  **www.FawnKey.com**
- *Seth Hishmeh*
  Co-Founder and COO
  USAS Technologies, LLC
  **www.usastechnologies.com**
- *Harry Husted*
  Creating Words
  **www.creatingwords.com**
- *Ruth Ann Karty*
  Taking Care of Business Consulting Services
  Clarkfield, MN

- *Karin Kolodziejski*
  Founder and Principal Consultant
  MetaSkills Consulting Group
  Portland, OR
  **www.metaskills.com**

- *Diane Lewis*
  Executive Dimensions, LLC
  Author of *Equal to the Challenge*

- *Jill Lublin*
  CEO, Promising Promotion
  Author of Networking Magic
  **www.jilllublin.com**

- *Eileen McBride*
  Senior Recruiter
  The Parthenon Group
  Boston, MA
  **www.parthenon.com**

- *Mara Osis, Principal*
  Amati Business Group
  Calgary, AB
  **www.amatibusinessgroup.com**

- *Lonnie Pacelli*
  Leading on the Edge
  International
  Author of *The Project Management Advisor*
  **www.leadingonedge.com**

- *Linda L. Paralez, Ph.D., MBA*
  President, CEO
  Demarche Consulting
  Group, Inc.
  **www.demarcheconsulting.com**

- *Linda Popky*
  President
  Leverage 2 Market Associates
  Redwood City, CA
  **www.leverage2market.com**

- *Nido Qubein*
  Business Consultant,
  Speaker, Author
  President, High Point University
  **www.nidoqubein.com**

- *Bill Speck*
  Consultant
  Demarche Consulting
  Group, Inc.
  **www.demarcheconsulting.com**

- *Richard Valiquette*
  Sales Consultant and Coach
  Creative Coaching Solutions
  Calgary, AB

- *Alan Weiss, Ph.D.*
  President
  Summit Consulting Group, Inc.
  East Greenwich, RI
  Author of The *Million Dollar Consulting™ Toolkit*
  **www.summitconsulting.com**

- *Martin Wilkins*
  PVA Consulting Group Inc.
  **www.pva.ca**

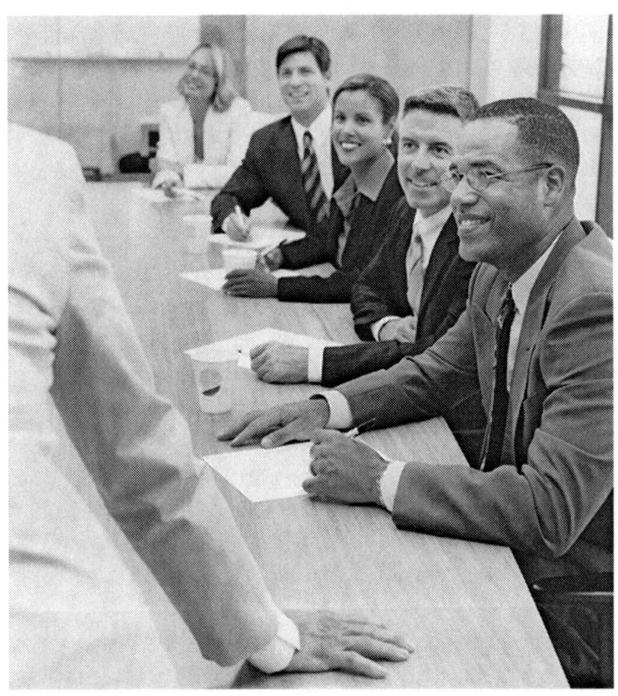

# 1. Introduction

## 1.1 Welcome to Business Consulting

Congratulations on your decision to join one of the fastest growing and most lucrative professions in North America. According to the U.S. Census Bureau publication *Statistical Abstract of the United States: 2012*, management consulting services generate more than $160 billion in annual revenues.

A rewarding profession intellectually as well as financially, consulting was ranked #3 in CNN Money's top 100 best jobs in America in 2010. In this FabJob guide, you will learn about life as a business consultant and how to use your problem-solving skills to enter this exciting profession.

### 1.1.1 What is a Business Consultant?

Like others who decide to become a business consultant (also known as a *management consultant* or *management analyst*), your first introduction to this career may have happened when you observed someone consulting at your employer's office. When the consultant was in the office, he or she likely had the full attention of management and was involved in asking important questions and reviewing key company data. Before long, the consultant disappeared, leaving a wake of changes and earning a tidy sum of money.

Chances are your employer felt the consultant's fee was well-deserved. That's because business consultants help businesses and other organizations identify problems, and recommend solutions to those problems. The University of Chicago's Career and Placement Services defines business consultants as:

> "Problem solvers and advisors who contribute an objective point of view. By using fact-based, analytically driven thinking to break problems down into components and solve each component, consultants reach a single perspective on a problem."

Corporations, small businesses, governments and non-profit organizations hire business consultants to draw on their experience, apply their critical thinking skills, analyze, and ultimately recommend and implement solutions.

Business consultants focus on one problem or a cluster of related problems in each *project* (also known as an *engagement* in the consulting world). At the completion of that engagement, the business consultant may take on another project to solve a different problem within the same organization or move on to a different organization and their problems.

### 1.1.2 A Growth Industry

Why has business consulting experienced such a surge? In the 1980s and 90s business streamlined to operate more cost-effectively. At that time, they let go many of the internal experts who had specialized knowledge outside the core business. But now, the complexity of doing business in today's global economy has forced many businesses to seek expert advice on those same issues. The ideal solution is to bring in, short term, a consultant with exactly the expertise required.

For example, an automotive manufacturer's expertise is building cars, but as the recent economic downturn has shown, there is much more to being successful in the automotive industry than production. The automotive business is a vast web of production, marketing and financial issues, just to name a few, and no one company can possibly excel at everything.

Fortunately for business consultants, the world has become increasingly specialized, requiring consultants who specialize in everything from call centers to human resources, from quality control to small business management. In fact, many corporations feel that it is not to their advantage to spread their expertise too thin, and prefer to concentrate on being the best at their core business. The result is that they turn to business consultants to bring expertise to essential but non-core areas of their business.

Another reason for the growth in business consulting is the continued trend of hiring employees on a contract basis. Despite typically paying business consultants a higher rate than an employee, companies feel that they receive a better deal with a consultant because they get expert advice without having to make a long-term commitment.

> *"Companies have limited staff and need to occasionally add additional labor and expertise to even out their low points. Also, the structure of many companies lends itself to cliques that tend to narrow perspectives. Hiring a business consultant forces companies to ask the tough questions that aren't being asked internally. In one sense, business consultants 'shake things up,' but in a controlled manner."*
>
> — Linda Paralez, Ph.D.
> Demarche Consulting Group, Inc.

This phenomenal growth and opportunity has not gone unnoticed by those graduating from top business schools. Approximately 30-35 percent of MBA graduates enter the consulting profession.

But it's not only MBAs taking advantage of this opportunity. According to a recent U.S. Bureau of Labor Statistics report on "Management, Scientific, and Technical Consulting Services," 28% of consultants do not have a degree of any kind. Individuals with diverse backgrounds are having tremendous success and are emerging as major players in the business consulting industry.

### 1.1.3 Business Consulting as a Profession

Business consulting is an exciting, dynamic profession that offers individuals with diverse specialities and experience the opportunity to showcase their talents and make a good living doing it.

Business consultants primarily work in one of two ways: as an employee or as an independent consultant. Employees generally work for consulting firms or for large corporations that keep business consultants on staff. Independent business consultants have the same skills as their salaried counterparts but they are entrepreneurs charging businesses for their expertise.

#### Work Hard, Play Hard

There's an old saying that goes: as a business consultant you'll only work half days – 12-hour days, that is. The contract nature of business consulting means that in order to meet client requirements, consultants must commit 100% of themselves to the engagement. This means long hours.

The upside of this hard work is that management in many consulting firms recognizes the intense nature of engagements, and subsequently offer their employees a minimum of four weeks paid vacation. As an independent consultant, you'll be in a position to take the jobs you want. For many, this means going all out for three to four months and taking weeks off in between engagements. In either case, you'll have the money to really enjoy your time off.

#### Where You'll Work

Where you work as a business consultant depends on whether or not you work for a consulting firm or independently. But it is also determined by the needs of your clients. Generally you'll find that your on-the-job will fall into one of two scenarios: on-site and off-site consulting. And more than likely it will be a combination of the two.

Whether you are an individual business consultant or employed by a business consulting firm, it is unlikely that you will go to the same desk to work each day. Where you are working on any given day will depend on the phase of the client project, the need for client meetings and your judgment about the balance between showing the client what you are doing versus focusing on concentrated work at your own desk.

Client meetings and the gathering of project information will likely be done on-site, with the client providing you with an office or appropriate place to work. In some cases, however, the client will not have enough space to provide you on-site accommodations, so much of your work will be conducted off-site at your own office, possibly a home office, or in your employer's office. Consultant Scott Braucht says: "We find that it's good to work part-time off-site, as consultants tend to get distracted by issues that don't pertain to the project when working on-site. Working off-site gives them a chance to collect their thoughts and get the necessary paper work done."

## 1.1.4 Benefits of the Profession

### Financial Rewards

Even if you believe money isn't everything, it's hard to ignore the fact that business consulting, even entry-level, is among the highest paid professions. A recent survey by the Association of Management Consulting Firms found entry-level consultants earn an average of $65,000 annually while senior partners earn an average of over $300,000 (including bonuses and profit sharing).

Independent business consultants can earn $35 to $400 or more per hour. Many factors go into determining fees, including the consultant's experience, geographic location, specialization, and type of client (e.g. large corporations typically pay more than small businesses or non-profit organizations). In many cases, however, the annual income for an independent business consultant is limited only by the individual's initiative and drive, with many consultants earning six figures.

Alan Weiss, Ph.D., President of Summit Consulting Group, says the most rewarding aspect of his consulting career is "the independence and the ability to earn 7-figures working from my home."

### Opportunity to Learn and Grow

The rewards of business consulting go well beyond the financial. As a business consultant, clients rely on your capacity to solve problems. So the rigors of being a consultant mean that you will stretch your intellectual muscle on a daily basis.

## Dynamic Profession

If you thrive on change and a dynamic work environment, look no further than business consulting. Business consulting by its very nature is based on change, or at least overseeing change. Also, contracts with clients are just that, contracts, and there's an end to each one. These can range from a couple of weeks to a year or more, depending on the project. As a business consultant, you'll get a chance to see a wide range of organizations at work.

> *"I enjoy the interaction and stimulation that comes from solving a broad range of problems for a variety of clients."*
>
> — Linda Popky
> L2M Associates, Inc.

Projects can take a consultant from city to city and even country to country depending on the firm and area of specialty. Indeed, travel is a big part of the allure for many who enter the profession. For those working with large firms or independently this could mean jet setting across North America and around the world.

## Prestige

Although you may not have known who that consultant was in your employer's business, you likely admired what he was doing. Why? The reason is simple: business consultants are highly respected individuals. They are relied upon in every industry in every country. They're admired for both their expertise and their independence.

## Personal Satisfaction

Another benefit business consulting offers is the opportunity to see the tangible products of their work more so than in other "white collar" professions. Just imagine: instead of the frustration of being unable to change problems that got in the way of your productivity, now it's your job to recommend changes. You are now working with the top-level people who will implement change and they are turning to you for direction on doing so.

*"I get a great deal of satisfaction in working with others to better their businesses, and seeing the fruits of my labor when I drive down the street and find that business still thriving 5 years after my recommendations and implementations."*

— Ruth Ann Karty
Taking Care of Business Consulting Services

## Make a Difference

The results of some of your work will improve life for workers and even customers. Sometimes this may impact large numbers of people. What better source of satisfaction than knowing you have made a positive difference in people's lives?

*"You chose a career in consulting because you have a burning desire to make a positive difference in the organization that may hire you. You believe that your talents and skills are such that you can teach others how to do things better and in the process make their organization more successful."*

— John Baldoni
Baldoni Consulting, LLC

## Meet People

Business consultants work with many people in many diverse industries. As a result, you will have the opportunity to make friends and connections across the country and around the world. It is a common complaint among those in corporate positions that they don't get the chance to showcase their talents. As a business consultant, you'll do this every day, and you never know who's paying attention.

## Low Risk to Start Your Own Business

You can start and operate a business consulting firm from home, without a bank loan. In fact, you probably already own the primary equipment needed such as a computer and phone. There can be some marketing costs when starting, but costs are minimal, as word-of-mouth and networking are powerful forces in this business.

You can start consulting on a part-time basis, while keeping a primary source of income. At the same time you can ease your way into the business by getting the word out that you are interested in consulting work. Then as the demand for your services grows, you can commit to consulting full time.

## 1.2 Inside this Guide

*The FabJob Guide to Become a Business Consultant* offers knowledge and insight of industry insiders to help you get started and succeed as a business consultant. According to the U.S. Bureau of Labor Statistics, competition is expected to remain keen in this industry through the year 2020. So your investment in this guide will pay off when you are competing with less informed individuals.

Chapter 2 describes in more detail the role of a business consultant. Following an overview of consulting specializations, the chapter takes you step-by-step through a consulting engagement – from determining the client's needs to the final evaluation. You will learn practical techniques for gathering information, how to identify possible solutions, and how to present your recommendations to clients.

Chapter 3 outlines the skills you will need in order to succeed as a business consultant, such as problem-solving and project management, and offers resources for developing those skills. Chapter 4 then offers ways to increase your business knowledge through educational programs and self-study. It also explains how to get practical experience.

If you want the stability of a full-time position, Chapter 5 focuses on consulting jobs. You will discover employers who hire consultants, how to find out about job openings, how to prepare an effective resume and cover letter, and what to expect in a case interview. You will even discover how to create a job.

If you want the freedom of starting your own business, you will find good advice in Chapter 6. You will find practical information on getting ready to open for business, including setting your fees and preparing client contracts. In Chapter 7, you will discover practical tips for getting clients for your business. It covers a variety of marketing tools and techniques, with advice on creating proposals.

The guide concludes with expert advice in Chapter 8 to help you succeed in your business. Also included is a list of professional associations. When you're finished with this guide you will know what step to take next and where to go from there. By applying what you learn here, it's just a matter of time before you'll be where you want to be – in a rewarding career as a business consultant.

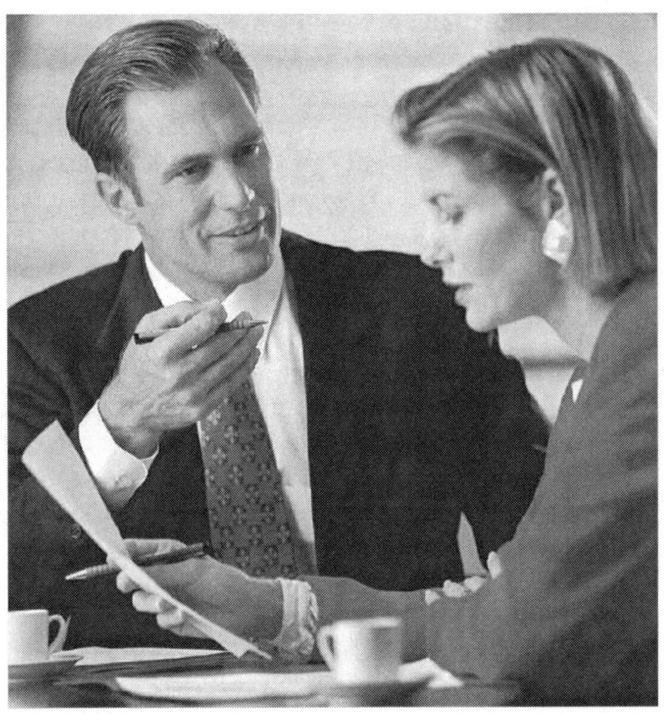

# 2. What a Business Consultant Does

You know that business consultants are hired problem solvers. They use analysis to break down problems and develop recommendations. But what does that look like day by day? What does a business consultant actually do on the job?

This chapter looks at the broad range of areas where consultants put their skills to work. It then takes you step-by-step through a consulting project. This information is applicable to all consultants, whether working independently, with a consulting firm, or for a corporation.

## 2.1 Business Consulting Specializations

### 2.1.1 Types of Specializations

What specific types of problems do business consultants recommend solutions for? The answer is any type of business problem. Some business consultant, somewhere, right now, is probably working on a business challenge in almost any area of business you can imagine. If it is part of running a business, sooner or later, it will need a consultant to fix it.

In fact, there really is no boundary to what a business consultant can do when it comes to advising organizations how to solve problems or do things better. What a business consultant chooses to specialize in depends on the consultant's particular area of expertise or experience, and a client's needs.

Some consultants specialize in working with businesses in particular industries, such as health care or manufacturing. Others work with clients in a wide variety of industries, but specialize in particular business functions or departments, such as marketing, human resources, or information technology. If you work as an employee of a large consulting firm, you will work on the types of projects the firm specializes in.

If you start your own consulting business, you will determine what types of consulting you want to do. You might choose a broad specialization such as "operations consulting" or "strategic consulting" for any type of organization that needs your help. Or you might choose a narrow specialization such as public relations consulting for theatre companies, safety consulting for oil companies, business start-up consulting for retail stores, or any other area that interests you and that organizations need help with.

In every specialization, you will carry out essentially the same steps which are described later in this chapter, including defining goals, determining a timeline, conducting research, identifying problems, and making recommendations. Throughout, you will be mindful that your solution will, in some way, impact the whole organization. In that regard, whatever your specialization, you need to be a generalist as well.

## 2.1.2 Popular Specializations

While you can consult on virtually any aspect of your clients' businesses, you will likely find some specializations are more in demand than others. Popular specializations which you may want to consider include the following broad areas:

- Operations Consulting
- Organizational Development Consulting
- Strategic Consulting

Popular specializations focusing on a specific department or type of business include:

- Communications Consulting
- E-business Consulting
- Human Resources Consulting
- Information Technology Consulting
- Marketing Consulting
- Small Business Consulting

Even if you already know what you want to specialize in, it's good to be aware of other popular specializations in case your clients ask you about them. It's important to note that specializations may vary depending on the type of organization, and there may be considerable overlap. For example, a single project might involve strategic consulting, small business consulting, and marketing consulting.

The following is an introduction to these specializations. You can learn more about particular specializations from the resources listed later in this book.

## Operations Consulting

As an operations consultant you will look for better ways for companies to do things. The University of Chicago's Career and Placement Services (CAPS) says operations consultants "examine a client's internal workings, such as production processes, distribution, order fulfillment, and customer service."

By the early 1900s, efficiency experts were looking for ways to streamline the sprawling results of the industrial revolution. One hundred years later, business consultants improve efficiencies in an increasingly automated environment while ensuring consistent, high quality products and services. You could be working in a hotel operation or a fish packing plant. In either case, the operation is the guts of delivering the goods.

An operations consultant may monitor processes, equipment, scheduling, costs, space, materials, and human resources to identify wastage and recommend improvements. It will be critical to your success to factor in the human element. You will also have to stay current with production innovations.

**Sample Project**

Mahoney Mobile Homes is considering significant changes. After 35 years of successful mobile home production, they want to expand. They have brought in a team of business consultants and you are one of them. Your role, working with the management team and other business consultants, is to examine the feasibility of updating parts of the assembly line to produce a luxury, mobile home line.

You will analyze the current performance of the assembly line and all its parts. You will interview staff about efficiencies, inefficiencies, skills and flexibility. You will learn about the replacement and additional equipment that would be necessary to purchase and explore how well the existing equipment would interface with the new. You will develop space requirements and redesign the assembly line. You will work closely with in-house and consulting HR to determine the new roles of staff, new staffing requirements and necessary training.

If you love sorting out schedules, working with details, reconfiguring, examining alternatives, smoothing processes, and have a good mind for spatial relationships, you may enjoy operations consulting.

## Organizational Development Consulting

"Organizational development" is a widely-used term in business consulting. Generally, organizational development is a broad consulting area that may encompass a variety of consulting specializations including strategic planning, communications, and human resources.

As organizations grow and add new divisions and expertise they may become inefficient, and departments may be working at cross purposes to each other. For example, a company's public relations department may want to promote the company and its products by getting publicity in the news media, while the company's legal department may aim to minimize the amount of information disclosed to the public.

An organizational development consultant may be brought in to houseclean the whole organization, reducing bureaucracy and increasing communication and flexibility. These consultants typically work closely with the human resources department to find the management problems that reduce effectiveness.

You will start with the company's mission and goals and then review each part of the organization and its policies to ensure efficiency and congruency. Your interviews with staff will probe for areas of overlap, turf wars and areas where no-one takes responsibility. In making your recommendations, you will guide management to a leaner, efficient organization by bringing people, policies, and reporting structures into line with each other. This may include changing the organization chart and the roles of people within it.

**Sample Project**

A power company was initially owned by the government and had a monopoly in the area. New legislation opens the local market to competition. Management needs to change the whole organization from a bureaucracy to a market responsive business.

You will examine the existing structure and reporting patterns. You will examine decision-making and delegation. This will involve surveys of specific groups within the company to determine habits and attitudes. Working with management, you will redraw the organizational structure to more efficiently respond to a changing marketplace. Working with the training department you will develop and deliver training programs to encourage an internal, entrepreneurial spirit. You will continually track the evolving transition to add additional training and behavior modeling as required.

If you are good at understanding individuals' strengths and weaknesses and uncovering the right fit for people, you may be an organizational development specialist at heart.

## Strategic Consulting

Strategic consultants, also known as *strategy consultants*, advise executives about the best way to carry out an organization's core priorities. According to the University of Chicago's CAPS, strategy consultants "aim to help a client's senior executives understand and face the strategic challenges of running their company or organization."

To guide a company in its strategic planning, a business consultant examines and summarizes the organization using tools such as SWOT Analysis to analyze strengths, weaknesses, opportunities and threats (see section 3.2.2). Armed with that information, the consultant facilitates the highest level of management, or the board of directors, in choosing the course of action that is most likely to lead to the best future for the organization. It is the responsibility of the consultant to provide the planning framework and facilitate a meeting, which may take place over the course of several days, at an off-site retreat location.

The ability to think conceptually and understand the practical implications of a strategy are essential for strategic planning. It involves a combination of creativity and practicality. Facilitating a planning session requires amassing all the data and reference material that may be drawn on during discussions. It also requires skill at diplomatically steering proceedings so that productive decisions are reached.

**Sample Project**

An educational institution that includes a trade school, English-as-a-second-language training and educational upgrading receives most of its funding from the government. The writing is on the wall that government funding is going to dry up but the demand for their services, particularly by new arrivals in the country, is expanding. The board hires you to guide them through strategic planning so that the whole organization can restructure to be financially viable after funding is cut.

In order to have information on which to base decisions during the planning retreat you will plot trends in enrollment in each program, do a cost-benefit analysis of each program, and gather information about the employer demand for graduates. You will also research additional sources of funding and elasticity of enrollment fees. You will instruct the internal operations manager to provide information on the flexibility of the space requirements. You will open the strategic planning meeting by explaining the posted guidelines for discussion and asking for agreement on them.

In addition to the broad areas described above, there are many consulting specializations that focus on specific business departments or types of businesses. The most popular of these include:

## Communications Consulting

Companies communicate with many audiences, including employees, customers, investors, government, the media, and the general public. This role is typically carried out by a corporate communications or public relations department (in some organizations corporate communications is carried out by the marketing department).

A communications consultant, also known as a *public relations consultant*, may be brought in to set up or guide the substantial overhaul of a communications department. This may entail a communications audit to research the impact of all current communication tools and identify those that are lacking.

A high-level communication consultant will examine the organization's mission and goals to ensure that effective communication is built into all business practices. Your goal in this role will be to establish the optimal target audiences, within and outside the organization, and the most effective communication strategies to reach and influence each of those audiences. You will evaluate communication tools, timing, and targeted messages. You may also delegate on-going communication responsibilities as a business consultant often plays a role in choosing the corporate communications manager to continue the work.

If you like working with people, clarifying information, and developing creative ideas, communications consulting may be a good fit for you.

**Sample Project**

Interior Airways and TransMountain Airlines are merging in two months. You are hired to develop a coherent internal and external communication plan before, during and after the merger. This will required a review of existing communication in both airlines, right down to luggage tags.

You will do research on perception of this merger, both internally among employees and externally among passengers and the public. Drawing on the results, you will create a unified plan that educates and inspires employees, passengers, media and the public. You will manage the design of logos, ads, and the media campaign. You may need to coach the new CEO on press conferences and set them up. You will track results of the new communication program and after six months, work with senior management to hire a permanent, corporate communications manager.

## E-Business Consulting

In this cutting edge business sector, business consultants are sometimes brought in to manage the transition from a kitchen table business to a lucrative enterprise that may be growing explosively. Like small business consulting, this may involve global work on every facet of the organization. Other e-business consulting projects involve working with large organizations to develop an e-business component to their business.

As an e-business consultant you will have to be completely at home with technology and the language of online business. You will need to be a marketer at heart because that is what success in an e-business is all about. However, you should also have a strong handle on administrative processes, as this is an area where many e-businesses need help. Strengths in developing procedures and processes, strategic planning, human resources, and finance can also be an asset.

**Sample Project**

SLAM produces games which participants pay to play online. The company has grown exponentially in the last five years. Management structure has been loose and there are no job descriptions, pay scales, written policies or financial controls. They expect to earn $10 million next year and know they need better controls.

As their business consultant, you will review all facets of the business, examine their financial records and work closely with the founders to learn their short and long-term goals. You will be challenged to establish an innovative business model that marries their creative style with solid business practices. Part of your work will be training management and staff in new business practices and procedures.

## Human Resources Consulting

Businesses bring in human resources consultants, also known as HR consultants, when they are undergoing a major change or when they have deep-seated employee problems that they have not been able to resolve. You could be working in a union or non-union environment. In either case you will examine existing policies and perform research among staff to learn the effect of those policies. For the current situation to make sense, you may have to learn some of the history and gather historical information from several sources to ensure you get a balanced view.

In developing solutions, you may review some case studies to explore ways that similar issues have been resolved. You will guide management on overall corporate strategies and best practices that build productive relationships between staff and management as well as different departments and regions. It may be part of solving the problem to train the supervisors on staff relations and even raise awareness of all staff on how to handle their relationships with each other.

Human resource work tends to attract consultants who are interested in the dynamic relationship between individuals at different levels in an organization. They also have an ability to view staff as a resource that can cost-effectively accomplish the goals of the organization.

**Sample Project**

A huge national company, Cycor Printing, is making a massive change to greater automation. When complete, their pressroom will rarely have people in it, their bindery will be fully automated. They are a union shop and the last time they took a step toward automation, they experienced an expensive and lengthy strike. You have been brought in to smooth the way for this change.

You will explore the history, current pay and benefits and industry standards. You'll look for case studies outside the printing industry to find creative best practices that reflect innovative thinking on automation. You will negotiate with the union to do research among the workers. You will establish an outplacement program that includes generous retraining and support for staff that want to start a business. You will also be recruiting new employees who will manage the technology in the new plant. You will work closely with the corporate communications manager to ensure that internal and external communications deal with rumors and showcase Cycor's commitment to the people in their communities.

## IT Consulting

Organizations have become increasingly dependant on information technology (IT) yet there may be problems and inefficiencies. Innovations may have been cobbled into the system in a patchwork way. Whole system conversion may be required, ideally with minimal service interruption. Your first task will be to understand the core business, how IT currently supports it and how it could be better. You need to know what is available to buy and what nature of internal, tailored programming is feasible to solve the problems.

If there has been a history of poor communication between IT and the rest of the organization, you will interview key participants and then create new systems to improve communications. Training may be required and user groups may need to be established.

If you are knowledgeable about software and hardware, and completely at home staying current with changes in the field, you may thrive in IT consulting. If you can speak the language of both the techies and the end users and can bridge the gap between them, you can be highly valued as an IT consultant.

**Sample Project**

A bank has a slow and cumbersome computer system that does not interface effectively with their ATM network. It is awkward for the tellers, slow on check clearing and crashes when overloaded. They are ready to buy and implement a new system. You are brought in to finalize the purchase, plan the transition, train senior staff and set up training for other staff.

You need to be fully familiar with the system they have currently, the one they are installing, and the challenges that will arise during conversion. This is an organization that requires IT functionality around the clock so during the early days of the conversion, you may be sleeping on site to be accessible for troubleshooting. You will need to be a top-notch communicator to avoid misunderstandings during this critical transition and you will work with HR and corporate communications to ensure that the transition is understood and supported.

## Marketing Consulting

The word "marketing" can mean everything from sales to advertising. It is ensuring the right product is sold in the right place for the right price at the right time to the right person. Your marketing goal is to ensure that the largest volume of products/services is sold for the maximum price to the largest number of buyers. Or to a small, select number of buyers, depending on your strategy.

To make that happen, you may examine all the parts of the dynamic relationship between purchasers and sellers such as target markets, distribution channels, raw materials, costs, competition, and products. You will track and compare promotions, advertising results, buying trends and emerging demands. There may be a completely independent, advertising function within marketing that strategizes and implements campaigns. Once you have examined all the factors, you will advise management on the strategies they should implement to maximize profits.

Marketing involves numbers and statistics in addition to creativity. If you have a head for numbers and like digging in detail, marketing consulting may be right for you.

**Sample Project**

A big box hardware store is arriving in Small City. Gardeners Heaven, a large, prosperous garden centre, retains you to work out the best marketing response to this challenge. Gardeners Heaven knows that the big box store will stock most of the garden equipment that they carry, but at greatly reduced prices. They will also carry a selection of the most popular plants during the summer. Your job is to determine a pricing strategy for each of Gardeners Heaven's product lines, and recommend any changes in the products carried, hours of business, and promotions and advertising they should do.

You will examine purchase patterns in similar situations to determine the customers most likely to switch to the big box store and those that you can retain. You will help management tailor the revamped operation to draw in and retain those targeted customers. You will explore new services such as gardening seminars and you will cost-out the value of a garden planning service for customers. You will work with their communication manager to ensure that your unique advantages are known to staff, the local media and eventually the customers. You will work with HR to establish a training program so that staff are friendly and helpful above expectations.

## Small Business Consulting

You will need to have a complete range of business experience and be able to scale it to a small operation when you are consulting for small business. Whether advising on start-up or growth, your work may cover everything from legal and accounting choices, to testing the viability of an idea, setting up systems, market research and launch promotion, staffing policies, inventory management, supplier choices, distribution options, branding, cash flow management, premises and even integrating the business owner's personal and business life.

This type of consulting work is ideal for the individual who believes small is beautiful. You like to see the whole picture and enjoy being able to influence everything about the organization on a small scale.

**Sample Project**

A golf enthusiast has inherited enough money to purchase the land for a driving range. He knows a great deal about golf and has many connections in the field. He has good common sense but knows little about market research, marketing, business start up and financials.

You will work with the client through a series of go/no-go decisions as he tests his idea, researches the market, determines whether to incorporate, explores financing options, generates building and parking plans, discusses costs with vendors, creates a comprehensive budget, drafts a human resources policy, captures his idea in an inspiring, written mission statement, explores the lifestyle implications of an intensive, summer-time business, and makes strategic choices about communicating this new business to the key individuals and markets in the geographic area. In other words, you will help with virtually every aspect of starting his business.

In addition, you will help him find strategic allies to offer golf holiday vacations with hotels and a kids program to attract young golfers.

No matter what specialization you choose, the basic steps involved in a consulting project are essentially the same.

## 2.2 Steps in a Consulting Project

Once you have been hired by a client (covered in Chapter 7), your work for the client begins. Of course, each project is different and will have unique challenges, but chances are your projects will include the following steps. Read on for advice on how best to approach each stage of a consulting project.

## 2.2.1 Conduct a Needs Analysis

Companies do not hire business consultants because they are satisfied with the way things are; consultants are called in when companies need to solve a problem or make things better. So the first stage of the process is to identify what your client needs so you can set goals for the consulting project.

In some cases company representatives have a clear picture of what they need, and may put it in writing in a "Request for Proposal" (RFP). A typical RFP is a document that provides information about the organization, their consulting needs, and what they require in a proposal to do the consulting work. RFPs are discussed in depth in section 7.4.1 of this guide.

But you may get consulting work without an RFP. Even if there is an RFP which outlines project objectives, you should clarify the problem through your own research because there may be a discrepancy between what the client thinks is wrong, and what's really wrong.

The importance of coming to a consensus with your client on project goals cannot be overstated. Having a face-to-face meeting with the primary players in the organization will be your first step to defining the client's problems and goals. You will clarify these through further meetings and research, but during the initial meeting, you will get the process started and you may be surprised at how many significant insights surface at this meeting.

### Preparing for the Meeting

Here is a list of items and considerations that should not be overlooked when entering this meeting.

#### Come Prepared

Professionalism at this meeting is paramount. Ensure that you arrive with the necessary documentation, pens, paper, laptop and a list of prepared questions.

### Dress Professionally

Even if your client runs a casual or business casual office, arrive for this initial meeting like you mean business, which means a business suit. Treat the meeting as though you're still in the interview stage, which to some degree you still are.

### Take Notes

Nothing ensures a client that you've retained what's been said at a meeting than the sight of someone taking notes. And do not be afraid to ask anyone in the room to repeat what was said; this just reinforces the first point. For journalists and other professions, a tape recorder is suitable. In the consulting world, however, it is not standard practice. And besides, you're only creating more work for yourself through the need to transcribe all of these notes.

### Arrive Prepared to Lead

Although this meeting will have been arranged at an agreed upon time and place, it may still be unclear who is leading this meeting. The client will have certain expectations in mind about what s/he is looking for you to accomplish, and therefore may want to take control of the meeting. The fact that the meeting will likely take place at their place of business reinforces this point. With this said, however, the client may be looking to you, as the expert, to take charge of the meeting. Therefore, be sure to arrive with the expectation that you may be presiding over this forum.

### Listen First, Ask Questions Later

Asking the right questions is crucial in determining the problems and goals of your client. If some of the project requirements have been outlined in an RFP, build on these when developing questions. If there is little information, you will use probing questions to bring the issues to the surface.

**TIP:** Remember, chances are that someone in the organization has something invested in your not discovering the real problem and in your not recommending the necessary changes.

However, try not to get ahead of yourself by blurting out several questions without offering the client an opportunity to speak. The best approach is to simply allow the client to present his/her issues, and respond with questions. This will also provide you with more material for relevant, insightful questions.

Below are sample questions that will help illuminate a client's issue or issues and help in the development of a recommended solution. The key in asking questions is to stay objective and diplomatic.

## Sample Questions

- What do you perceive as the problem?
- Why do you think this is happening?
- What specific areas do you want me to address?
- Do you know when this started happening?
- What overall changes would fixing this issue bring?
- Have you tried to correct this internally? If so, what happened? Do you have the project notes?
- What are the results you expect?
- What measurables will indicate we have solved the problem?
- What are the obstacles right now?
- Is there anything else you think I need to know?

These are just a few ideas to help you develop your own questions. Many of these, however, could fit any project. As you will see, clarifying issues and goals can provide you with the necessary information to understand the gap between what business owners want to have happening and what is really, currently happening.

However, the problems that surface at this time may, further into the project, prove to simply cover up other problems. So remain open as you move forward. In section 2.3 you'll discover how to conduct further research into the situation.

## 2.2.2 Determine Project Specifics

During your initial meeting, you will also begin to determine the project scope, deadline, team, and budget.

### Project Scope

The project scope defines the services that will be provided. Unless you plan to work on a particular consulting project for the rest of your life, at some point you and the client will have to agree that the work is complete. The time to establish the project scope – i.e. the tasks and deliverables that are, and are not, included in the project – is at the project start.

For example, you need to determine such matters as:

- How much work the project will cover (e.g. will it involve a review of all branch offices or just the head office, North American or international operations, etc.)
- Who will be responsible for key tasks
- What you are responsible for to implement the solutions (e.g. will you be involved with training or follow-up meetings).

Once you and the client have agreed to the scope of the project, you will put that information in writing in a letter of engagement or services agreement (covered in section 6.3). Then if the client wants to increase the scope of the project, you can negotiate a higher fee for your services.

### Project Timeline

A project timeline is a schedule of milestones leading up to the completion date, which may be weeks or months after the project begins.

A project timeline gives the client dates to report milestones and project findings to a board of directors or shareholders. It also indicates when project solutions will begin to impact the rest of the organization. For example, if one of the solutions is the introduction of a new product line, that will affect numerous departments ranging from marketing to operations to finance.

The client will either give you a deadline that they want the project completed by or will ask you to tell them when it will be finished. Often, a client will present an estimated deadline and it's up to you to decide if you can stay within these parameters. Determining the length of a project will be a mutual decision between you and the client.

To assist you in scheduling your work throughout the project, you will complete a detailed timeline. Creating a timeline is an invaluable exercise for the business consultant because it helps to break down the project into manageable tasks, and provides "steps" and small victories on the road to client satisfaction. You can report these interim successes to management to reassure them that the project is on track and that you are doing your job.

Many consultants use project management software to facilitate the process of creating and keeping track of project timelines. These applications provide graphs and charts that make it easy to track progress. An example is Microsoft Project which offers online information and tips at **www.microsoft.com/project/en-us/project-management.aspx**. Project management software is discussed in more depth in section 3.4.1.

To determine a timeline, estimate how long each primary task will take you to complete and add on time for miscellaneous items and smaller tasks. Make sure you include any deadlines for items that the client must provide, and that you supply this information to the client so you are not held responsible if the client misses deadlines.

On the next page is an example which lists the various sub-tasks involved in conducting a group interview.

## Project Team

When creating your timeline, you will identify the human resources you'll need to complete each part of the project. The initial meeting is the appropriate place to discuss who you think should be part of your team and who your client thinks should be part of the team.

Depending on the client's goals and budget, you may work with other individuals from your consulting firm, or you may be the single outsider on the project. In this scenario, you will often be part of a team made up of employees from every level of the client's operation.

## Sample Project Timeline

| | |
|---|---|
| **Task** | Group interview |
| **Work Involved** | • Get permission<br>• Determine how/when/where to communicate interview to employees<br>• 1 hour group interview<br>• Transcribe notes, analysis<br>• Administrative |
| **Time** | 120 minutes<br>(60 minutes is estimated for administrative and production work) |

A team can be anywhere from 1-20 individuals, depending on the size of the project. You don't, however, have to accept the team provided by your client. Use your own process and judgment to build the team that you need. For example, if your instincts tell you that a problem might be with certain individuals not being suited for their current positions, request that a representative from the Human Resources department be on the team.

To assist you in building your team, ask for an organizational chart. If you will need employees to carry out administrative tasks, let the client know what staff resources you will need from them in terms of FTEs (full-time equivalents).

### Project Budget

Once you know the scope of the project and the resources required to complete it, you will be able to prepare a budget.

The budget will include your salary, as well as expenses. Don't cut yourself short and find yourself digging into your own pocket in order to complete the project. Follow the advice in section 6.2.5 for setting your fees and in section 6.2.7 for invoicing your clients.

**TIP:** Time and budget are areas in which business consultants can slip up and get a bad reputation. They are also, in some projects, one of the few yardsticks of success. Any potential concerns should not be left until you're halfway through the project and 50% over budget. To impress the client, be disciplined about projecting timeline and budget, communicate clearly about them and stick to them.

## 2.2.3 Gather Information

While you will begin gathering information the first time you talk to a prospective client, most of your information gathering will take place as part of the project.

Business consultants understand that having the right information is at the heart of being able to solve any problem. They use a variety of research methods to capture valuable data from every aspect of the organization.

This key element of consulting is covered in detail in section 2.3 of this book.

## 2.2.4 Do a Gap Analysis

A *gap analysis* is a process used to identify gaps that exist between the current and desired situations in an organization. For company representatives, the gap is the space between "where we are" and "where we want to be."

Before you can do a gap analysis, you must know the desired outcomes. These may have been clearly identified in the initial meeting with your client. However, chances are you will clarify and quantify precise desired outcomes only after further research and discussion.

For example, the person who hired you may have told you in your initial meeting that they want to "reduce employee turnover" because their current rate of attrition is causing production slowdowns and increased human resources costs. However, they might not have clearly specified what they want the attrition rate to be. Or they may have identified a desired attrition rate that your later research finds to be unreasonable for their industry.

To assist you in defining desired outcomes, you can use the S.M.A.R.T. method, a well-recognized model for setting strategic objectives. To be S.M.A.R.T., your objectives should be:

- **Specific:** What is the specific result desired? (Instead of just saying you want to "reduce employee turnover," state a specific level you want to reduce it to.)
- **Measurable:** Can the outcome be measured in a reliable way?
- **Attainable:** Given staffing, budget, timing and other restraints, is the objective attainable?
- **Relevant:** Do the people involved have the authority, the skill and the resources needed to meet the objective? And is the objective important to the organization or individual?
- **Time-Based:** Is there a start and end point to the objective?

Once you know the desired outcomes, and have researched the current situation, you can then do a gap analysis. An easy but effective way to approach a gap analysis is to place all the information gathered from the client and your own research into a gap-analysis matrix. You can use the following sample as a guide to develop a suitable matrix for the unique features of your project.

## Sample Gap Analysis Matrix

| Issue | Desired Outcome | Why Is It Happening? |
|---|---|---|
| Not producing enough widgets to meet demand (currently making 800 units per day) | 1,000 units per day | Process is manual. |
| Material costs are high | Reduce by 5% | Supplier has monopoly on the local market. |
| Attrition rate has been rising and is now 15% | Keep it under 10% | Competitor has introduced 4-day, 12-hour-a-day work week. Losing staff to them. |

### 2.2.5 Identify Possible Solutions

Once you have identified the gaps and why they are happening, you can start to identify possible solutions to bridge the gap between the current situation and the desired one. Filling the gaps becomes an exercise of "what if." This is the thinking, creative, planning part of your project. Look at all the knowns you have gathered. Then ask questions: "If we tried this, what would happen?"

For example, in the first issue shown on the matrix (the company is not producing enough widgets to meet demand because the process is manual), you might recommend introducing automation into the company's widget production. With the second issue shown on the matrix (material costs are too high because the supplier has a monopoly on the local market), you might recommend pricing out-of-town suppliers.

In developing solutions, you need to consider what specific actions must be taken and what resources (money, time, people, materials) will be needed to implement the solutions. The advice in section 3.2 can help you develop your problem-solving skills so you can identify possible solutions for your clients.

### 2.2.6 Present Your Recommendations

The solution is provided to the client in both a meeting presentation and a written document. It may be tempting to work on the solutions on your own, then step into the boardroom, and deliver your recommendations like a hero riding to the rescue of the company. However, if you take this approach, you may be surprised at the amount of opposition you encounter.

Remember that the company's problems have developed under the management of the same people that you want to buy into the solutions. Therefore, as answers begin to emerge from your analysis, it's wise to discuss them with hand-picked management members so you can begin to get buy-in for your recommendations. Keep the person you report to aware of emerging trends as well. You don't want them to be caught by surprise.

The final recommendations are often presented to the client in both a formal presentation and a written document. Both the written and oral presentations of your proposed solution should be presented in an easy-to-follow format and stated as simply, and clearly as possible. Clients want to see how you came to the conclusions that you did, and if the recommendations are capable of being implemented. Your recommendations must also be practical to implement, so that the client has confidence that your solutions can be implemented and carried out even after your contract has ended.

**TIP:** Throughout your informal discussions with management and your formal presentation, remain sensitive to reactions. Continue to acknowledge what they have done right and build their commitment to supporting the solutions.

To successfully sell your business solutions, you will give the client facts supported with quantifiable evidence. You will include anecdotes that illuminate what the numbers say. You will demonstrate confidence in your work and in your conclusions.

You will divide your presentation into relevant key areas, such as:

- Objective
- Methodology (how you collected information)
- Research Findings
- Recommendations
- Next Steps (what is required to implement recommendations)

Optimal presentation length depends on the size of the project and the style of the organization. Generally, the bigger the project, the longer and more lavish the presentation should be. Some organizations, particularly bureaucratic ones, expect formal presentations and they may book every meeting in a one-hour block. In that case, to leave room for discussion, time the presentation for 20 minutes maximum.

To prepare your presentation, begin with an outline. An outline gives you a chance to capture your main points while you ensure logical flow and consistency. It will help you detect if your points are parallel and help you find gaps.

## Sample Presentation Outline

**Audience** – Franklin Plumbing, senior management team

**Audience perspective** – serious about problem, innovative, skeptical about "touchy-feely"

**My goal** – to sell the implementation of employee retention ideas

**Context** – for discussion and reference, written report handed out immediately after verbal presentation of recommendations at a specially convened, management team meeting

**Title** (chosen after outline drafted):
*FRANKLIN PLUMBING: EMPLOYER OF CHOICE*

**I Introduction:**

A. Original problem
   1. History
   2. Financial impact
   3. Trend

B. Importance of solving
   1. Emerging market opportunities
   2. Franklin growth plans
   3. Competitive environment

**II Executive Summary (written after report drafted)**

**III Research**

A. Primary
   1. Policy review
   2. HR records review

3. Survey
    a. Methodology
        i. Wording
        ii. Respondents
        iii. Administration
        iv. Analysis techniques
    b. Results
        i. Problems
        ii. Opportunities

B. Secondary
1. Industry trends
2. Demographic trends
3. Case study solutions

**IV Recommendations**

A. Policy revisions
B. Compensation adjustments
C. Annual reviews
D. Delegation/responsibility
E. Management training

**V Implementation**

A. Timeline
B. Budget
C. Champions

**VI Summary**

A. New vision
B. Projected impact

Jot down your thoughts in freehand or on screen, whatever affords the greatest creative and analytical latitude for you. Create major headings, subheadings, minor sub headings and so on. This will give you time to develop your ideas in a logical way and think about the transition from one section to another. The table of contents of this book constitutes an outline.

When you start your own outline, as with any communication, begin with the *audience*. Consultant Marg Archibald says: "I start every outline with points about the audience, goal, and context at the top of the page. When I feel I am drifting, I go back to those points."

By studying your outline you can figure out where support from visuals would be useful and when you should encourage discussion. Also look for places you can add vivid anecdotes to help drive your points home. Quote some comments completely, if you can do so without revealing your sources. Doing so can turn dry numbers into a reality to which your audience can relate.

Presentations are often made with Microsoft PowerPoint. More information about making presentations can be found in section 3.3.5.

## 2.2.7 Implementation

You or your client put your recommendations into action at the implementation stage. This is often a collaborative stage in the project. The business consultant acts as a project manager, overseeing the operation. A successful implementation requires the same strategic and structured approach taken at the beginning of a project.

Some examples of these steps include:

### Break Down Implementation Into Sub-Projects

Breaking down the solutions into manageable sub-projects will not only aid you in getting the job done, it will also provide the client with an understanding of the tasks at hand and budget/priority options. This step is necessary for delegation to several people and various departments.

## Build an Implementation Team

This team does not have to be the same players that you used at the beginning of the project. Use your judgment in assessing who the right people are for each of the tasks. Pick the internal people required for buy-in to the solution who are capable of taking the necessary steps.

## Develop an Implementation Timeline

This may have been addressed at the beginning of the project, but new findings may necessitate change. Either way, it is a good idea to review and update this in detail for the final phase.

## Define Benchmarks for Success

In many cases, this is what the client is most interested in – how they're going to be able to recognize that you've been effective. The key is to provide measurable benchmarks that demonstrate improvement, such as improved time, quantity or savings. Your benchmarks will include *key performance indicators* (KPIs) so the company can evaluate progress in implementing the solutions.

A good overview of KPIs was developed by the U.K. government and Cranfield School of Management. An excerpt appears below; you can find more information at **www.businesslink.gov.uk** (do a search for "key performance indicators").

> A key performance indicator (KPI) helps a business define and measure progress toward its goals. KPIs are quantifiable measurements of the improvement in performing an activity that is critical to the success of a business.
>
> KPIs should complement a business' overall targets and relate to its core activities. As a result, they will differ depending on the business. In a telesales business, for example, answering customer calls before they ring off will be a key business activity. The percentage of calls answered within one minute may be one of its KPIs.

There must be a way to define and measure KPIs if they are to be useful. For example, a business wanting to increase sales needs to consider whether to measure this by units sold or by value of sales, and whether to deduct returned goods from sales in the month of the sales or the month of the return. You also need to set a target, such as increasing sales by five per cent per year.

Financial KPIs focusing on sales, costs or working capital are popular as they enable businesses to monitor and control the profitability and cashflow of the business. For example, a KPI for monthly sales enquiries will warn you about peaks and troughs that will affect cashflow.

KPIs can also be used as a performance management and improvement tool by focusing your employees on achieving the business' goals. KPI monitoring enables management to spot and correct weaknesses in the business, for example in terms of cashflow.



## 2.2.8 Post-Project Review

The post-project review is an informal meeting that takes place anywhere from two days to two months after the project is completed. This serves two purposes:

### Knowledge Transfer

A post-mortem is the time and place for one of the primary roles of a business consultant – the transfer of knowledge. Simply put, you are telling the client what you've learned and giving them the tools they need to deal with a similar issue should it ever occur.

At first this might seem counter-productive. You are turning away potential work. That view is short sighted. It is human nature to value a person who empowers us. The result: it makes you look good, gains allies and wins new clients and positive referrals. Some business consultants view this knowledge transfer as the primary responsibility of a consultant. You are empowering a client.

*"We all should have an adversity to hoarding knowledge; at the end of the engagement the client should know as much as we know. And they should have learned to do what we do and create a similar engagement for themselves without us the next time."*

— Linda Paralez, Ph.D.
Demarche Consulting Group, Inc.

### Getting Client Testimonials

Once the project is complete, take the time to gather quotes from your clients. Testimonials from happy clients can be used in future sales presentations, in proposals, or in promotional materials such as brochures, letters, and your website.

Throughout and after a project, clients may spontaneously express that they are pleased with your work, impressed with your skill and grateful for the results you are achieving. You may not have a pen in hand at the moment but remember the essence of what has been said. Get it down on paper at the earliest chance you have, quoting as accurately as possible.

Do not be shy about asking if you could make use of these comments. Tell your clients how much their praise means to you and the ways it can be helpful in letting others know about your work. Everyone is busy so make it easy for your clients. Jot down their praise, print it on plain paper at your office, and present it to them for approval. Ask to have it photocopied onto their letterhead and have them sign it. Many clients who are pleased with your work will be happy to give you a testimonial.

## Client Feedback

Another key purpose of the post-project review is to get feedback from the client that will help you improve upon your next assignment. It also provides an opportunity to capture positive feedback and subtly sell your next project.

It is an informal meeting that looks at issues such as:

- What went right?

- What went wrong? Why?
- Did the project stay within budget?
- Was it on schedule?
- Was your implementation successful? If so, how?
- What concrete results have been measured?
- Next steps, if any?

For broader input, you can ask various people within the company to fill out a brief questionnaire that asks specific questions about the project.

**Sample Client Feedback Questionnaire**

**(on your letterhead)**

**Date:** ____________________

**Your Client's Name:** ____________________

**Company:** ____________________

**Address:** ____________________

____________________

Dear Valued Client:

The (name of project) is complete. It has been a pleasure working with you and your team. Please take a minute to complete this brief questionnaire concerning your overall impression of our service. This will help to improve our services and increase the level of quality in future projects.

1. Were the goals and objectives easy to understand?

   ❑ Excellent ❑ Good ❑ Fair ❑ Poor

2. How would you rate the data collection methods?

   ❑ Excellent ❑ Good ❑ Fair ❑ Poor

3. How would you rate the analysis?

   ❑ Excellent ❑ Good ❑ Fair ❑ Poor

4. Was written documentation concise and complete?

   ❑ Excellent ❑ Good ❑ Fair ❑ Poor

5. How would you rate the overall results of the project?

   ❑ Excellent ❑ Good ❑ Fair ❑ Poor

6. How would you rate your Return on Investment for this project?

   ❑ Excellent ❑ Good ❑ Fair ❑ Poor

7. In a sentence or two, what did you like best about the service?

8. What aspects of the service did not meet your expectations?

9. Rate your feelings about hiring my company for future projects.

   ❑ Excellent ❑ Good ❑ Fair ❑ Poor

If you have any additional comments, please feel free to write them on the back of this questionnaire.

Thank you for taking the time to complete this survey.

Regards,
I.M. Aconsultant
XYZ Business Consulting Services

## 2.3 Information Gathering Techniques

As discussed in the overview of a consulting project, having the right information is at the heart of being able to solve a problem. In deciding which information gathering methods to use for your project, keep in mind that there are two major approaches to research methodology: *qualitative* research and *quantitative* research.

*Quantitative* research methods deal with quantities or numbers. They provide measurable results. In business consulting, a typical method of quantitative research is a survey with answers that can be tabulated statistically.

*Qualitative* research methods study participants' opinions, behaviors and experiences. Qualitative research methods used in business consulting include interviews and observations of people and documents.

To help you decide which methods should be for specific tasks during a consulting project, consider the purpose of your research. Here are a few distinctions between the two methods:

### Qualitative

- Emphasis on understanding issues from respondents' point of view
- Observations in natural settings
- Interpretative
- Subjective view

### Quantitative

- Emphasis on testing a theory
- Controlled measurement
- Focus on numbers and facts
- Objective view

Qualitative analysis might be applied to projects in which the client is aiming to achieve changes in the structure of an organization, such as how employees interact with each other and the customers, and the processes in place around this interaction. For example, a client might hire a business consultant to determine a more effective method of reducing the amount of sick time taken. To find a solution, you might use qualitative research methods that focus on understanding why employees call in sick.

Quantitative analysis is typically used in projects for clients who want to improve the bottom line by increasing profits or cutting costs. For example, a client might hire a business consultant to find ways to save money in a production plant. Through collection and measurement of data, the consultant might determine that it's more efficient to move the production staff to 12-hour days, with four days on and three days off, thus saving both time and money by running the equipment at maximum efficiency.

Although qualitative and quantitative research methods are typically used for gathering information about and resolving different types of problems, most consulting projects will require the business consultant to use a combination of the two methods. As the online encyclopedia Wikipedia explains, "qualitative research is often used to gain a general sense of phenomena and to form theories that can be tested using further quantitative research." So your number crunching about the 12-hour shift could also include some qualitative analysis of employee reaction to the idea.

Some common methods of information gathering and tips on getting the most out of them are described below. You can learn more about how to use these information gathering techniques in the resources provided later in this book.

### 2.3.1 Observation

Observation is an excellent qualitative method for business consultants to learn about a variety of aspects of a client company. As a consultant, you might observe people, processes, or documents.

A main advantage of observation is that it allows you to gather first-hand knowledge. For example, to observe company processes you might watch as products are being assembled in the manufacturing plant. Or, depending on the project, a representative of your consulting company might take on the role of a "mystery shopper"and pose as a typical shopper to gather information about such matters as employees' customer service, sales ability, product knowledge, and procedures.

A particularly effective way to discover what is really going on in an organization is to listen to employees or customers as a bystander. Casual conversation in lunchrooms, elevators, hallways – all the places where people speak freely and make offhand remarks are good places for a consultant to spend some time. What you hear can help you understand people's perceptions and identify potential issues. You may find similar candid remarks on employees' blogs.

Another form of observation is to review company documents such as memos and reports. Start with records directly related to the problem but follow your hunches into other areas. Watch for trends and noteworthy events. See what actions have been taken in the past, and what the outcomes were. That way you can avoid recommending "been there, done that" solutions that the company has already tried. If you do propose a solution that has been tried unsuccessfully in the past, you can explain how different circumstances make this a good course of action to take at this time.

One of the greatest challenges in observing is that most people believe they are completely objective about what they see and hear. Few people question the accuracy of their perceptions. However, police officers routinely find that when more than one person witnesses an accident or crime, there will be more than one version of what happened.

To be a skilled observer, you must be able to pay attention, understand what you are seeing, and remember or record it accurately. It is also wise to question the accuracy of your perceptions, and whether you are seeing the entire picture. An article on "How to Increase Your Powers of Observation" offers interesting advice about observing people, activities, and documents. Although written for private investigators, you may find some useful information to use in consulting projects. You can find the article online at **www.pimall.com/nais/n.obser.html**.

## 2.3.2 Case Studies

In addition to reviewing documents of the company you are consulting for, you can gather a tremendous amount of useful information by reviewing documents about other companies that have faced similar situations. These documents are known as *case studies*.

*The American Heritage Dictionary of the English Language* defines case study as "A detailed intensive study of a unit, such as a corporation or a corporate division, that stresses factors contributing to its success or failure."

Case studies of other corporations, or of other divisions within the company you're consulting for, may help you identify the best solutions for your client. For example, if you are consulting for a dot-com whose owners want to take the company public, you could examine what has happened in the cases of other dot-coms going public.

Harvard Business School has a library of business case studies available online. Many of these case studies focus on business innovations and provide helpful insight into the implementation of solutions to specific problems. For a few dollars per case study, you can learn details about experiences of companies such as Apple Computer, Cirque du Soleil, Coca-Cola, Disney, Staples and many others. To give only one example, if you have a client that is looking to expand to Japan, you can learn how Toys 'R Us entered the Japanese toy market.

At the time of publication of this book, the case studies could be found by following these instructions: go to **http://hbsp.harvard.edu**, then click on "Begin Search for HBS Cases." This will take you to a list of real-life business cases used in Harvard's undergraduate and MBA courses. From here, you can refine your search of cases by discipline, industry, geography, etc.

Despite the "For Educators" heading at the top of the page, you don't need to be a teacher to register as a user and place an order. In 2006, we were able to purchase a case study for $6.50 (they are now $6.95) and when we contacted Harvard Business School Publishing to ask whether they permitted business consultants to share the information from their case studies with clients, they told us that "individuals can certainly order case studies to use when consulting with clients."

### 2.3.3 Interviews

An interview is a one-on-one structured conversation between a business consultant and an employee, customer, supplier, or other individual who can provide information or opinions about a company. As Rudolph F. Verderber and Kathleen S. Verderber note in their textbook *Communicate!*, "interviewing is a powerful method for collecting first-hand information that may be unavailable elsewhere."

Before conducting an interview, you must:

- **Determine the purpose of the interview:** For example, are you looking for information about how a particular department operates, do you want to learn how employees in that department feel about their work, or do you want their suggestions for how to improve productivity?

- **Decide who to interview:** Once you have selected people to interview you will need to schedule a time to interview them. In most cases, interviews are conducted on-site if you can get a secure location where the conversation will not be overheard. Having a secure location may help the interviewee feel at ease and respond more honestly.

- **Develop the interview format:** This includes deciding how long the interview will be, what questions you will ask, and the order of questions. Generally, it's a good idea to start with an easy or factual question at the beginning, and ask more difficult or controversial questions after you have established rapport.

In determining the amount of time you'll need, the Verderbers say "A rule of thumb is to allow four minutes for each open-ended or qualitative question and one minute for each close-ended or quantitative question." (Close-ended questions are those that can be answered in one or two words, such as "yes" or "no" questions.)

However, be prepared for the possibility that an interviewee may bring up additional issues. If they are within the scope of your project, ask follow-up questions to learn more about those issues.

For best results in interviews, use the effective communication skills described in the next chapter. For additional tips on developing questions, see the next section on Surveys.

**TIP:** If you want employees to give candid feedback, it is important that you have agreement from management that your sources will remain anonymous. You need the self-discipline to keep any comments that could tip off management about a source out of your conversation with them.

## 2.3.4 Surveys

This method utilizes questionnaires and helps with recording the opinions and attitudes of employees, customers, suppliers or industry colleagues, all of whom may have useful insights, depending on the nature of the problem. The data can be valuable for assessing the cause-and-effect relationship of a problem and for gaining new insights. In each case you need to reassure respondents of complete confidentiality.

### Creating the Questionnaire

Here are steps to creating a questionnaire, followed by a sample survey.

Management should send a letter to all staff, prior to the survey, introducing you, identifying the problem and your role in fixing it. This is usually a good idea whether or not you do a survey as it paves the way to co-operation with your work.

1. Determine exactly what you are trying to learn. Be clear what you are going to do with that information.

2. Draft the introduction, assuring respondents of confidentiality and explaining why their opinion counts.

3. Draft the questions, keeping in mind that they should be neutral (i.e. stay away from questions to which respondents would feel compelled to answer a certain way). Although quantitative or closed questions (i.e. those answered "yes/no" or numerically) are the easiest to collate, you may also gain valuable insights by including a qualitative "anything else" question at the end.

4. After management revisions of your draft survey, test your questionnaire on a small sample of employees you can trust to keep quiet about the contents. Invariably you will find areas for clarification and improvement. Make your improvements quickly and get it out to all before any talk among employees dilutes the validity of the survey.

5. Either meet with staff or set up a way to communicate that this questionnaire is coming, why, and when you need the completed surveys back. This communication comes from you. You

separate this survey from management and assure staff or any other respondents of confidentiality. Impress on employees that you want their individual opinions. Request that they complete their own questionnaire without discussion with colleagues.

6. Set up a tight schedule for completion to minimize discussion while employees are still working on them. You might arrange to have the questionnaire completed over a lunchtime or even extended coffee break as long as respondents feel it is fair. Another option is to have an online survey.

If you prefer not to develop your own surveys, you can find a selection of surveys to use in your consulting business in *The Consultant's Big Book of Reproducible Surveys and Questionnaires*, by Mel Silberman.

## Sample Survey

On the next few pages you will find an example of a simple survey. This survey is designed to determine employee skills and knowledge, and therefore their ability to help the customer.

### Sample Survey

**We want your opinion!**

Hello Staff:

As you know, we are working with your management team to ensure that it is easy for you to serve your customers. From casual conversation, we have detected that there may be gaps in the information you need to do so. But we want to make sure that we are on the right track. You are the only people who can tell us what we need to know. Your input is uniquely important.

We guarantee it will remain completely confidential. Supervisors and management will never see these questionnaires and they will be stored off site forever. The management team, and you, will only see the compiled results.

Once we have all the questionnaires back, they will be collated and summarized. We will be looking for trends and insights so please read these questions carefully and answer honestly.

Remember, your answer is not a reflection on what you should know and will never be connected back to you. It simply lets us measure the level of knowledge among all staff, collectively, and how they acquire that knowledge.

Thank you for your time and opinion. This will take you approximately three minutes to complete.

### Access to Knowledge & Training

Please answer each question by circling the number that best applies.

| | Never/No | | | | Always/Yes |
|---|---|---|---|---|---|
| I feel confident in my ability to help with any customer query | 1 | 2 | 3 | 4 | 5 |
| In order to get answers I escalate customer issues to team leaders or managers | 1 | 2 | 3 | 4 | 5 |
| I was provided with adequate training when I started working at the company | 1 | 2 | 3 | 4 | 5 |
| There is appropriate reference material to aid me in dealing with customer issues | 1 | 2 | 3 | 4 | 5 |
| I am able to anticipate customers' needs | 1 | 2 | 3 | 4 | 5 |
| I feel that I have clear guidelines in how to deal with unusual customer issues | 1 | 2 | 3 | 4 | 5 |
| I dread customer calls because I know that I won't be able to help them myself | 1 | 2 | 3 | 4 | 5 |
| I feel empowered to deal with customer problems | 1 | 2 | 3 | 4 | 5 |

If you have any additional comments, please write them on the back of this survey.

## Compiling the Results

Here are some suggestions for collating, analyzing, and summarizing the results of a survey.

A small number of questionnaires can be collated by hand, using a blank questionnaire. After somewhere between 50 and 100 surveys, particularly if they are long, this gets tiring. However, even with larger numbers surveyed, you can gain significant insight into the results by collating some of the questionnaires by hand.

Take time to harvest everything you can from the original questionnaires and write out all the subjective comments word for word. Add up your numbers and convert them to percentages. Then sit with the information and think about what it is telling you. Come back to it a few times to make sure you are picking up on all the tell-tale findings. Sometimes the subjective information explains why you are getting the numbers you are so look for similar comments within the subjective responses.

Draft a summary that lists the good things that management will be glad to hear. Couch the bad news in a constructive way but do not fudge the information. For each problem area, include your recommendations on what they should do about it. The questionnaire may be just one small part of a bigger project so you may need to consider the results with information from other sources.

Complainers are the canaries in the mine. Take them seriously. Whether you are polling staff or customers, a dissatisfaction rate as low as 10% reflects a problem worth addressing.

## Online Surveys

There is a growing number of online services that support your questionnaire development and collation. By putting your survey online results, charts and graphs can be generated, at any point in the survey, right from the time the first survey is entered. Examples include Survey-Host at **http://surveyhost.apian.com** and Opinio at **www.objectplanet.com/opinio**.

You can find links to demonstration models, freeware and shareware for a range of research software at **www.researchinfo.com/docs/software**. You may also want to look into SPSS at **www-01.ibm.com/software/analytics/spss** which has long been respected by professional researchers but had not been easy for the novice to use. Now they support the business user whose primary business is not research.

## 2.3.5 Focus Groups

Focus groups are an inexpensive and efficient way to gather qualitative information from a group of people. They bring a small group of people together for a facilitated discussion on one topic or several related topics. The interaction within the group produces insights far different from that of a single interview or survey.

Focus groups may be asked to discuss a wide range of topics, from giving impressions of an advertising campaign or a new food product that participants have just been given to eat, to examining why an organization is losing its youngest and most capable employees.

Be aware that there are limitations to a focus group. A focus group does not replace quantitative data from a survey of large numbers of people. In fact, focus group results cannot be generalized to the wider population. They only tell you about the opinions and ideas of the people who participated.

### When to Use (and Not Use) a Focus Group

When you have questions that are too complex or subtle for a survey, consider a focus group. When you want to nurture the evolution of ideas from different perspectives, consider a focus group. When the information you are getting from individual interviews and surveys is not answering the questions, or has raised an issue that requires more detailed examination, consider a focus group.

A focus group can be held prior to a survey to finalize the questions that will be asked and determine how to ask them so that you don't bias the results. It can be held after a survey to explore the ambiguous results you got from the survey. It can be held between two surveys to do both.

In the end, what you will have gathered is a depth of insight about causes, reactions and motivations that you simply cannot get in a survey. You gain ideas that the group has brainstormed, together, that you cannot get from a single interview. If that's what you are looking for, a focus group is worth the investment.

### How to Run a Focus Group

The focus group facilitator welcomes participants, introduces them to each other and explains the rules of the discussion. He clarifies where the washrooms are, if any refreshments will be served, and what time the focus group will end. He asks participants to turn off cell phones.

Then he outlines the code of conduct for all participants and may post these. They will include listening respectfully, only one person talking at a time, a warning of how he will end discussion on one topic and introduce another one, that he will ask particular participants for their opinions, change topics and halt a fruitless discussion if necessary.

He will have a list of things he is trying to find out before starting. During the focus group, he will explore these by asking who, what, when, where and especially, why.

The facilitator will have some immediate comments at the end of the focus group. He will probably articulate the most noticeable or surprising results and then study the recorded session to develop additional ideas, insights, and suggestions. He will know how to interpret results in light of the personality of each participant. He will also be aware of the interplay of participants and how that has affected what any individual may have said.

He will prepare a report outlining the answers to your questions and any additional information that he believes is relevant. He will insert key quotations in his report to illustrate his analysis. He may attach a transcript of the whole focus group although that can be lengthy.

Stay away from a focus group if management insists on running it or wants to approach it as just any other meeting, because it isn't. You should also stay away from a focus group if the people from whom you would pick participants have a hidden agenda or are emotionally entrenched at either end of the spectrum.

Let's explore some of the factors you need to be aware of to set up a productive focus group and manage the results.

## Picking Group Participants

Once you have clarified and documented what you are trying to learn from a focus group, pick people who have the knowledge and insights necessary to provide information on that topic. This does not necessarily mean experts. This may mean users, casual observers, or average citizens. Optimal focus group size is between eight and twelve people. You want a range of ideas and perspectives plus maximum participation of everyone there.

While picking participants, be sensitive to the chemistry that could occur among them. Human behavior is hard to predict and you will make mistakes. People who are domineering, passive or followers do not make useful participants. You want people who are thoughtful, good listeners and critical thinkers. Look for people who take their responsibility seriously. This helps prevent a runaway group that blindly follows a single, forceful participant. Challenging interaction can be useful but it is not productive to have the group degenerate into a squabble.

If your focus group participants are employees, you need to explain that management will see the transcripts and ensure that they are comfortable with that. If confidentiality needs to be maintained, you need to get management buy-in on that. Likewise, you need to be doubly careful about the dynamics of interplay among employee participants. Some facilitators would suggest the group be either all management or all employees. A mix can be useful but be sensitive to the dynamics.

## Practicalities

Telephone and online focus groups are emerging as a new way to gather far-flung participants. However, most focus groups still involve getting a group together in one location.

Most focus groups conducted by professional researchers are held in a focus group suite, designed for comfortable discussion around a table where audio and even videotaping can be handled unobtrusively. Most of these suites have a gallery for real-time viewing by senior officials which both allows them to gain vivid insight into people's feelings but also provides a chance for them to bring forward additional questions while the group is still together.

Experienced facilitators with their own equipment can free you up from having to attend to all the details of running a focus group. They can handle reception, nametags, recording equipment operation, refreshments, lighting, note-taking materials, thank-you payment (for example, if you're inviting customers to participate), transcribing the results, picking out worthwhile insights, and running the show.

Be careful about taking on the facilitating yourself if you have no experience at it and the stakes are high. To find someone that can do focus groups for you, look online or in the Yellow Pages for local companies that offer market research services. When you bring in another facilitator you want to manage him and the focus group process as part of your research for the client. Pick a facilitator with whom you feel comfortable and can talk openly about your hunches and concerns.

More information about focus groups can be found online. The World Bank offers a clear, simple, useful how-to on focus group management at **http://siteresources.worldbank.org/WBI/Resources/213798-1194538727144/6Final-Focus_Groups.pdf**. A useful series of online articles that address several focus group challenges can be found at: **http://mnav.com/focus-group-center.**

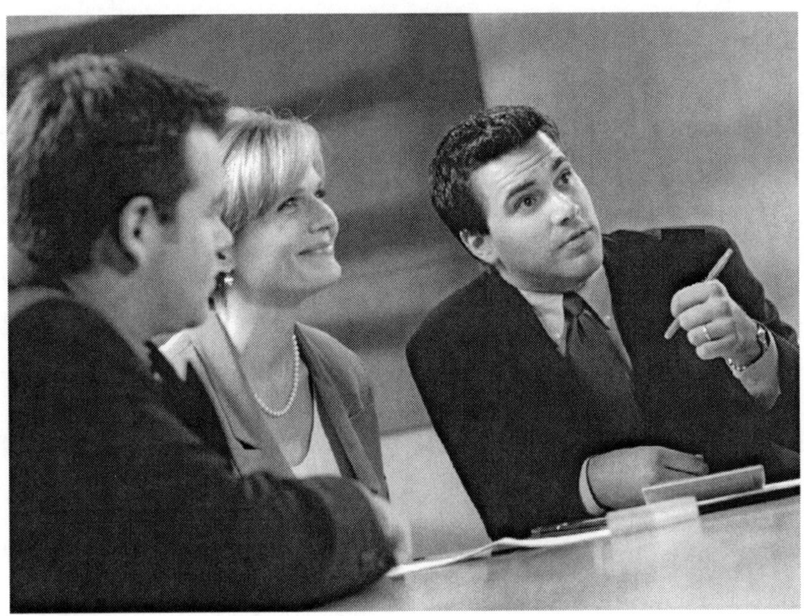

# 3. Developing Your Skills

Before you begin applying for consulting jobs or start a consulting business, there are several steps that may make it easier for you to transition to this career. In this chapter and the next, you will discover how to develop your skills, knowledge and experience. By following this advice, you could make yourself much more attractive to prospective employers and clients.

## 3.1 Skills Assessment

Business consultants need to use a variety of skills to do their job well. As you will read in this chapter, the skills you need to succeed as a business consultant can be learned. However, if you already have relevant business experience or an aptitude for consulting, entering this career will be even easier for you.

Here are some questions that reflect traits shared by many business consultants. Make a mental note or put a checkmark next to all that are a "yes" for you.

1. _____ Do people frequently ask for your advice?
2. _____ Do you enjoy finding solutions to problems?
3. _____ Are you a critical thinker?
4. _____ Do you know a variety of problem-solving techniques?
5. _____ Do you enjoy doing research?
6. _____ Do you have a good vocabulary?
7. _____ Do you avoid using jargon or technical terms that others may not understand?
8. _____ Do people consider you to be a good listener?
9. _____ Do you understand non-verbal communication such as body language?
10. _____ Do you have excellent written communication skills?
11. _____ Are you comfortable speaking in front of a group?
12. _____ Do you have project management experience?
13. _____ Can you see the big picture and break it down into manageable components?
14. _____ Are you well organized?
15. _____ Do you meet deadlines?
16. _____ Do you have experience leading teams?
17. _____ Are you ethical in all your business practices?

These 17 questions offer insight into characteristics typical of individuals who enter and succeed in the world of business consulting. How did you do? If you answered "yes" to all of these questions, you already have qualities found in successful business consultants. Now look at any you answered "no." Questions 1 to 5 relate to problem-solving skills, questions 6-11 relate to communication skills, questions 12-16 relate to management skills, and question 17 concerns business ethics.

As we said at the start of this chapter, the skills you need to succeed as a business consultant can be learned. So let's take a look at the specific skills that can help you succeed in business consulting. Later in this chapter you'll find plenty of resources to develop these skills through education and self-study.

## 3.2 Problem-Solving Skills

> *"We can't solve problems by using the same kind of thinking we used when we created them."*
>
> — Albert Einstein

It's a common assumption that human beings are better at creating problems than solving problems. Arguably, this goes double for companies, and it's a good thing too, because this is precisely why they hire business consultants.

Fortunately, business consultants are excellent problem solvers. They identify and verify the problems, determine what data needs to be collected and decide how it is going to be collected. Then, they figure out how to use this data in order to make a recommendation that ultimately solves the organization's problem. Data collection techniques were discussed in the previous chapter. However, data alone does not solve problems. It is the business consultant's analysis of relevant data that leads to a solution.

This section introduces a variety of problem-solving techniques and describes personal traits that assist in analyzing information. In the next section of this book, you will find a variety of resources to help you develop the traits and learn the techniques involved in problem-solving.

### 3.2.1 Critical Thinking

Business consultants use critical thinking when analyzing information. If you are a critical thinker, it means you have a healthy dose of skepticism when you hear or read something. You don't take everything at face value or automatically assume it's true. Instead, you are open to the possibility that even information that is presented as "factual" may not be true, or at least that it may not be the entire truth. Other factors that make a good critical thinker include:

- Natural curiosity
- Logical thinking
- Tendency to ask questions
- Reading between the lines

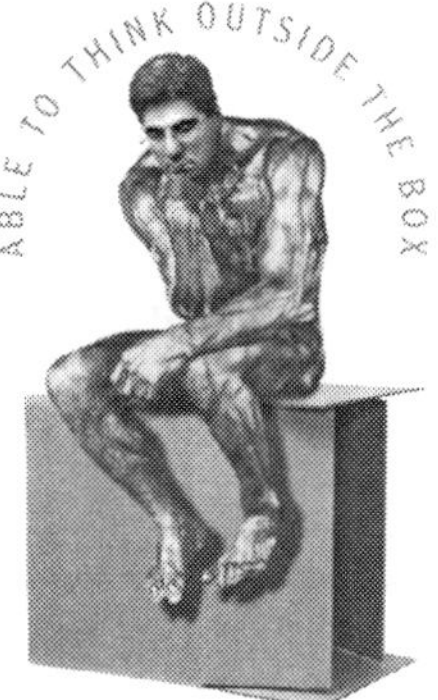

© Peter Cyngot

The term "thinking outside the box," which is now widely used to describe thinking that goes beyond the standard obvious answers, certainly applies to the work of business consultants.

You can develop this skill through training and experience (described later in this chapter). In addition, you can start strengthening your critical thinking skills right away simply by asking questions. Dr. Wayne Wickelgren, one of America's most eminent problem-solving experts, recommends asking the following questions when you are considering a set of facts:

- Have I identified all the facts, including those that are implied by other facts?
- Have I identified or taken into account any ambiguity in the facts that could be putting me on a false path?
- Have I correctly understood the information provided by the facts?

Here are some additional questions you can ask whenever you see or hear new information:

- What is the source of this information? Is it reliable?

- What evidence supports this claim? Is it tangible or just hearsay?
- Is there any other possible explanation for this? If so, what are some other possible explanations?

**Example**

You have been hired to help Company A identify the cause of a significant drop in sales of widgets. When you start investigating the situation you discover that Company A's widget sales started to decline shortly after Company B began selling widgets in Company A's geographic market. On the surface, it appears that Company B's actions are the cause of Company A's falling widget sales. However, an effective business consultant will question whether there might be something else that is causing the decline in Company A's widget sales.

Possibly the market for Company A's widgets is saturated (everyone who wants one already has one) or possibly a new product has replaced widgets – just as CDs replaced vinyl records and DVDs replaced VHS tapes. Because there may be many other possible explanations for the decline in widget sales, the effective business consultant recognizes that even an answer that appears "obvious" (in this case a competitor entering the market) may be incorrect or incomplete.

Critical thinking is essential for avoiding a wrong answer, but your goal as a business consultant is to find the best answer for your clients. To do so, you'll need to use a problem-solving technique such as those described in the next section.

**TIP:** Don't forget that other people may not think as logically as you do. You may have to deal with problems created by people (such as customers, the general public, or even your clients) who are not critical thinkers. For example, if you are a marketing consultant, you may have to deal with hoaxes or rumors about companies you are consulting for. For a fascinating look at current "urban legends" about companies and products visit **http://urbanlegends.about.com/library/blxcompanies.htm**. This site is a good resource for correcting any misinformation about a client.

## 3.2.2 Problem-Solving Techniques

It would be nice if there were always only one "right" solution to every problem that you could find by collecting enough data. In fact, there are often numerous possible solutions. Edward de Bono, who is regarded as the world's leading expert in creative thinking, illustrates this point in an article titled "Creative Problem-Solving" at **www.thinkingmanagers.com/management/creative-problem-solving.php** (scroll past the ads to read the article). Using the example of traffic congestion, he shows that there may be many ways to solve a particular problem. Thus, rather than trying to find the only solution to a problem, your goal will likely be to find the "best" solution in a particular situation.

There are a variety of problem-solving techniques you can use to help you do so. You might already have your own system, such as the one on the next page developed by consultant Marg Archibald, a contributing author of this book. Or you can use one of the many popular problem-solving techniques commonly used in business consulting. The excellent website MindTools.com gives a practical overview of techniques for solving complicated and difficult business problems.

They explain:

> By using these techniques you can start to tackle problems which might otherwise seem huge, overwhelming and excessively complex. These tools give you a starting point in problem solving where other people would just feel helpless and intimidated by the situation. These techniques help you conduct a rigorous analysis of the problems you face, helping you look at as many factors as possible in a structured and methodical way.

The problem-solving techniques include the following:

- Appreciation (Extracting maximum information from facts)
- Cash Flow Forecasting (Analyzing the financial viability of an idea)
- Cause & Effect Diagrams (Identifying possible causes of problems)
- Drill-Down (Breaking problems down into manageable parts)

- Porter's Five Forces (Analyzing the forces that affect a company's ability to make a profit)
- Risk Analysis (Evaluating and managing the risks you face)
- Systems Diagrams (Understanding the way factors affect each other)
- SWOT Analysis (Analyzing Strengths, Weaknesses, Opportunities and Threats)

## Sample Framework for Business Problem-Solving

*Step 1:* Clarify the problem.

*Step 2:* Find out if others have solved this problem or similar ones. This is where experience becomes invaluable, and you will be building experience all the time. In the future you will be able to refer back to a situation you dealt with first hand or recall an article that applied. For now, get good at researching sources of information in your specialty and engage in dialogue with other business consultants so that you know who to draw on when needed. Stay current with developments in your field, and spend some time browsing business case studies online.

*Step 3:* Break the problem down into components. Solve the simplest part first.

*Step 4:* Throughout the problem solving, watch for hidden assumptions. That's what stumps us when we are challenged with brainteasers with simple solutions. Using critical thinking, keep asking why and challenging what you find out.

*Step 5:* Be creative in your search for solutions. Sometimes looking outside your field altogether will provide solutions. The apple falling on Newton's head did it for physics.

*Step 6:* Watch for multiple sources of the problem and the interaction among them.

| *Step 7:* | As you develop your theory on the cause of and solution to the problem, test your theory on a small scale. Watch results with a critical eye. Try it with different variables. Discuss it. Inch toward solutions that will apply in all the conditions that pertain in this specific problem. |
|---|---|

You would not use all of these techniques on a single problem, but choose the ones that fit best with the types of solutions you need to come up with for your clients. Here is an example of a popular technique which you are likely to encounter during your career as a consultant.

## Sample Technique: SWOT Analysis

A SWOT Analysis is a problem-solving technique that evaluates the Strengths, Weaknesses, Opportunities, and Threats involved in a business objective. It can help you determine if an objective is achievable and, if so, what factors may help or hinder the company's achievement of that objective.

Strengths and weaknesses are internal to the organization, while opportunities and threats are external to the organization. Strengths and opportunities can help the organization achieve the objective, while weaknesses and threats can get in the way of success. Leon Winer, Ph.D., MBA, Emeritus Professor of Marketing and Entrepreneurship at Pace University, developed the following visual definition of SWOTs:

**Definitions of SWOTs**

| | **Helpful** to achieving the objective | **Harmful** to achieving the objective |
|---|---|---|
| **Internal** (attributes of the organization) | **Strengths** | **Weaknesses** |
| **External** (attributes of the environment) | **Opportunities** | **Threats** |

To do a SWOT analysis, you'll begin with the specific objective you have identified. (Section 2.2.1 has information on setting objectives.) You will then identify and list the SWOTs. You would consider all factors, both internal and external, that can help or hinder achieving the objective.

Some examples include:

- Management
- Financial resources
- Staff
- Product quality
- Price
- Location
- Hours of operation
- Economic conditions
- Foreign currency exchange rates
- Market saturation
- Competitors' actions
- Distribution channels
- Technological innovations

Your own analysis will likely have additional or different items than the ones listed above. When creating your own list, be as specific as possible, and break down each item as needed. For example, rather than trying to determine whether the company's "staff" is a strength or weakness in connection with your objective, you might identify "customer service staff" as a strength and "sales staff" as a weakness.

As Leon Winer explains, "A particular factor is relevant only with reference to a specific objective. For example, a large cash balance is a strength if the objective is expansion. If the objective is to discourage a hostile take-over, a large cash balance is a weakness."

Once you have listed the SWOTs, you'll develop strategies for each of them by asking:

- How can we use each strength?
- How can we remedy or minimize each weakness?
- How can we take advantage of each opportunity?
- How can we defend against each threat?

After analyzing this information, you may decide that a particular course of action is not as strong compared to alternatives. However, if a particular strategy looks like a good one, especially if you have evaluated it using additional problem-solving techniques, then you can proceed to recommend specific steps to move forward.

Investopedia.com recommends that you "keep your SWOT analysis short and simple, and avoid complexity and over-analysis since much of the information is subjective. Thus, use it as a guide and not a prescription."

## For More Information

For more information on SWOT Analysis and the other techniques listed above, as well as additional techniques for solving business problems, visit **www.mindtools.com** and choose "Problem Solving" from the drop down menu under the "Toolkit" tab. In addition to articles describing each problem-solving technique, the site offers a free newsletter, self-study courses, and books for further learning.

MindTools.com also has information about decision-making techniques such as Decision Trees, Edward de Bono's Six Thinking Hats, and Cost-Benefit Analysis. You can visit de Bono's site directly at **www.edwdebono.com**.

For a quick overview and links to additional resources, search for techniques you are interested in learning about at the online encyclopedia **www.wikipedia.org**.

Here are some additional resources you may want to check out:

- *The Path to Critical Thinking: HBS Working Knowledge*
  This article at the Harvard Business School site is highly recommended. If you check out only one resource on this page, make it this one.
  **http://hbswk.hbs.edu/archive/4828.html**

- *Fifty Problem Solving Strategies Explained*
  Although this collection of problem-solving tips does not focus specifically on business issues, it may spark some ideas.
  **www.une.edu.au/bcss/psychology/john-malouff/problem-solving.php**

- *The Foundation for Critical Thinking Articles*
  **www.criticalthinking.org/pages/index-of-articles/1021**

## 3.3 Communication Skills

Many believe a business consultant's primary job is to sell. First you sell your services and then you sell your solution. In between you sell multiple individuals and committees on trusting you, working with you, and answering your questions. In order to sell, you must be able to communicate effectively.

Whether you take this definition to heart or not, communication skills will play an enormous role in your daily business consulting activities. Many communication skills required to succeed as a business consultant are the same as those needed to meet the demands of many corporate positions. However, they may need to be taken to a higher level so they can be applied to an entire organization and its operations.

As part of your job, you will be communicating verbally and in writing, with individuals and groups. This book covers essential components of those communication skills. In this section we look at the skills that can help you effectively communicate all types of messages as a business consultant. The specifics of how to sell (from what to say in a sales call to writing a winning proposal) are covered in Chapter 7.

### 3.3.1 Basics of Communication

A study of face-to-face communication conducted by Albert Mehrabian at the University of California, Los Angeles, found that the percentage of the meaning conveyed through each channel of communication was as follows:

*Verbal* (the actual words used) .................................... 7%
*Vocal* (tone of voice and other vocal qualities)........ 38%
*Visual* (primarily facial expressions)........................ 55%

While these figures do not apply in communication situations outside the research lab, this now famous study helped make people aware of the importance of vocal and visual communication.

Most people intuitively know that vocal qualities, facial expressions, and body language can communicate more than words alone. For example, imagine asking someone "How are you?" If that person replies "fine" in a curt manner, with a frown on her face, and her arms crossed, chances are that person is not really "fine."

### 3.3.2 Verbal and Vocal Communication

Although in the UCLA study only seven percent of a message's meaning was conveyed through the words alone, a business consultant's choice of words are important. This is particularly true in communication situations where there are few or no visual clues, such as written communications or telephone conversations.

In all communication situations, your vocabulary is important. You're not communicating effectively if the reader or listener doesn't understand you. Speaking over the heads of your clients using industry-specific and technical business terms might sound impressive but it's not effective. If you must use business terms and acronyms that your client may not be familiar with, explain them as you speak.

On the other hand, a client may occasionally use a term that you're not familiar with if you haven't brushed up on business vocabulary. If there are specific terms you want to look up, the following sites contain lists of business terms and definitions:

- *AllBusiness.com Business Glossary*
**http://bit.ly/MEMKq3**

- *New York Times Glossary of Business and Financial Terms*
**www.nytimes.com/library/financial/glossary/bfglosa.htm**

- *Washington Post Business Terms Glossary*
(Free membership is required.)
**www.washingtonpost.com/wp-dyn/business/specials/glossary/index.html**

All industries also have their own set of business terms or corporate lexicons, and it's a good idea to have a basic understanding of these terms. Make it your job to learn their inside terms and concepts and use them as often as you can. No single characteristic wins you friends and trust as does talking their language.

You may begin picking up their lingo in their printed materials, on their website, and in discussions with company personnel. It's also a good idea to visit industry websites. For example, consultants specializing in human resources may hear clients using training terms such as "experiential" or "accelerated learning" and acronyms such as "WBT" (web based training), "HPI" (human performance improvement), and "SME" (in HR training SME means "subject matter expert" not "small and medium-sized enterprises"). In this case, information about these and other terms can be found through the American Society for Training and Development site at **www.astd.org**.

In addition to vocabulary, there are many other verbal and vocal traits that may affect the way a business consultant is perceived. People may make judgments about a consultant's competence, knowledge, and trustworthiness based on the consultant's accent, pronunciation, grammar, use of fillers (such as "uh" and "um"), and vocal qualities such as volume, tone, pitch, and rate of speaking.

To give one example of how vocal qualities can affect how you are perceived, consider some common stereotypes based on speech rates. In the *FabJob Guide to Become an Image Consultant*, the image experts said:

> A fast-talking person may appear to others to be shifty or untrustworthy. Some people feel that fast talkers do not really know what they

are saying, and their thoughts are not well reasoned out. Those who speak more slowly may be slower, more methodical thinkers. They may think carefully about what they say. The impression, however, can be that these people lack intelligence because they are "slow."

To improve your vocal communication skills, ask people you respect for feedback on any areas that could be improved. For professional assistance consider hiring a voice coach or speech coach. You may be able to find a local coach in the Yellow Pages or through the Voice and Speech Trainers Association at **www.vasta.org**.

## 3.3.3 Non-Verbal Communication

As the UCLA study found, non-verbal communication can be particularly powerful in face-to-face communication. Generally, if there is conflict between the words being said and the message communicated by the body, the body is more likely to be believed. It is essential that you control your non-verbal communication so that you do not inadvertently communicate negative messages.

Non-verbal communication (also known as "body language") happens through facial expressions, eye contact, posture, gestures, and other body movements. Negative body movement such as fidgeting and crossed arms, and negative facial expressions such as narrowed eyes and furrowing the brow, send off signals of uneasiness and a lack of confidence, both of which are unattractive qualities in a business consultant.

The first step to sending positive non-verbal messages is to become conscious of your body language. Notice when you make particular gestures out of habit or as a reaction to what's happening around you. Then choose to use positive body language.

For example, you can control the amount of eye contact you make when interviewing someone or conversing with a client. In North America, the person doing the talking in a conversation typically makes eye contact 40% of the time, while the listener typically makes eye contact almost 70% of the time. Those who make more eye contact without staring are perceived as more confident and interested, while those who make less eye contact may be seen as uncomfortable, bored, or hiding something. More signs for conveying confidence are included below under "Presentation Skills."

It is worth developing the habit of being sensitive to your non-verbal communication before you are actually in a communication situation such as a presentation or interview; then using appropriate body language will come naturally to you when the pressure is on.

It is not only your own body language that is important. Reading other people's non-verbal cues can help you in your work. Although body language can't tell you precisely what someone is thinking, it can give you clues so you can ask follow-up questions, even as basic as "How do you feel about that?"

If you want to improve this skill, you can find some excellent advice in books such as *Reading People,* by Jo-Ellan Dimitrius and Wendy Patrick Mazzarella and *How to Read a Person Like a Book,* by Gerald I. Nierenberg and Henry H. Calero.

## 3.3.4 Listening

Writing for the *Harvard Business Review on Effective Communication,* Ralph G. Nichols and Leonard A. Stevens assert in an article titled "Listening to People," that "the effectiveness of the spoken word hinges not so much on how people talk but mostly on how they listen." As a business consultant, understanding the needs of your clients is crucial to a successful project. Therefore, effective listening skills are a must.

While listening seems like an easy skill to master, most of us experience challenges in at least one of the following areas involved in listening: paying attention, understanding, and remembering. You can improve your listening skills by focusing fully on someone when they are speaking. Here are some ways to do that:

- Don't be distracted by what is going on around you. Such factors as loud noises, the other person's misuse or mispronunciation of a word, or an uncomfortable room temperature can all affect your listening.
- Avoid interrupting the other person. Allow the other person to finish speaking before jumping in with a comment or question.

- Keep listening to the other person, even if you think you know what they will say next. If you make assumptions, you may miss the point they're making.
- Pay attention to non-verbal signals (tone of voice, facial expression, body language) which may provide additional information about a speaker's emotions.
- Consider the perspective of the person talking and the context of their comments. For example, a new employee may speak in much more positive terms about a company than other employees because they are excited about being hired for their new job.
- Ask questions if you need any points clarified.
- Paraphrase what the other person has said. This allows you to confirm that you understood what they said correctly to avoid misunderstandings later.

You can improve your recall by taking notes during the conversation. If information must be recalled exactly, then the conversation should be recorded if the other person consents.

Additional advice to help you improve your listening skills is available online at **www.businesslistening.com**.

## 3.3.5 Presentation Skills

A presentation involves speaking in front of an audience. Business consultants normally make presentations at both the beginning and end of a project – first to present their proposal to land the consulting contract, then to present their project findings.

Consultants may also speak in front of groups during a consulting project, for example, to explain to a group of employees how to complete a questionnaire. Some consultants also give presentations as a way to market their consulting services and attract new clients.

Credibility is an important factor in determining how successful you are in your presentations. Credibility is an audience's perception of how believable or trustworthy a presenter is. To be credible, a speaker must be seen as someone who is both an expert on the topic and a likeable person. Someone who appears to be a "know it all" is not likely to be seen as likeable by their audience.

As a business consultant you will of course be expected to provide excellent information in your presentations. This can be done visually as well as verbally, and many consultants use software such as Microsoft PowerPoint to illustrate key points of their presentation.

However, to communicate effectively, your presentations must also have excellent delivery (speaking style). Poor delivery can make the most interesting topic sound boring, while excellent delivery can make even a dull topic come alive.

Two things that can help business consultants have excellent delivery when making presentations are naturalness and confidence. Naturalness involves speaking in a conversational manner, with appropriate enthusiasm and vocal variety. Presenters who speak naturally are much more likely to be perceived positively by their audience than presenters who speak in a monotone or as if they are delivering a lecture.

Effective presenters also appear confident. Business consultants may sometimes feel nervous, especially when presenting a proposal to a prospective client, but they don't let it show, and they don't tell the audience they feel nervous.

**Non-Verbal Signs of Confidence**

Ways to convey confidence through your body language include:

- Make eye contact
- Give a firm handshake
- Walk like you know where you're going
- Smile when appropriate
- Maintain a straight but relaxed posture
- Hold your head high
- Make a steepling gesture with your hands
- Look the part by dressing professionally

Confidence is often judged on the basis of non-verbal factors. Speakers look and sound more confident when they make eye contact with the audience, move naturally, use audiovisual equipment effectively, and speak fluently (avoiding too many "uhs" and "ums"). If you are feeling nervous before an important presentation, the key is to act as if you are not nervous.

## How to Improve Your Skills

Start by reading the advice on giving presentations in sections 2.2.6 and 7.5 of this book.

As with any skill, one of the best ways to improve is by just doing it. With public speaking, this means getting yourself in front of as many audiences as possible. One excellent way to do this is by volunteering to present talks on business to community groups. This is discussed in section 7.3.4.

You can also get speaking practice by taking a continuing education course. Many colleges offer courses in public speaking, from intensive two-day seminars to courses held several hours a week over an entire semester. Check the Yellow Pages for local colleges and universities. If you can't find a listing for "continuing education," call the school's main switchboard.

Another way to improve your skills is to join Toastmasters, an international non-profit organization that helps people develop presentation skills. Toastmasters clubs usually meet for an hour per week, and provide the opportunity to practice speaking. To join, attend a meeting at your local chapter and get a membership application. Dues are $36 every six months. Local Toastmaster clubs may also charge small fees to cover their expenses. To find a chapter near you, check the phone book, visit the Toastmasters website at **www.toastmasters.org** or call their headquarters at (949) 858-8255.

While simply practicing speaking in front of audiences can help you become a more confident speaker, you can also use these occasions as an opportunity for feedback. An easy way for audience members to give you feedback is by filling out an evaluation form. You can create a form to ask for general feedback (e.g. What did you find most useful about the presentation? What suggestions do you have for improvement?).

Another option is to ask for feedback on specific aspects of your presentation such as your vocal volume, eye contact with the audience, use of visual aids, clarity of information, use of jargon, or any other areas you want feedback about.

The following sites offer good advice to help with your presentations:

- *Improve Your Presentation Skills*
  (Scroll down to "Presentations and Pitches")
  **www.inc.com/guides/growth/23032.html**

- *Presentation Magazine*
  **www.presentationmagazine.com**

- *117 Ideas for Better Business Presentations*
  **http://tomkirbyseminars.com**

## 3.3.6 Business Writing

As a business consultant you will be presenting ideas in writing on a regular basis. Your proposal will open a project and your final recommendation report will end it. In between, you may write memos, letters, emails, status reports, and other documents. Being able to write well can help you get the job and ensure client satisfaction.

Being an effective business writer does not require a grand literary style like that of a novelist. What it does require is clarity of thought, precise language, and logical flow. Readers must be able to understand what you have written. A few simple guidelines, plenty of practice and someone to critique your writing and give you honest feedback will insure that your written work leaves a positive impression.

- **Begin with an outline:** Jot down your ideas and thoughts before starting to write. Use the format of a draft outline with major headings, subheadings, minor sub headings etc. This will give you time to develop your ideas in a logical way and connect them together. See section 2.2.6 for an example of an outline. At this point you can watch for material that needs visual support.

- **Cover the 5 Ws:** This isn't just for journalists. Communicating who, what, where, when, why, plus how, applies to all writing.
- **Use the active voice:** This means that the noun or subject in your sentence comes before the action. Here's an example: "The contractors were hired by Bill" (passive), which should be written "Bill hired the contractors" (active). Watch for the preposition "by" as a warning of a passive sentence.
- **Keep your sentences short and simple:** Avoid long, run-on sentences. Break your ideas down into smaller parts if you need to.
- **Edit and proofread it:** Few people can write a perfect first draft. If you have time, put your writing aside for a while so you can return later for a fresh look. See if it is clear and rearrange sentences and paragraphs, if you need to, so it flows logically. Also try to eliminate any unnecessary words or concepts. After you have edited it, proofread for spelling and grammar. The spell check on your computer doesn't know that you meant to write manager instead of manger.
- **Get someone else to proofread it:** Many people notice others' mistakes before they notice their own.

These few tips will get you started. To improve your writing skills consider enrolling in a business writing class at a college in your area or check out the following resources to learn more:

- *The Elements of Style, by William Strunk Jr.*
  **www.bartleby.com/141**

- *Paradigm Online Writing Assistant*
  **www.powa.org**

## 3.3.7 Second Languages

The global nature of business consulting makes a second language a distinct advantage. The traditional second languages of the United States and Canada, Spanish and French, will extend your business opportunities inside these countries.

It can also benefit you to have a rudimentary, if not fluent, knowledge of the languages of any of the powerful G8 countries of the world, such as Japanese, Chinese (the two main dialects of which are Cantonese and Mandarin), and German. Plus, now that business consultants are working in nations from Latvia to Madagascar, any language you grew up around can be polished and put to use.

Most colleges offer night courses on language, but there are also a variety of online and home-study language courses. Here are a few examples of the types of resources available for learning a second language:

- *Berlitz*
  **www.berlitz.com**

- *Rosetta Stone*
  **www.rosettastone.com**

- *Language Learning Audiobooks*
  **www.audiobooksonline.com/Language_CDs_audiobooks.html**

- *Word2Word – Links to Free Online Language Courses*
  **www.word2word.com/course.html**

## 3.4 Management Skills

To be an effective business consultant, you must be an effective manager. As discussed in Chapter 2, consultants oversee projects and manage resources including time, money, and people.

### 3.4.1 Project Management

Project management involves the planning and coordination of a project from start to finish. The online encyclopedia *Wikipedia* defines it as follows:

> Project management is the discipline of defining and achieving targets while optimizing (or just allocating) the use of resources (time, money, people, materials, energy, space, etc) over the course of a project (a set of activities of finite duration).

Project management is carried out by someone designated as the *project manager*. In consulting projects, the business consultant assumes this role. Effective project managers ensure projects are completed on time, within budget, and accomplish the goals established at the start of the project. As described in section 2.2.2, in carrying out the project, consultants primarily use the clients' resources, including employees of the client company.

As the project manager, the specific activities you will carry out may include the following:

- Define project objectives and scope
- Identify specific tasks that need to be done
- Create a project timeline
- Establish the budget
- Identify the resources that will be needed
- Assemble the project team
- Acquire other needed resources
- Assign specific tasks to project team members
- Supervise project team members
- Resolve any issues that arise
- Ensure deadlines are met
- Control costs
- Report progress to your client
- Analyze the results
- Prepare and present a final report

There are a number of planning tools that can assist you in this process. On the next page is a worksheet adapted from the *FabJob Guide to Become a Professional Organizer* by Grace Jasmine.

To assist you in keeping track of everything that needs to be done, it's a good idea to create a visual representation of the project in the form of a Gantt chart.

## Gantt Charts

A *Gantt chart* is a type of bar chart that shows tasks as bars, with the beginning and end of the bars corresponding with the beginning and end of the task. Here's a simple example illustrating a small part of a consulting project:

| | | October 2013 | | | | |
|---|---|---|---|---|---|---|
| **Task** | 31 | 1 | 2 | 3 | 4 | 5 |
| **1. Group Interview** | | | | | | |
| Get permission | | | | | | |
| Select participants | | | | | | |
| Book interview room | | | | | | |
| Hold group interview | | | | | | |
| Transcribe notes | | | | | | |

A Gantt chart can help you track the project's progress over time. At a glance you can see which tasks need to be done first, what ones overlap, and what deadlines are coming up, so you can ensure team members are on track and the work is getting done.

Gantt charts are the industry standard for showing project management tasks and timelines. However, there are other methods for keeping track of project tasks, ranging from simple schedules and to-do lists to more complex planning tools, the most common of which are the CPM (Critical Path Method) chart and the PERT (Program Evaluation and Review Technique) chart.

## Project Task Worksheet

### Task Description:

______________________________________________

______________________________________________

### Person(s) to Complete Task:

| Name | Qualifications or training needed? | Hours | Cost |
|---|---|---|---|
| ________ | ________ | ____ | ____ |
| ________ | ________ | ____ | ____ |
| ________ | ________ | ____ | ____ |

### Materials Needed:

| Description | Amount | Cost |
|---|---|---|
| ________________ | ____ | ____ |
| ________________ | ____ | ____ |
| ________________ | ____ | ____ |

### Equipment Needed:

| Description | Amount | Cost |
|---|---|---|
| ________________ | ____ | ____ |
| ________________ | ____ | ____ |
| ________________ | ____ | ____ |

### Facilities Needed:

| Description | Amount | Cost |
|---|---|---|
| ________________ | ____ | ____ |
| ________________ | ____ | ____ |
| ________________ | ____ | ____ |

Start Date: ____________________

End Date: ____________________

Estimated Time to Complete: ____________________

Total Estimated Cost: ____________________

**TIP:** While it's useful to know what PERT charts are, it's unlikely that you will use them for consulting as they are typically used for complex projects involving multiple departments or organizations where it may be difficult to predict how long tasks will take. You can see an example at **www.smartdraw.com/examples/project-charts**.

While you can create a Gantt chart with a program such as Excel, or even by hand, many project managers use project management software.

## Project Management Software

Project managers typically use software to assist in planning and overseeing the project.

The most popular project management software is Microsoft Office Project (MS Project). At the time of publication of this book, MS Project 2010 is the most recent version of the software. Visit **www.microsoft.com** or check out the following links to see which version is currently available:

- *MS Project Product Information*
  (Click on "Free 60-day Trial" under the heading "Product Information")
  **www.microsoft.com/project/en-us/project-management.aspx**

- *MS Project Free Trial & Demos*
  **www.microsoft.com/project/en-us/try-buy.aspx**

While MS Project dominates the project management software market, there are other software products you may want to look into, such as Project KickStart and Intuit's QuickBase. Like MS Project, both offer free trials of their software so you can decide which project planning software, if any, is best for you.

- *Project KickStart*
  **www.projectkickstart.com**

- *QuickBase*
  **http://quickbase.intuit.com/overview/trial/**

## Resources for Learning More

In addition to the resources in section 3.2, there are many online resources for learning project management skills. The following are among the best:

- *Project Management Institute*
  **www.pmi.org**

- *A Short Course in Project Management: MS Project 2007 Step by Step*
  (The current link to this book excerpt appears below. As an alternative, go to the Microsoft Office home page at **http://office.microsoft.com** and search for "a short course in project management." Include the quotation marks.)
  **http://office.microsoft.com/en-us/project/HA102354821033.aspx**

- *PM Boulevard*
  (Click on the "Project Management" tab to find articles on project management. Although you must be a member to access articles, at the time of publication, membership is free.)
  **www.pmboulevard.com**

- *Project Management Planning Tips*
  **www.projectkickstart.com/downloads/tips.cfm**

- *MS Project 2010: Project Management Resources*
  **www.microsoft.com/project/en-us/project-management-resources.aspx**

## 3.4.2 Organization

Organizational skills will help you as a project manager and in your consulting business. If you're not in the habit of using a paper or electronic organizer, now's the time to start. An organizer will help you to remember the numerous meetings and tasks you'll be involved with throughout the day. Your options include:

- A day planner such as a Day-Timer

- Computer software such as the calendar that comes with Microsoft Outlook

- A Personal Digital Assistant (PDA) such as an iPhone or Blackberry

However, it's important to maintain only one calendar. If you use a digital handheld organizer and desktop computer software calendar, be sure that they are synchronized daily. In addition to creating daily to-do lists, some other lists to help you stay organized include:

- **Client List:** This is a list of all your currently active clients.
- **Prospect List:** These are all the people and organizations you are actively courting.
- **Expenses:** What's going out is as important as what is coming in. Keep track of your daily expenses and which client they are for. This helps you stay current with expenses and gives you actual numbers for fine-tuning your next budget.
- **Contact List:** You should have a phone book or electronic organizer with phone numbers, emails and addresses for clients, business associates, suppliers, prospects, and anyone else you may need to contact.
- **Project List:** Keep track of what aspects of the project have been completed and what deliverables are outstanding.

But beware of going overboard with paper lists. According to Grace Jasmine, author of the *FabJob Guide to Become a Professional Organizer,* "Paper can be overwhelming in an office. Not only can disorganized papers be stressful, but in a business environment disorganization can mean missed deadlines, missed appointments and meetings, and poor work quality." Some typical pitfalls are:

- Allowing a "to-be-filed" stack of folders to pile up
- Keeping materials past their need date
- Keeping files "just in case"
- Failing to review and purge on a regular basis
- Filing duplicate materials
- Not communicating filing procedure to all users

To help you organize your paperwork, she offers these tips:

- The arrangement of the files should support the processes of the file users. As appropriate, file alpha-numerically by subject or category, or chronologically by date.
- An information map showing the layout of the files and the logical relationships between the sections should be plainly displayed.
- Use visual helpers, such as color-coded files and well-labeled cabinets. Special-handling files (sensitive, urgent) are clearly identifiable.
- Unnecessary information should not be stored. Active files should be routinely purged and inactive files archived to long-term storage. "To-be filed" stacks are frequently cleared out.
- For large files, break the file down into more manageable sections. A helpful product is the six-section classification folio that is a multi-section file folder with brad-type fasteners to hold documents in place.

## 3.4.3 Time Management

Do you ever feel frustrated because there don't seem to be enough hours in the day to do the things you need to do? Is too much of your time taken up with phone calls, emails, or other matters which are "urgent" but not "important"? Do you frequently find yourself working late to get everything done? If you answered "yes" to any of these questions, you may be able to greatly increase your productivity and reduce your stress with effective time management techniques.

### Keep an Activity Log

The first step in effective time management is to identify what your time is currently being spent on. One way to do this is by using a notebook to keep a log of your activities. For a few days, jot down things you're doing as you do them, and note the time when you change activities. After a few days, you can analyze the log. Chances are you will notice some time-wasters. To get real insight from this activity, make sure you don't change your normal behavior.

If your schedule varies, as it does with most business consultants, you may want to consider keeping a simpler log over a longer period of time. On the next page you'll find a *Time Activity Log* from the *FabJob Guide to Become a Professional Organizer*, by Grace Jasmine. You can use this form to keep track of your major activities in hourly increments throughout the day. Grace Jasmine recommends logging your daily activities for two weeks so you can see variances in your current schedule.

To get the most benefit from this tool, make sure you fill it in throughout the day, and not at the end of the day when it's more difficult to remember all the day's activities. Assuming it's important to you to have balance in your life, in addition to your daily work schedule, you can track personal time for family, relaxation, exercise, etc. At the end of the two weeks you can analyze the log to see where your time is going.

## Tips for Managing Your Time More Effectively

Once you have completed an activity log you should have a sense of what is consuming your time. There are four categories of tasks based on urgency and importance:

- urgent and important
- non-urgent and important
- urgent and non-important
- non-important and non-urgent

While it would be logical to focus first on tasks that are both urgent and important, many people spend a lot of time on tasks that are not important, either because those tasks are urgent or because they are easy. Completing a lot of easy tasks, even if they are not important, can give a sense of accomplishment. Of course, putting off the more difficult tasks that are important but non-urgent, eventually leads to those tasks becoming urgent! So the first tip is to focus on what's important.

The next tip is to focus on results, not being busy. If you have ever had the experience of working hard, but achieving little, it may be due to something known as the Pareto Principle, also known as the 80-20 rule. For most people, 20% of their activities lead to 80% of their results. The other 80% is "busy work" – we're doing something, but getting relatively less (20%) results.

## Time Activity Log

| | SUN | MON | TUE | WED | THU | FRI | SAT |
|---|---|---|---|---|---|---|---|
| **A.M.** | | | | | | | |
| 12:00 | | | | | | | |
| 1:00 | | | | | | | |
| 2:00 | | | | | | | |
| 3:00 | | | | | | | |
| 4:00 | | | | | | | |
| 5:00 | | | | | | | |
| 6:00 | | | | | | | |
| 7:00 | | | | | | | |
| 8:00 | | | | | | | |
| 9:00 | | | | | | | |
| 10:00 | | | | | | | |
| 11:00 | | | | | | | |
| **P.M.** | | | | | | | |
| 12:00 | | | | | | | |
| 1:00 | | | | | | | |
| 2:00 | | | | | | | |
| 3:00 | | | | | | | |
| 4:00 | | | | | | | |
| 5:00 | | | | | | | |
| 6:00 | | | | | | | |
| 7:00 | | | | | | | |
| 8:00 | | | | | | | |
| 9:00 | | | | | | | |
| 10:00 | | | | | | | |
| 11:00 | | | | | | | |

A key for insuring you get results on a daily basis is to set daily goals for yourself. But what if you have dozens of items on your to-do list? Grace Jasmine says the answer is simply to put first things first. Prioritize. Go through the to-do list and mark each item with an A, B, or C:

- "A" things must be done first in chronological order, or are those items that potentially will deliver the greatest benefit.
- "B" things are important to do, but in the larger picture, they are not urgent.
- "C" things can logically happen later or are merely "nice-to-have" instead of "must-have now."

**TIP:** Remember that priorities change over time. The A-B-C markings should be reviewed monthly to see if they still reflect your goals.

Now you can control what happens in your day. You can use the *Time Activity Log* as a weekly planner. Start by filling in the parts of your daily routine that are unavoidable, such as commuting, standing meetings, and scheduled events. Start filling in the blank time with A-list to-do items. When the A-list items are complete, move on to the B-list items, and then eventually take on the C-list tasks. Once you have your own time under control, you will be in a much better position to manage other people.

### 3.4.4 Leadership

Clients hire business consultants to lead their organizations out of unfavourable situations. If you start your own consulting business you will also be leading your own staff.

The common thread among leadership gurus is that a good leader gives others the confidence and motivation to follow. People need to trust you, have confidence in your judgment and be motivated to exceed your expectations. Inspiration is part of leadership, even when you are just inspiring people to do the best job they can.

## Leadership and Consulting

As a consultant, most of your leadership will be short-term. You will be leading project teams to gather information. You will be leading management into solutions, new ideas, and fresh ways of perceiving problems. You will be leading their employees through change.

As an outsider coming in, threatening to some, perceived as "in the pocket of management" by others, you need to display, very quickly, your integrity as a leader. In the first few days that people are forming their opinions of you the small gestures count (even washing and replacing your coffee mug). The impressions you make at this time will pay off for you when you need support.

Some ways to act like a leader right from the start of a project are:

- Greet everyone warmly and respectfully.
- Learn people's names then make an effort to remember them and call people by name.
- Ask the tough questions.
- Pay attention when people are talking.

Throughout the project, there are a number of additional behaviors that can help you lead effectively, including:

- Give clear directions. Few things are as frustrating to employees as getting incomplete or confusing direction.
- Remain calm when the pressure is on.
- Adjust your leadership style depending on the individual or group you are leading. That means knowing when to delegate and empower individuals to make decisions and when to direct. See the resources on the next two pages to help you determine which leadership style to use in different situations.
- Express appreciation to each member of your project team. Acknowledge the performance of team members individually, among that group, and to management as well.

You should also clearly communicate the importance of each person's role. Dr. Ken Blanchard, coauthor of business best-sellers such as *The One Minute Manager*, is a leadership expert as well as one of the world's leading business consultants, with blue chip clients such as General Motors, The Hershey Company, IBM, Ritz-Carlton, and the U.S. Chamber of Commerce. He says:

> "People want to make a difference; they want to know they perform important work. The key to making this happen is sharing information with people so they understand why things are done a certain way and what part their work plays in the overall scheme."

## Developing Your Leadership Skills

While it's true that some people are born leaders, that does not mean you can't learn how to become one.

To help you identify the type of leader you are now, and what areas can use some improvement, you may enjoy an online leadership quiz developed by The Price Group. It is fun to do and assumes you are already leading someone, somewhere. Try it at **www.pricegroupleadership.com/tl_quiz.shtml**.

Stacks of management books have been written on leadership. Browsing these can be worthwhile when you are gaining insight on your own natural tendencies. Most of them will also help you clarify how to expand your leadership strengths and improve on your weaknesses. With so many excellent leadership books to choose from, where do you start reading? Here are several recommended books:

- *First, Break All the Rules: What the World's Greatest Managers Do Differently*, by Marcus Buckingham and Curt Coffman

- *How to Win Friends and Influence People*, by Dale Carnegie

- *The 7 Habits of Highly Effective People*, by Stephen Covey

- *The E-Myth Revisited: Why Most Small Businesses Don't Work and What to Do About It,*
  by Michael E. Gerber
  *(A must-read if you are planning to consult for small businesses)*

In addition to reading, you can take leadership training seminars such as those offered by Dale Carnegie Training (**www.dalecarnegie.com**) or The Ken Blanchard Companies (**www.kenblanchard.com**). Both sites offer some free resources in addition to training programs.

You can see a summary of Ken Blanchard's situational leadership model for changing your leadership style to adapt to the individual you are leading online at **www.12manage.com/methods_blanchard_situational_leadership.html** or do a Google search for "situational leadership."

While resources can certainly help you develop your leadership skills, a key part of being an effective leader is having a strong sense of business ethics.

### Exploring Leadership Styles

Think about the leaders throughout your life that have inspired you: the teachers who motivated you to excel; the athletic coach that inspired you and your team to perform beyond your expectations; the boss you gladly went the extra mile for.

Examine your memory of these people. How did they relate to you? What did they know and understand? How did they handle risk and the unknowns? How did they change when they led different people? Did they encourage you to make decisions? Did they allow you to make mistakes? Did they trust you?

Now think about the people who were flops as leaders. What was wrong with the leaders you resented, didn't trust, or fought all the way? What were the obvious things they were doing wrong? Did you find fear and uncertainty under the surface? Did they micromanage? Were they quick to anger? Did they take credit for your work? What were their relationships like with their staff?

Jot down some of your insights about both good and bad leaders and examine your own style in light of that.

## 3.5 Business Ethics

Twenty years ago, the term *business ethics* was rarely spoken. Today, perhaps more than ever before, companies are keenly aware of the importance of operating ethically and being socially responsible. Executives know that their employees, customers, and shareholders – as well as the media – are watching out for signs that a company may be the next Enron or WorldCom. While consulting for a large organization, one of the staff members you may be working with is the company's *ethics officer*. You may also need to adhere to the company's *code of ethics*.

*The American Heritage Dictionary of the English Language* defines ethics as: "A set of principles of right conduct. The rules or standards governing the conduct of a person or the members of a profession." Or, to put it more simply, ethics are the moral values that guide us when people are not looking. Clients place a great deal of trust in the consultants that they hire. They offer them free reign of their business, entrust them with proprietary information and company secrets.

The importance of ethics has been addressed by organizations such as the Institute of Management Consultants USA. IMC USA requires adherence to a code of ethics as a condition of membership and certification as a CMC (Certified Management Consultant). According to the IMC USA website, the code requires that Certified Management Consultants:

- Safeguard confidential information
- Render impartial, independent advice
- Accept only those client engagements they are qualified to perform
- Agree with the client in advance on the basis for professional charges
- Develop realistic and practical solutions to client problems.

You can find more information about the IMC USA's ethical code, and find links to excellent resources for learning more about business ethics at **www.imcusa.org/?page=ETHICS**. Among other resources, you can read case studies of ethical issues involving business consultants.

## An Expert Recommends Ethics Resources

*Laura de Jonge served as Vice Chair of the Social Responsibility Working Group of the International Petroleum Industry Environmental Conservation Association and currently sits on the Conference Board of Canada's Ethics Management Council. We asked her what business ethics resources she would recommend to someone who wants to get started in a career in business consulting. Here's what she told us:*

"A really good free weekly newsletter is published by the Institute for Global Ethics which can be found online at **www.globalethics.org**. You can sign up on the home page and find copies of past newsletters which provide ongoing information on current happenings. A free newsletter is also offered by the Ethics Resource Center at **www.ethics.org**.

Most universities, Chambers of Commerce and other business groups offer sessions or workshops from time to time. Chambers are more likely to bring in a business leader to speak on the topic. Also, there may be a local network of practitioners that you can get linked into by showing up at an event like this and chatting with others to find out more.

I think if someone is going to be a business consultant they should also be informing themselves on CSR (corporate social responsibility) and/or sustainability as risk mitigation tools for business particularly if the consultant will be dealing with the senior leadership of a company or the company is in a sector that has high impacts (i.e. energy, manufacturing).

Business for Social Responsibility was my greatest resource when I first started in my role and you can find some excellent free issue briefs on a lot of CSR topics including ethics at **www.bsr.org/en/our-insights/research**. The information that BSR provides was fantastic for me in developing my own practice, implementing programs and being able to develop my own briefings for our management and operations people who may not be as familiar with some of the issues. Spending some time on that website would give a business consultant a general understanding of ethics and CSR."

While it's important to have a personal and professional code of ethics, it's also important for clients to see you as ethical. You need to clarify your own code of ethics for yourself, make it clear to clients, and let them see it for themselves.

Here are some ways to assure clients of your ethics:

- If you are a member of an organization with a professional code of ethics (a list of consulting organizations is included in the Resources section at the end of this book), tell clients about the code of ethics that you adhere to.
- If you have experience with other jobs or projects in which you were responsible for large budgets and proprietary information, let the client know – but only if you can do so without disclosing any confidential information.
- Provide your client or potential client with references. Nothing says you maintain a strong code of ethics as convincingly as a personal and professional recommendation from someone who entrusted you with their company's money and corporate secrets.
- Let clients see your ethics in action. Don't talk about other clients. Don't divulge confidential information. Don't take particularly sensitive material out of their office. Do be meticulous about your time and expenses. All this communicates you have integrity and can be trusted.

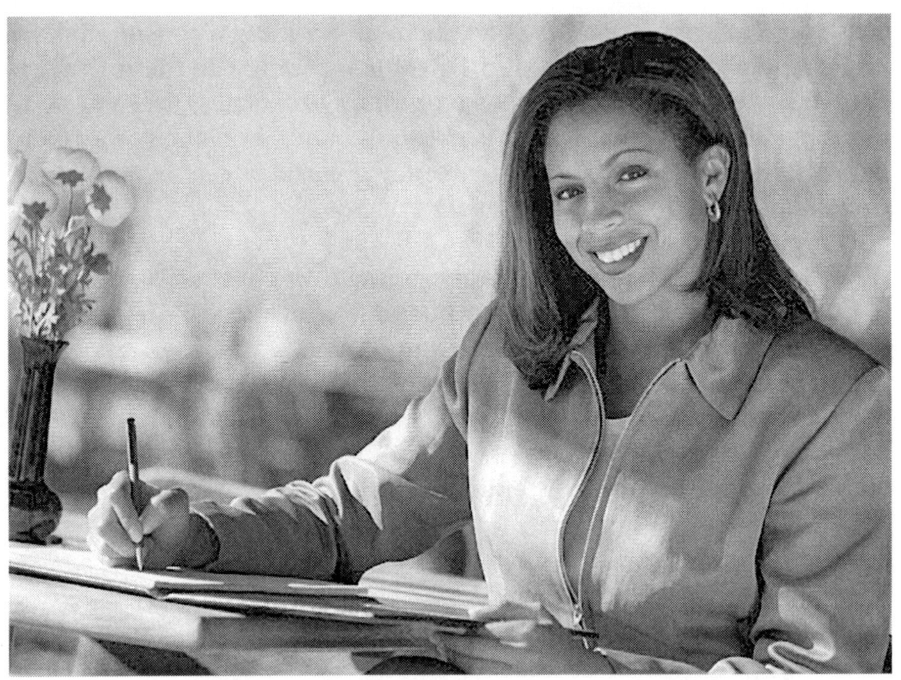

# 4. Ways to Learn Business Consulting

Unlike professions such as accounting or engineering, there are no specific educational requirements to become a business consultant. According to a recent U.S. Bureau of Labor Statistics report on "Management, Scientific, and Technical Consulting Services," 28% of consultants do not have a degree of any kind.

However, that certainly doesn't mean that it's easy for someone with no credentials to become a successful business consultant. Those who are most likely to succeed in business consulting usually have either a formal business education or a wealth of business experience.

It might be said that the growth and focus on MBA programs over the last 20 years has categorized the global consultant base into those with a MBA and those without. Generally, if you want to get hired by a large consulting firm, you'll need a business degree, preferably a Master's of Business Administration (MBA).

If you want to start your own consulting business, educational credentials can certainly be useful, however, they are not essential. That's because many clients are more concerned with finding a consultant who has real world experience solving problems similar to theirs. For example, if the client company has a problem with sales, they will look for a consultant who has a sales background and has helped other companies with their sales. These clients may not ask, or care, whether that consultant has a degree.

What an MBA does for one's business consulting career is offer a potential firm or client proof of your business education. It's a guarantee that you have had exposure to current business practices, ideologies and methodologies. In essence, it's a personal marketing tool. However, there are many successful business consultants who do not have MBAs. For example, Martin Wilkins of PVA Consulting (**www.pva.ca**), has a business degree but did not pursue an MBA. He says:

> *"I don't believe that education makes a good consultant. Someone with natural ability, confidence and people skills that doesn't have an MBA will go further than a MBA without these skills."*
>
> — Martin Wilkins
> PVA Consulting

Those without an MBA must market themselves in a way that shows: "I've got experience or skills that equal or surpass the MBA designation." In the end, getting the job or the client becomes a matter of them trusting in your ability to perform and succeed at the required tasks for the projects.

Whether or not you wish to pursue an MBA, this chapter will provide you with a wide variety of options for learning business consulting. The chapter includes many helpful resources, whether your goal is to develop your knowledge or add to your credentials. It covers:

- **Educational programs:** In addition to information about traditional MBA programs, this section covers options for busy working people to get educational credentials more quickly or conveniently through accelerated, part-time, and executive MBAs, online degrees, and business seminars.
- **Self-study:** This section provides information about books, periodicals, and websites that can help you get a business education. Through self-study you can quickly brush up on a particular subject or stay on top of current business practices.

- **Learning by doing:** For those who do not have much hands-on business experience, this section explains how to get experience and learn about business through activities such as internships, information interviews, and volunteer work.

# 4.1 Degree Programs

Hundreds of colleges and universities offer business degrees at the Bachelor's and Master's level. Because of the popularity of business programs (and no doubt their importance to our society in developing future business leaders), a number of top publications, such as *U.S. News & World Report, The Wall Street Journal, Forbes*, and *Business Week*, have produced guides to what they judge to be the "best" business schools. In addition, there are numerous books and websites offering information and advice on business programs.

With so many thousands of pages of resources about whether a business education is right for you and, if so, which particular programs will suit you best, it can be overwhelming to try to review all the available information. In this section we hope to make your information-gathering easier by introducing you to various options for obtaining a business degree, and pointing you in the right direction for learning more.

## 4.1.1 Undergraduate Programs

Although a degree is not necessary for self-employed business consultants, those who want to get hired by a consulting firm need at least an undergraduate degree. According to *The Princeton Review* (**www.princeton review.com**):

> "Employers generally prefer candidates who majored in one of the following areas: business, economics, statistics, mathematics, computer science, and logic. An Ivy League education is a distinct plus..."

When looking for a business degree program, one consideration is whether the school is accredited. Accreditation can ensure that a school meets a particular standard of educational quality. Princeton University's Wordnet defines accreditation as "the act of granting credit or recognition (especially with respect to educational institution that maintains suitable standards)."

The premier accrediting agency for business degree programs is the Association to Advance Collegiate Schools of Business (AACSB). As of July, 2012, 655 institutions in 44 countries hold AACSB business accreditation. You can find AACSB accredited schools listed by name or country and state or province at **www.aacsb.edu/accreditation/accredited members.asp**.

However, some good business programs are not AACSB accredited. In an article titled "Business school accreditation: pros and cons," David Williams writes, "the fact that a business school is unaccredited... does not mean that the quality of its education is deficient." That's because accreditation can be expensive and time-consuming.

You can find a comprehensive list of all business schools, including those that are unaccredited, at Peterson's. Visit **www.petersons.com/college-search.aspx** to search for undergraduate programs. If you're in a position where you can choose to pursue a business degree at any school of your choice you can find lists of the top U.S. business schools, as determined by *Business Week*, *Forbes*, *The Wall Street Journal*, and *U.S. News and World Report*, at **www.bschool.com/library/the-top-mba-programs-links-to-authoritative-mba-ranking-results**.

### 4.1.2 MBA Programs

While a bachelor's degree may help you get an entry level position with a consulting firm, for most management consulting jobs, the best degree you can have is an MBA (Master's of Business Administration). As *The Princeton Review* says, "many employers look extremely favorably on MBAs, which are necessary requirements for upward mobility in this profession."

According to the Graduate Management Admission Council:

> "Although no two business schools offer the same curriculum, all MBA programs expose students to a common body of knowledge in basic accounting, economics, finance, human resources and organization design, marketing, operations, policy, and quantitative methods and statistics."

Following are your options for pursuing an MBA:

## Traditional MBA

Until recently, the only way to obtain an MBA from most educational institutions was through two years of full-time study. Traditional MBA programs are still available, but they have been joined by a variety of other options for obtaining an MBA which are described below.

## Accelerated MBA

Accelerated MBA programs enable you to get an MBA more quickly and less expensively than through a traditional MBA program. Most accelerated MBAs are intense 12 month programs that run year-round, beginning in the summer, although some run over an 18 month period. In order to complete an MBA program so quickly you should expect to devote yourself full-time to it. Because these programs don't cover business basics, but more advanced subjects, they are best for individuals with a combination of undergraduate business education and some work experience.

## Part-Time MBA

If you want to continue working while pursuing your MBA, consider a part-time program. Classes for part-time MBA students are usually held on evenings or weekends. Some schools refer to their programs as "Weekend MBA Programs." These programs are typically completed in three years, although schools may allow students to take more or less time to complete the program (e.g. two to seven years). Some part-time programs have a curriculum that is identical to full-time programs offered by the same educational institution (in other words, both programs cover the same material), while other part-time programs may offer fewer courses than their full-time counterparts.

## Executive MBA

An executive MBA (EMBA) program is ideal for you if you are a mid- to senior-level manager or entrepreneur who wants to develop your leadership and senior management skills. To be accepted into an EMBA program you will need to show that you have a particular number of years of work experience. Exact requirements vary from school to school but typically range from four to 10 years of professional experience, with current employment in a management position.

Because EMBA students work full-time, classes are usually held on weekends (or Fridays and Saturdays), although some educational institutions offer evening courses as well. EMBA programs vary in length, but typically are completed in two years. You can find information about EMBA programs which Bloomberg Business Week compiles every year at **www.businessweek.com/bschools/rankings** (click on the "EMBA" tab). The top ranked EMBA program in 2012 was the University of Chicago's Booth School of Business Executive MBA Program which you can read about at **www.chicagobooth.edu/execmba**.

### Mini MBA

Despite the "MBA" in the title, mini MBA programs do not offer an MBA degree. Instead, these short intense business education programs are either non-credit or offer a certificate upon completion. An example is the Robins School of Business (**http://robins.richmond.edu**) at the University of Richmond in Virginia, which describes their program as follows:

> The Mini MBA®, a non-credit program, provides a practical foundation in current business theory and practices in an intensive, 14-week format. Through case studies, lecture, problem-solving exercises and interactive class sessions, you will obtain the knowledge you need to succeed within your organization.

Other mini MBA programs may range from one week to several months, with longer programs requiring as little as one evening class per week.

## Distance Learning

If you want a flexible program that allows you to earn an MBA from a school in another city while you keep your current job, a distance learning program may be right for you. Most programs deliver information online, allowing you to work from home. Some allow you to completely determine your own schedule, while others give you the opportunity to interact live online with other students and faculty.

While some distance learning MBA programs cost less than $10,000 to complete – considerably less expensive than earning a traditional MBA – prices range up to more than $100,000 for MBA programs at top schools.

Relatively few schools currently offer distance learning, but their numbers are growing each year. Look for programs that are offered through a recognized educational institution or are certified by the Distance Education and Training Council or by your department of education.

A list of more than 100 programs, plus advice on choosing the best program for you is offered in the book *Bears' Guide to the Best MBAs by Distance Learning*, by John B. Bear and Mariah P. Bear. Degree.net also offers good free advice on choosing an MBA program at **www.degree.net/resources/degree-level/mba-degree-guide_201002182375.html**. Another good resource is **www.GetEducated.com** which has a list of top ranked best buys in accredited online MBA programs.

## Finding MBA Programs

In addition to the resources listed above, you can find MBA programs through the following which offer free searchable databases:

- *Petersons.com*
  **www.petersons.com/mba**

- *SchoolFinder - Canadian MBA and Business Schools*
  **www.schoolfinder.com/schools/schoolindex.asp?CountryCode=CA&ProfileType=MBA**

- *USnews.com Business School Directory 2013*
  Go to **www.usnews.com** and click on "Best Graduate Schools" under "Education" to start your search or go directly to: **http://grad-schools.usnews.rankingsandreviews.com/best-graduate-schools/top-business-schools**

- *Canadian MBA Schools and Programs*
  **www.canadian-universities.net/MBA**

The U.S. News site includes a lot of useful free information including links to the top 50 MBA programs and an online directory of 426 MBA programs. More detailed information about the programs, including admission requirements, deadlines, and financial aid can be found in U.S. News Business School Guidebook and Compass Access available for $34.95. Go to **www.usnews.com** and click on "Best Graduate Schools" under the heading "Education."

Another source of information about MBA programs, including rankings of MBA programs and links to websites of 372 business schools and MBA programs around the world can be found at **www.foreignmba.com/schools**.

## Getting into an MBA Program

When deciding which applicants to accept into an MBA program, schools consider a variety of factors:

- Academic transcript of your courses, grades, and degrees
- Work experience
- Recommendations
- Essays
- Score on the Graduate Management Admission Test (GMAT)
- Interview (in person or by telephone)

You can find the admission requirements for a particular MBA program at the school's website. While an undergraduate business degree may be helpful, it is not a requirement. Even Harvard Business School advertises in their admission criteria at **www.hbs.edu/mba/admissions/admission criteria.html**:

> "There is no particular previous course of study required to apply; you must, however, demonstrate the ability to master analytical and quantitative concepts."

## Top MBA Programs

According to U.S. News & World Report, the top 10 MBA programs in the United States for 2012 are as follows:

1. *Harvard University (tie)*
   Harvard Business School
   Boston, MA
   **www.hbs.edu/mba**

1. *Stanford University (tie)*
   Graduate School of Business
   Stanford, CA
   **www.gsb.stanford.edu**

3. *University of Pennsylvania*
   The Wharton School
   Philadelphia, PA
   **www.wharton.upenn.edu/mba**

4. *Massachusetts Institute of Technology (tie)*
   Sloan School of Management
   Cambridge, MA
   **http://mitsloan.mit.edu/mba**

4. *Northwestern University (tie)*
   Kellogg School of Management
   Evanston, IL
   **www.kellogg.northwestern.edu**

4. *University of Chicago (tie)*
   Booth School of Business
   Chicago, IL
   **www.chicagobooth.edu**

7. *University of California Berkeley*
   Haas School of Business
   Berkeley, CA
   **www.haas.berkeley.edu**

8. *Columbia University*
   Columbia Business School
   New York, NY
   **www4.gsb.columbia.edu/mba**

9. *Dartmouth College*
   Tuck School of Business
   Hanover, NH
   **www.tuck.dartmouth.edu/mba**

10. *Yale University*
    School of Management
    Harford, CT
    **www.mba.yale.edu**

The rest of the U.S. News & World Report list of top 50 MBA programs can be found by going to **www.usnews.com** and clicking on "Education" then "Best Graduate Schools." Different MBA programs rate highly in other rankings. For example, you can find a chart of 26 top Executive MBA programs in the U.S. at **http://online.wsj.com/public/resources/documents/st_EMBARank_20080929.html** that allows you to see how each school is ranked according to a wide variety of different categories (faculty quality, corporate ranking, cost, etc.).

For a list of top MBA programs based on rankings from Business Week, US News & World Report, Wall Street Journal, Financial Times, Economist Intelligence Unit, America Economia, and Asia Week visit **www.foreignmba.com/schools**.

## Top International Programs

The following MBA programs are among those recognized as leading programs in Canada and around the world.

A number of international schools have campuses or offer classes in other countries. For example, IESE offers its programs in Silicon Valley, California and China as well as Spain while the Richard Ivey School of Business has campuses in the Toronto area and Hong Kong.

You can find other top international MBA programs at **www.b-school-net.de/topmba.htm**.

- *University of Toronto*
  Rotman School of Management
  Toronto, Ontario Canada
  **www.rotman.utoronto.ca**
- *University of Western Ontario*
  Richard Ivey School of Business
  London, Ontario, Canada
  **www.ivey.uwo.ca**
- *IESE Business School*
  Barcelona, Spain
  **www.iese.edu**
- *INSEAD*
  Fontainebleau, France
  **www.insead.fr**
- *IMD (International Institute for Management Development)*
  Lausanne, Switzerland
  **www.imd.ch**
- *London Business School*
  London, U.K.
  **www.london.edu**
- *Melbourne Business School*
  Melbourne, Australia
  **www.mbs.edu**
- *University of Oxford*
  Saïd Business School
  Oxford, U.K.
  **www.sbs.ox.ac.uk**

Before applying to an MBA program in the United States or Canada, you will need to take the Graduate Management Admission Test (GMAT). Many international schools also require applicants to take the GMAT. The GMAT measures verbal, quantitative (mathematical) and analytical writing skills. You can find information about the GMAT test and how to register through the Graduate Management Admission Council (GMAC) website at **www.gmac.com**.

**TIP:** Submit your application to an MBA program as soon as possible. A business school may begin accepting applications in October for an MBA program which starts the following September.

The following online resources offer excellent advice to help you successfully apply to an MBA program.

- *MBA.com – Apply to Schools*
  Advice from the Graduate Management Admission Council.
  **www.mba.com/schools-and-programs/apply-to-schools.aspx**

- *Princeton Review – Business School*
  Offers advice on topics such as writing application essays, the GMAT, and more.
  **www.princetonreview.com/business-school.aspx**

- *Bloomberg Business Week – Business Schools*
  **www.businessweek.com/business-schools**

## 4.2 Business Courses and Seminars

Courses and seminars are another way to build your business knowledge, add to your credentials, and improve your skills in areas such as writing and project management. Literally hundreds of colleges, universities, associations, and training companies offer programs ranging in length from one day to one evening a week over several months.

These not only provide information for those looking to enter business consulting, but many practising consultants consider taking regular courses a necessity. They help to keep them informed on the latest trends, tools and strategies.

### 4.2.1 Colleges and Universities

One of the first places to look for local business seminars and courses is through educational institutions such as colleges and universities. From Ivy League universities such as Harvard and Columbia, to local community colleges, virtually every institution of higher learning offers programs through their business school. Most also offer programs through a continuing education department (which may be called adult education, continuing studies, extension, or further education).

For example, one of the authors of this book is a part-time instructor in the Business and Professional Programs at the University of Calgary. Among the courses offered in those programs are: Business Finance, Business Law, Business Management, Business Strategy, and dozens of others. These 40 hour courses are spread out over 13 weeks (3 hours per week). For those who want to quickly add a completed course to their credentials, there are one and two-day seminars on topics ranging from "Financial Analysis and Planning for Non-Financial Managers" to "Project Management: The Fundamentals."

Phone or visit websites of business schools and continuing education departments at local colleges and universities to see what they offer.

### 4.2.2 Seminar Companies

National and local seminar companies offer seminars from one to several days. Following are some national companies that offer seminars on many of the subjects covered in this book, such as project management, strategic planning, leadership, finance, communication, time management, business writing, and more. Prices vary widely, and you might spend $199 for a one-day Career-Track seminar or $2,195 for a three-day American Management Association seminar. Visit their websites for a complete list of seminars, locations, and prices.

- *American Management Association*
  AMA is highly respected as a leader in business training. AMA offers 120 two-day to four-day seminars in more than 40 cities, as well as conferences, books, and self-study courses
  **www.amanet.org/seminars**

- *AMA Worldwide*
  Visit this webpage to find links to AMA affiliates in 14 countries from Australia and Canada to China and Turkey.
  **www.amanet.org/aboutama/worldwide.htm**

- *Career Track and Fred Pryor Seminars*
  **www.pryor.com**

- *Lorman Education Services*
  **www.lorman.com**

- *National Seminars Group and Padgett-Thompson*
  **www.nationalseminarstraining.com**

- *Skillpath Seminars*
  **www.skillpath.com**

### 4.2.3 Other Learning Opportunities

Most cities have a variety of opportunities to learn from business speakers and seminar presenters at breakfast meetings, luncheons, and presentations held during or after working hours. These events have the added benefit of providing an ideal setting for networking. Groups that offer such programs include:

- Alumni Associations
- Business Clubs
- Chambers of Commerce
- Civic Groups
- Corporations
- Government Agencies
- Industry Associations
- Networking Groups
- Professional Associations
- Service Clubs

To find out about upcoming events, read your local business publications and check with your city's Chamber of Commerce. You can search for U.S. Chambers of Commerce at **www.chamberofcommerce.com**.

Also look into events organized by consulting associations. For instance, the Institute of Management Consultants USA offers national conferences and local events such as workshops through its 25 chapters. In addition, IMC USA says on its website that it offers its members:

> ...skill and knowledge building teleseminars, electronic courses and classroom seminars produced and presented by credible universities, consultants, trainers, member consultants, associations, IMC USA developers, chapters and member institutes of ICMCI.

You can learn about IMC USA at **www.imcusa.org**. A list of other professional associations for consultants can be found in section 8.3.

**The Million Dollar Consulting™ College**

For those who want to quickly establish, operate, and grow a consulting practice, The Million Dollar Consulting™ College offers over 35 hours of intensive, interactive class work, followed by six months of individual coaching by Alan Weiss, Ph.D. of Summit Consulting. Tuition is $14,500 with discounts available for members of IMC and the Society for Advancement of Consulting. For information about the college visit **www.summitconsulting.com/consulting-college/consulting_college_2012-12.php**. Alan Weiss also offers mentoring programs with fees starting at $3,500. For details visit **www.summitconsulting.com/mentor.html**.

## 4.3 Learning By Reading

Reading relevant material about business consulting is one of the most effective and accessible ways to build your knowledge about business and stay current with the latest trends. Keeping pace with the latest literature will help you develop the vocabulary used in the business, as well as gain an understanding of how other consultants and clients are approaching business problems. Here is a list of books, periodicals, and websites that provide information of interest to business consultants.

### 4.3.1 Books

#### MBA Knowledge

A number of excellent business books are referred to throughout this guide. However, if you are looking for a single book that can help you acquire as much MBA level knowledge as quickly as possible, here are some possibilities.

- *MBA in a Nutshell,*
  by Milo Sobel
- *Complete Idiot's Guide to MBA Basics,*
  by Tom Gorman
- *The Complete MBA for Dummies,*
  by Kathleen Allen and Peter Economy
- *The Fast Forward MBA in Business,*
  by Virginia O'Brien
- *The Ten Day MBA: A Step-by-Step Guide to Mastering the Skills Taught in America's Top Business Schools,*
  by Steven Silbiger
- *MBA In A Day: What You Would Learn At Top-Tier Business Schools (If You Only Had The Time!),*
  by Steven Stralser
- *The Portable MBA,*
  by Robert F. Bruner, et al.
- *What the Best MBAs Know,*
  by Peter Navarro

## Current Business Bestsellers

To keep on top of new trends, it's a good idea to browse the business bestsellers on Amazon.com on a regular basis. Chances are that clients will ask for your advice when they hear about a new management system or technique for improving the bottom line.

For example, if you had been working as a business consultant in the mid to late 2000s, you would have been expected to know about Six Sigma. The July 24, 2006 issue of *Fortune Magazine* described what happened when General Electric CEO Jack Welch devoted a chapter of his book *Winning* to Six Sigma (a set of methods GE used for improving quality and reducing costs). "More than a quarter of the Fortune 200 followed suit," reports the magazine. However, since then, more than 90% of those companies have fallen behind the S&P 500 Index for stock performance.

You can read about Six Sigma and other existing business methods in the books and websites listed in this section. However, new concepts are introduced to the business world all the time, often through best-selling books. As the "business expert," your clients will expect you to know about what's hot, and whether it's something they could use in their company.

When the first edition of this guide was written, the #1 business book on Amazon was *The Long Tail: Why The Future of Business is Selling Less of More,* a book about niche marketing by *Wired Magazine* editor Chris Anderson. At the time of publication of the current edition of this FabJob guide, the #1 business bestseller was *Unintended Consequences: Why Everything You've Been Told About the Economy Is Wrong*, by Edward Conard. By the time you read this, there will very likely be a different business bestseller with a different hot concept that clients will be asking about.

**Other Subjects**

In addition to business books, consultants should read a variety of books on other subjects says business consultant, speaker, and author Nido Qubein, whose client list is "a 'who's who' of blue chip corporations," according to *Money* magazine. In an interview for this book, he suggested that consultants "read books beyond our field, such as books on reason, philosophy, positioning, branding, problem solving and decision making." This can provide consultants with innovative approaches to their work and help them pick up on trends. "For $20 or $30 if you pick up one idea [from a book] it's worth it," says Qubein.

## 4.3.2 Periodicals

The following periodicals are some of the most relied upon in business for their up-to-the minute information and in-depth coverage. Although business magazines and newspapers are not consulting focused, the broad spectrum of business-related topics they offer makes the information important to anyone in any business.

**TIP:** Some of these publications are pricey. For example, the cover price for an annual subscription to Harvard Business Review is over $100. Look for sample articles and subscription discounts online. Also consider purchasing single issues on newsstands or reading them at your local public library.

## Publications for Consultants

Many of the following publications for consultants offer at least one free sample issue.

- *Kennedy Consulting Research & Advisory Wire*
  **http://bit.ly/LK9CKK**

- *Consulting Magazine*
  **www.consultingmag.com**

- *Consulting Times (U.K.)*
  **www.consulting-times.com**

- *Top-Consultant.com Management Consultants' Newsletter*
  **http://news.top-consultant.com/weekly_newsletter_signup.aspx**

### Case Studies and Articles by Consultants

- *Bain and Company Publications*
  **www.bain.com/bainweb/publications**

- *The Boston Consulting Group Publications*
  **www.bcg.com/publications**

- *Harvard Business School Cases*
  See section 2.3.2 of this book for ordering information.
  **http://hbsp.harvard.edu**

- *McKinsey Quarterly*
  **www.mckinseyquarterly.com**

## How to Identify Business Trends

There are good reasons for you to know about business trends. Clients will expect you to advise them about trends that may affect their businesses. Keeping on top of the latest trends can also be helpful in your own consulting business.

For example, you know that a dominant trend in recent years has been the increasing globalization of the economy. With a diverse range of North American companies venturing into emerging markets, this has resulted in opportunities for consultants in a wide variety of industries. The McKinsey Global Institute's Emerging Global Labor Market Report reported on this trend as early as 2005, which you can read about at **www.mckinsey.com/Insights/MGI/Research/Labor_Markets/The_emerging_global_labor_market_demand_for_offshore_talent**.

To keep on top of emerging trends, read as much as possible. This section of this guide has a list of business magazines and websites that can help you identify new business issues, technological developments, consumer demands, and other trends. You can also get some good tips at trendwatching.com which has "Top 15 Trend Questions (and Answers)" at **www.trendwatching.com/trends/top15questions**. For small business trends see **www.smallbiztrends.com** and the article "Five Ways to Spot Business Trends" at **www.smallbiztrends.com/2006/02/five-ways-to-spot-business-trends.html**.

In addition, watch for predictions from Faith Popcorn, who is considered by publications such as *Fortune* and the *New York Times* to be America's foremost trend expert. In her best-selling books, including *The Popcorn Report*, she has offered advice on how to recognize and generate profits from emerging consumer and economic trends. Among many other trends, she predicted the demand for four-wheel drives and was the first to anticipate the explosive growth in home delivery, home businesses and home shopping (the Cocooning™ trend).

In January 2012, Faith Popcorn offered her predictions for the coming year. Following are some of the trends identified for the year described as "The SHE CHANGE." Faith Popcorn predicts that 2012 will bring a "pervasive revolution" where characteristics usually associated with women will become more desired in the business world:

> "The SHE-CHANGE is exactly what society needs right now. We need to rely on compassion more than competition and innovation more than invasion. The introduction of this new feminine power into all aspects of our lives will bring about a new era of productivity and peace."

The full predictions are available at **www.faithpopcorn.com/ContentFiles/PDF/FPBR%20Predictions%202012.pdf**. If you're reading this after 2012, you can see how accurate her predictions were. To find current predictions do a Google search for "Faith Popcorn's Predictions " plus the year (e.g. "Faith Popcorn's Predictions 2013").

## The SHE CHANGE

### 1. Very Young Women Are Leading the Way

Young women are working, making and spending money, and they're well educated. What to look for: Young women purchasing homes, earning more, getting more accolades. By the end of the decade there will be more businesses started by women than men. What it means: Women are key to economic growth and recovery.

### 2. The Nuclear Family 2.0

Marriage is losing its status as a mandatory life goal and more women and couples are having children outside of marriage. Also, more men are taking on childcare roles. What to look for: Alternative, non-traditional forms of birthing, marriage, childrearing and family structuring will become commonplace. What it means: There will be a rise in services that provide flexibility to all different family structures, such as 'co-parenting' (coparent.co.uk, WeCanParentTogether.com) and day and night care centers.

### 3. The New Chivalry

There's no longer any such thing as "the weaker sex". While men and women have different strengths and weaknesses women's strengths are becoming more viable. Women are protecting and looking after themselves while at the same time men are confronting some negative side effects of adjusting to this transformation. What to look for: Increase in depression and lack of performance among those males having trouble adjusting to profound social changes. Employers will be looking for men to show more 'feminine' traits. What it means: It will be up to women to teach men how to survive and thrive in a society that puts more value on feminine characteristics. Men will need education, support systems and counseling to help deal with what will be perceived as "unchecked masculinity" and develop their emotional intelligence.

**4. Women Are Closing the Gap in the Economy**

Women are seen as secure and patient investors, traits that have become more desirable in the current economy. Companies with women on the board are more profitable, and investors will be less likely to invest in companies that do not have any women in decision-making positions. What to look for: Behaviors seen as "traditionally female" will become preferred in business situations. Companies will value employees of both genders who demonstrate conscientiousness over aggressive decision-making. What it means: Employers will be looking for emotional intelligence in employees. Expect personality tests and newly emerging positions like "Chief Consciousness Officer".

**5. Women From the East are Setting the Example**

Asian women are finding their natural skills as transformative leaders crucial to the development of their respective countries. Because of this, companies in Asia are doing everything to retain their female talent. What to look for: Once other countries around the world see the benefits of incorporating women into business, they will begin to follow the same models for seeking out and retaining women. What this means: The influx of qualified female managers is and will be one of the most important changes going on in global business for the next decade. Companies who leverage this to their advantage will see massive rewards.

SOURCE: Faith Popcorn's BrainReserve

## Business Magazines and Newspapers

Below is a list of magazines and newspapers that provide current information to many business leaders and business consultants.

- *Business 2.0*
  **http://money.cnn.com/magazines/business2/**

- *Bloomberg Business Week*
  **www.businessweek.com**

- *The Economist*
  **www.economist.com**

- *Harvard Business Review*
  **www.hbr.org**

- *Fast Company*
  **www.fastcompany.com**

- *Forbes*
  **www.forbes.com**

- *Fortune Magazine*
  **http://money.cnn.com/magazines/fortune/**

- *The Wall Street Journal*
  **http://online.wsj.com/public/us**

## 4.3.3 Websites

In addition to the numerous websites listed throughout this chapter, the following sites offer comprehensive information on many aspects of business that consultants should know about. At the following sites you may discover everything from information about strategic planning to problem-solving techniques.

- *NetMBA Business Knowledge Center*
  **www.netmba.com**

- *QuickMBA*
  **www.quickmba.com**

- *MBA Toolbox*
  **www.mbatoolbox.org**

- *Management Portal*
  **www.themanager.org**

## 4.4 Learning by Doing

Most people who are attracted to a career in business consulting already have a wealth of hands-on experience in the business world. They may have invested years working "in the trenches," learning how businesses operate, and moving up the ladder to progressively more senior positions. They have seen firsthand what works, and what doesn't, in different business situations and want to share their experience and knowledge as a consultant to other businesses.

If you are bringing years of business experience to this career, and plan to work with companies facing challenges similar to those you have encountered in the past, you have already "learned by doing" and the information in this section is less likely to help you increase your already vast hands-on knowledge.

> **TIP:** Even if you have years of business experience, check out the information in this section on volunteering for non-profit organizations if you are looking to branch into new areas of consulting or if you're looking for opportunities to expand your network of contacts.

Those who are most likely to benefit from the advice in this section are college students without a tremendous amount of business experience who are hoping to find an entry-level consulting position. According to the Bureau of Labor Statistics:

> "Employment of management analysts is expected to grow 22 percent from 2010 to 2020, faster than that average for all occupations. Demand for consulting services is expected to grow as organizations seek ways to improve efficiency and control costs… Jobseekers may face strong competition for management analyst positions because the

high earning potential in this occupation makes it attractive to many jobseekers. Job opportunities are expected to be best for those who have a graduate degree or a certification, specialized expertise, and a talent for salesmanship and public relations."

Because consulting is such a competitive career to get into, having some hands-on business and consulting experience could give you the edge over other applicants. So here are some ideas to help you build your experience and knowledge.

## 4.4.1 Volunteer Experience

### Friends and Family

One way to get hands-on consulting experience is to offer your services free of charge to friends and family members who own businesses. For example, if your mother is looking at expanding her business into a new market or introducing a new product line, you could conduct research using techniques described earlier, such as reviewing case studies, then prepare a report on your findings.

When a friend or family member wants to use your business consulting services, try to treat them the way you would treat a "real" client. Schedule a meeting at their place and go through every stage of the consulting process (sections 2.2 and 2.3 explain how to do each of the following):

- Conduct a needs analysis
- Determine the project scope, deadline, team, and budget
- Gather information through techniques such as observation, case studies, interviews and surveys
- Do a gap analysis
- Identify possible solutions
- Present your recommendations
- Conduct a post-project review

A key part of the post-project review is getting feedback. Every time you do business consulting for someone – even a friend or a family member with a different last name from yours – ask for a letter of recommendation on letterhead. Advice on getting outstanding testimonials and recommendation letters is covered in section 2.2.8 .

To avoid misunderstandings, it's also a good idea to prepare a simple contract even if you're working with family members. (Let them know you need the practice.) See section 6.3 for a sample contract.

## Non-Profit Organizations

You can get practical experience in areas involved in managing an organization by volunteering your services to local non-profit organizations and community associations. You'll get the benefit of helping a worthy cause while you hone your skills, plus volunteering can be an excellent way to make contacts which could lead to future employment opportunities.

Assuming your goal is to get business experience, you should leave non-business tasks (such as walking dogs for the humane society or making decorations for parties) to other volunteers. Instead, volunteer to serve on committees involving marketing, fund-raising, operations, or other areas that you want to learn about. Depending on the organization, you may even have an opportunity to serve on its board of directors, which can expose you to all facets of an organization's operations, from human resources to finances to strategic planning. You don't have to be a board member for a large organization. You could even sit on the board of the local little league team. The purpose of being a board member is to gain valuable experience and contacts.

> **TIP:** Before accepting a board of directors position, conduct research and talk with an attorney if needed in order to be fully informed about whether you could be personally liable for board decisions.

Another option may be to offer your services as a business consultant on a *pro bono* basis (i.e. free of charge). The best approach to offering your services is to try to arrange a meeting with the executive director of the organization. You would gather information about the organization's needs and present a proposal to provide business consulting services. If this can't be arranged, call and get your message to the most senior people you can. Ask them what's the best way for you to send the proposal.

In some cases, volunteer organizations seek out the help of business consultants through advertising or RFPs. Below is a volunteer opportunity posted by the United Way of Massachusetts Bay on **www.volunteersolutions.org** seeking the help of business consultants:

### Be a Business Consultant

Neighborhood Business Builders (NBB) aspires to help entrepreneurs start and expand businesses. Our goal is to serve entrepreneurs and business owners in economically disadvantaged communities who are underserved by the traditional capital market and other support services.

Business consultants help to develop and strengthen the skills, attitude and knowledge of our pre and post-loan clients or our Self-Employment Trainees. NBB offers its volunteers several levels of involvement. A consultant can help: develop a business plan, review a marketing plan, prepare a loan package, conduct a process or financial analysis, or run a workshop in a particular area of their expertise. It all depends on the consultant's interests, availability, and skill level. Depending upon the project, a consultant may anticipate donating one hour of time per week.

Volunteers will work with the following groups

- Adults (26-54)
- Women
- Minorities

This opportunity addresses the following social interests:

- Mentoring Services

We are looking for volunteers with the following skills:

- Finance / Accounting
- Public Relations / Outreach
- Leadership Development
- Sales / Marketing
- Legal Services
- Teaching
- Management

While ads for such volunteer positions may be rare, and you must have business expertise and skills in order to volunteer, this illustrates the types of services you could provide to help business owners in need. You might propose something similar to a non-profit organization in your community.

You can find help in locating your community's non-profit groups through the Internet. GuideStar is a searchable database of more than 1.5 million IRS-recognized non-profit organizations in the United States. Visit **www.guidestar.org** then click on "Advanced Search" to search by your city or state. CharityVillage has a similar database of Canadian non-profit organizations at **www.charityvillage.com** (click on "Find Volunteer Listings" under "Directories" tab).

You might also contact your local Volunteer Center or Chamber of Commerce. Both of these organizations usually run a volunteer matching program and can help provide the information you need to get involved.

### 4.4.2 Information Interviews

In addition to providing opportunities for hands-on consulting experience, friends and family can help you arrange *information interviews* with people currently working in business consulting.

An information interview is defined as a brief meeting with someone who is working in a career you are interested in learning about. The goal of the information interview is to collect information that will allow you to make informed decisions about your career as a business consultant. The personal and professional benefits of an information interview are numerous:

- Help expand your professional network
- Increase your confidence
- Gain access to the most up-to-date career information
- Identify your strengths and weaknesses
- Get a look at a consulting firm/organization from the inside

To arrange information interviews, start with your network of contacts including family and friends to ask if they know anyone working in business consulting or management consulting. If possible, go beyond getting a name and telephone number. Ask if they would get in touch with people they know in the industry to see if you can contact them to ask a few questions.

If no one in your network knows anyone who works in consulting, you can try to arrange meetings by making cold calls. First do some research to come up with a list of local consulting firms that conduct business in your area of interest or specialization. The more research done prior to an interview, the more efficient it will be and the better impression you will leave.

You can find consultants that belong to the Institute of Management Consultants USA by visiting **www.imcusa.org** (click on "Find a Consultant" in the drop down menu under "About IMC USA", then do a search for your city). The Canadian Association of Management Consultants also has a member directory which you can search at **www.cmc-canada.ca**. To find other small consulting firms, consult your Yellow Pages or local Chamber of Commerce for firms in your area.

Once you have selected some local firms, it becomes a matter of picking up the phone and calling. Large and small firms will often have receptionists or administrative assistants answering the phones. They can be a valuable source of contact information. Ideally, you want to reach a senior person and directly ask them for a meeting. But as James Ege, owner and president of CM Consulting (**www.cmconsultingonline.com**), says "You don't necessarily need to talk to the person in charge. Sometimes the person in the field is the better fit, because they're in the field doing the job on a day-to-day basis."

Although you are conducting an "information interview," it is usually better to avoid using that term when you first call. Many professionals assume someone who wants to set up an information interview is actually looking for a job, not simply looking to learn about the profession. So they may decline to meet with you if they do not have any current job openings.

Instead, it may be better to say that you are doing research and politely ask if you can arrange to meet with them for 20 minutes to learn about the career. People are much more likely to agree to a meeting if they know it won't take too much time. However, others in the business say that it's not unreasonable to suggest a lunch-hour meeting.

It's important to remember that while some people are generous with their time and encouraging to newcomers, others may simply be too busy to meet with everyone who wants career advice. Anyone who works in a career field that many people are trying to break into may be inundated with requests for information interviews every week. If someone you contact says they don't have time for a meeting, politely ask if they know anyone who might be available to talk with you.

If someone agrees to a meeting, arrive on time and come prepared with a list of questions such as the following:

- How did you get started in consulting?
- What do you wish you had known when you were first getting into consulting?
- What are typical duties in your job? What are typical duties in entry-level consulting positions?
- What are the things you look for when you are hiring consultants for your firm?
- Based on a quick review of my experience to date, what training or experience do you think I should pursue next?
- What advice do you have for someone just getting started in consulting?
- Is there anyone else you can refer me to who is looking for someone with my skills, or who might be willing to meet with me?

If you have agreed to meet for a limited time, such as 20 minutes, let the consultant know when the time limit is up, say you know they're busy, and offer to leave. If they are willing to continue that's fine, but don't stay longer without permission. Thank them for their time and any referrals they were able to provide.

After the meeting, send a thank you note to the person you met with and, if someone referred you, thank that person as well. Making a good impression in an information interview could lead to future opportunities such as an internship or even a job.

> **TIP:** Ideally, an information interview should be a face-to-face meeting, but if this can't be arranged a telephone interview still has benefits. You may even get valuable advice from someone who isn't available to talk but is willing to answer questions by email.

## 4.4.3 Internships

### What They Are

Internships are an excellent way for those interested in careers in consulting to gain valuable experience and industry connections.

An internship is a short-term, entry-level position that gives you hands-on work experience. Internships are typically offered full-time during the summer, although you may be able to find a part-time internship at other times of the year. (These may also be called "co-op" programs.) Most consulting internships are paid, but some are *pro bono* or pay a stipend.

Even if you are volunteering your services as an intern, you get work experience that can be very helpful once you start applying for consulting jobs or start looking for clients for your own business. As an intern you can make valuable industry contacts, learn new skills, and build your resume. The company you intern with may even offer you a job. According to a Michigan State University career site:

> Research has found that students who had completed internships found employment more quickly following graduation, were more likely to be employed within their fields of study, and were more satisfied in their jobs. Your odds of getting a job in today's competitive marketplace are much greater if you have relevant experience.

### Finding an Internship

If you are a full-time MBA student, your college likely offers an internship program and can help you find an internship for the summer between your first and second year. In some cases, completing an internship may be a requirement of the MBA program.

**TIP:** Internships are normally not available for students in non-traditional MBA programs (such as part-time or executive MBAs) because participants in non-traditional programs are typically already in the workforce. If you are interested in doing an internship, find out whether the college you are considering attending offers an internship program which you would be eligible for.

Online you may be able to find internships posted at employers' websites. Check websites of local consulting firms, non-profit organizations and businesses. According to About.com, the following are among the top internship programs for MBA students. Even if you are not interested in applying to intern with these particular organizations, you may pick up some information to help you decide whether an internship is right for you and ideas to help you apply to other companies.

- *Mattel MBA Internshps*
  **http://corporate.mattel.com/careers/recruiting.aspx**

- *Progressive MBA Internship*
  **www.progressive.com/jobs/students-grads.aspx**

- *Sony MBA Internships*
  **www.sony.com/SCA/jobs.shtml**

- *Oracle Internships*
  **www.oracle.com/us/corporate/careers/college/index.html**

- *Toyota MBA Summer Internship*
  **www.toyota.com/html/talentlink/hr/graduate/mbasi.html**

- *U.S. Department of Labor MBA Internship Program*
  You can find a link to MBA Internship Programs at **www.dol.gov/dol/jobs.htm**. At the time of publication, the direct link was: **www.dol.gov/oasam/doljobs/MBA_Internship_Program/MBA_Internship_Program.htm**

- *Verizon College Intern/Co-Op Program*
  **http://www22.verizon.com/jobs/campus_internships.html**

Major career sites also list internship programs which you can find by doing a search for "internships". Monster has an excellent site specifically for student jobs and internships at **http://college.monster.com**. Other websites that focus on internships for students are:

- *InternshipPrograms.com*
  **www.internshipprograms.com**

- *Idealist.org*
  Internships with non-profit organizations.
  **www.idealist.org**

- *InternJobs.com*
  **www.internjobs.com**

- *Rising Star Internships*
  **www.rsinternships.com**

- *The Washington Center*
  Internships with government.
  **www.twc.edu**

Getting an internship will require you to face the same tough interview situation you would deal with if you were interviewing for a full-time position. Some suggest that getting an internship is actually more difficult than getting a permanent position, because there may be only one or two openings, with many qualified candidates in the running. The advice in Chapter 5 on applying for a job can help when applying for an internship.

## Creating an Internship

Another option for landing an internship, particularly if you are not a student, is to set one up yourself. First, decide which companies you would like to work with. (See sections 5.1 and 5.2 for information about different types of companies that hire business consultants.) Then start phoning. If it's a large company, you can ask their human resources department if they have an internship program. If they do have such a program they will tell you how to apply.

If you want to work with a small company such as a local consulting firm, ask to speak with one of the owners. (To find out the owner's name, try looking up the company on the Internet first.) Whether you get through to the owner, or speak with someone else in the company, explain that you would like to volunteer your services as an intern.

While you might think any company would jump at the chance for free labor, some companies are so busy the owner may feel they don't have time to train an intern. In some cases a business consultant may not want to help train a potential competitor, either. So be prepared to sell yourself and explain why you will bring value to the company.

One thing that most companies need is help doing the tasks that no one else wants to do. If you are willing to answer telephones, run errands, do filing, or whatever it takes to help them out, say so. It could give you a foot in the door you might not otherwise get.

If someone is interested in having you intern for them, they will ask you to come in for an interview and may ask to see your resume. As mentioned, in many ways, applying for an internship is similar to applying for a job. You will learn more about that in Chapter 5.

## Making the Most of an Internship

Here are some ways to get the most value from your internship:

- Do a first-class job with every task you are given, even the menial ones. Everyone pays their dues when they are starting a new career, and those who do it with a positive attitude can make a great impression.

- Look for any opportunities to get actual consulting experience even if it means working a few more hours than you originally agreed to. If a project comes up that you would like to work on, ask your supervisor if you can get involved.

- Consider keeping a journal of your internship activities to document every project you work on. Keeping track of everything you've learned can help you when you apply for a job in the future. Also make sure you keep track of any networking contacts.

- At the end of the internship, ask your supervisor for a written letter of reference.

### 4.4.4 Work Experience

#### Consult for Your Current Employer

You don't necessarily need to quit your job in order to get work experience as a consultant. For example, if the company you now work for is starting a new project in which they are considering hiring an outside consultant and you have a good relationship with your employer, you might offer to take on this task as a project consultant, perhaps offering your services free of charge and taking on the extra work in your "spare" time.

You may have to be willing to work through your lunch break, evenings and weekends but it's worth it if you are serious about using the opportunity to land your first real consulting job. If company management feels that the time requirements are too much then ask if you can work with the consultant they hire. This will give you invaluable experience and may make your employer choose your services over those of an outside consultant next time around.

#### Get a New Job

Another way to get related experience is by getting a new job (full-time, part-time, temporary, summer, or contract) in industries or corporate departments you want to consult in. Even if a job doesn't focus on consulting, it could give you an opportunity to develop contacts and learn valuable skills to help with your future career in consulting.

Depending on your interests and goals, departments that may be useful to work in include:

- finance
- human resources
- investor relations
- operations
- sales
- marketing

When it comes to making a good impression on future employers and clients, the particular job you're hired for may be less important than the reputation of the company that hires you. That was one of the surprising findings when an author of this book attended a session during which 70 recruiters met at the University of Calgary's Haskayne School of Business to discuss what can make or break a resume. The recruiters represented a variety of industries including natural resources, tourism, technology and financial services.

In writing about the event at Microsoft's MSN.com, Tag Goulet said one of the best ways to catch an employer's eye is to include names of well known companies you have worked for:

> "As one recruiter explained, if you previously worked for a reputable company, it enhances your application 'because they have some standards.' Employers are likely to assume you will be a good employee because you successfully passed that company's hiring process and were well trained."

**TIP:** Having blue chip company names on your resume can be a definite asset to your consulting career. Does "corporate name-dropping" (mentioning major corporations) really work? You may be an exception to the rule, but if you're like most people you probably found the above quote more credible because it came from Microsoft's MSN.com instead of a "no-name" website.

"Remember, most employers are only skimming your resume at first to make a preliminary decision," said Derek Chapman, Ph.D.professor of industrial organization and psychology at the Haskayne School of Business. So look for opportunities with Fortune 500 companies (you can find a list online at **http://money.cnn.com/magazines/fortune/fortune500**) or other organizations that are highly respected in your community.

Also consider entry-level or assistant positions with companies in fields directly related to consulting, such as consulting firms and market research companies. The next chapter offers detailed advice on how to get hired.

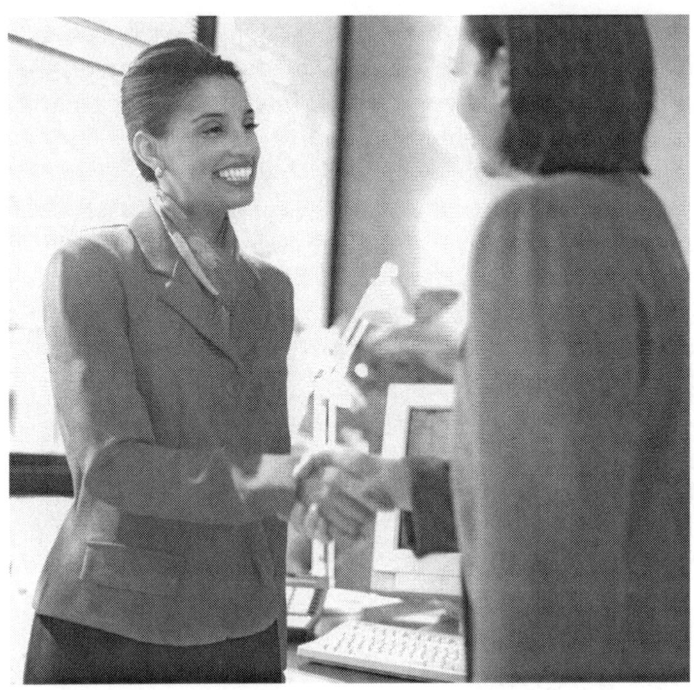

# 5. Getting Hired as a Consultant

Business consultants typically earn a living in one of two ways: as an employee or as a self-employed consultant. This chapter looks at the first of these, and describes your options for getting hired as an employee of a consulting firm or other organization. In the next chapter, you will learn how to start your own consulting business and "get hired" by clients.

As explained in Chapter 4, although a degree is not necessary for self-employed business consultants, if you want to get hired by a consulting firm you will need at least an undergraduate degree, and preferably an MBA. If you want the security of employment, but don't have the educational credentials that consulting firms look for, you may be able to find a job as an internal consultant to a corporation or other organization as described in section 5.2.

If you have the educational credentials to get hired by a consulting firm but are considering starting your own consulting business, you may want to consider getting experience as an employee before going on your own. Many consultants, like Michael Boschitsch, a CGA and owner of the consulting firm Misam Canada in Vancouver, see working for a firm or a company in your area of interest as a pragmatic step that opens doors to independent consulting.

> *"A lot of consultants have a business designation or MBA that provides the background and theory, which is good and lends credibility. But until you've actually worked in the industry that you're consulting in or for a firm, you won't have the real-world experience that's needed to become an independent consultant. Working for a large firm was really a stepping stone for me to starting my own practice."*
>
> — Michael Boschitsch, CGA
> Misam Canada

Whether you see a consulting job as an end in itself or as a stepping stone to starting your own consulting business, the information in this chapter can help you land that job.

## 5.1 Jobs at Consulting Firms

Consulting firms offer business consultants one of their most reliable sources of employment. Large firms (defined as those with more than 100 employees) are estimated to employ more than three-quarters of business consultants. Many large firms are multi-national, with offices around the world, and some employ thousands of consultants.

There are many benefits to working for a large firm. As discussed, the starting salary and signing bonuses are among the highest in any profession. Also, the global scope of many large firms means that travel or relocation is an option. With access to a wide range of employees around the world, these firms have the capacity to take on several complex projects at once, across many disciplines of consulting.

This is good news for business consultants, as it creates a need for specialists from all backgrounds, and creates opportunities to work on projects you're interested in. You may do consulting work for Fortune 500 clients, and the experience you gain at a large firm can open the doors to future opportunities with other employers or clients.

While the environment is exciting and challenging, and offers opportunities to learn and develop your skills as a consultant, it is not for everyone. Unless you already have consulting experience, you will start at the bottom. Plus, you should expect to work long hours in a highly competitive environment.

### 5.1.1 Career Paths at Consulting Firms

Consulting is a business not unlike that of a law firm, where many start in a junior position and climb the ladder to reach levels such as principal or senior partner.

Business consultants assume many different titles when they start work with a firm, depending on such factors as experience, specialization, and education. Here is a list of some of the titles found in a typical consulting firm and the responsibilities that may go with these positions. Exact titles and responsibilities vary depending on the firm, but the progression is generally analyst to junior consultant to senior consultant to principal or partner. The higher the position, the greater the client interaction and responsibility.

#### Analyst/Research Associate

This is an entry-level position that focuses on research and some analysis. There is little client contact in this position, but a strong understanding of the clients' business is required. Duties, responsibilities and salary will generally increase after the first year. Most applicants without a graduate degree will start with this position.

#### Associate/Junior Consultant

Associates and junior consultants participate in most aspects of a consulting project, but are under the direction of the senior or lead consultant. Associate is a typical entry-level position for applicants with an MBA or other graduate degree. Applicants without a graduate degree may start as an analyst or research associate before being promoted to a junior consultant position.

#### Senior Business Consultant

These individuals are responsible for taking the lead on major engagements for the firm. They oversee every aspect of the project and report directly to senior management or partners. Senior business consultants typically play a key role in finding and selling to clients. It is at this phase of the career track that many consulting firms begin to offer profit sharing or advanced bonus incentives for their employees.

### Junior Partner

Being given the title of a Junior Partner is more than just a promotion, it's an invitation to be not only a key player in a firm, but to become a stakeholder in the corporation. Responsibilities in this position include new business development, client relations and management of consulting projects for major clients.

### Senior Partner/Principal

This individual takes on the responsibilities of ensuring that the firm is profitable by overseeing the direction and development of the entire company. Senior Partners and Principals may also take the lead on major consulting projects. As you can see, there is plenty of room to get your foot in the door of a consulting firm, as well as tremendous potential to reach the top rungs.

## 5.1.2 Top Firms

There are a variety of rankings of consulting firms ranging from *Consulting Magazine*'s list of "The Ten Best Firms to Work For" to publications such as *Vault Guide to the Top 50 Management and Strategy Consulting Firms*. In addition, consulting firms appear on other "top" lists including the Fortune 500 and *Fortune*'s "Top 100 Companies to Work For."

While some companies (such as Accenture, Booz Allen Hamilton and McKinsey & Company) appear on virtually every list of "top consulting firms" there are many other companies that offer tremendous career opportunities for consultants due to their size or reputation. This section includes a list of more than 30 top firms where you might start your job search. You may find other top firms through the resources in this book.

These firms may have dozens of offices in countries around the world, so the place to start looking for information about local offices and current job openings is at their websites. Most large firms' websites include a "Careers" link on the home page. Many provide valuable insights into the company's corporate culture and what they look for in employees.

- *Accenture (formerly Andersen Consulting)*
  **www.accenture.com**
- *Aon Consulting*
  **www.aon.com**
- *A.T. Kearney*
  **www.atkearney.com**
- *Arthur D. Little*
  **www.adl.com**
- *Bain & Company*
  **www.bain.com**
- *Booz Allen Hamilton*
  **www.boozallen.com**
- *The Boston Consulting Group*
  **www.bcg.com**
- *Buck Consultants*
  **www.buckconsultants.com**
- *Capgemini*
  **www.capgemini.com**
- *CGI*
  **www.cgi.com**
- *DeloitteConsulting*
  **www.deloitte.com**
- *Ernst & Young*
  **www.ey.com**
- *Gallup Consulting*
  **www.gallupconsulting.com**
- *Hay Group*
  **www.haygroup.com**
- *KPMG*
  **www.kpmg.com**

- *Kurt Salmon Associates*
  **www.kurtsalmon.com**
- *Marakon Associates*
  **www.marakon.com**
- *McKinsey & Company*
  **www.mckinsey.com**
- *Mercer*
  **www.mercer.com**
- *Monitor Group*
  **www.monitor.com**
- *Navigant Consulting*
  **www.navigantconsulting.com**
- *Oliver Wyman*
  **www.oliverwyman.com**
- *Parthenon*
  **www.parthenon.com**
- *Pricewaterhouse Coopers*
  **www.pwc.com**
- *PRTM*
  **www.prtm.com**
- *Roland Berger*
  **www.rolandberger.com**
- *Towers Watson*
  **www.towerswatson.com**

### 5.1.3 Large Firms That Consult to Small and Medium-Sized Businesses

While the top firms tend to have large clients such as Fortune 500 companies, the firms in this category focus on providing consulting services to small and medium-sized businesses. As we discuss in section 7.1.1, small businesses can be a difficult market to sell consulting services to. Consequently, companies that focus on selling to small and medium-sized businesses may employ many salespeople and do more active recruiting for employees than the top firms do.

While it's unlikely that you'll see numerous ads seeking consultants for a top firm such as Accenture or McKinsey in your local classifieds, large firms that sell consulting services to small and medium-sized businesses may repeatedly advertise the same positions in cities throughout North America. Successful applicants may then fly to another city for a group training.

One of the best-known of the large firms that consult to small and medium-sized businesses in North America is International Profit Associates, also known as IPA (**www.ipa-c.com**). It has impressive-sounding credentials.

## Large IT Consulting Firms

Information Technology consulting is the largest and fastest-growing segment of the consulting industry. While many of the large firms listed on the preceeding pages offer IT consulting in addition to other services such as strategic consulting, there are a number of top firms that specialize primarily in IT consulting. They include the following:

- *Computer Sciences Corporation*
  **www.csc.com**
- *PWC Diamond Management & Technology Consultants*
  **www.pwc.com/us/diamond**
- *Electronic Data Systems*
  **www.eds.com**
- *Gartner*
  **www.gartner.com**
- *IBM IT Services*
  **http://www-935.ibm.com/services/us/en/it-services/gts-it-service-home-page-1.html**
- *Keane*
  **www.keane.com**

Here is a brief excerpt from a company press release:

> "International Profit Associates, Inc. (IPA) is the largest privately held provider of management consulting services to small and medium-sized businesses in North America. IPA and its more than 1,100 professionals offer a wide range of proven and innovative methodologies to help businesses grow and prosper regardless of the economic cycle."

This company may provide a good training ground and workplace for some people, but you should be aware of what you are getting into before accepting a job. If you are looking at working for a large firm that consults to small and medium-sized businesses, do research and ask questions such as:

- How often does this company run ads seeking consultants or analysts? Is it because the company is growing or is it because of high employee turn-over?
- What is the job description? If I go to work for this company will I actually be working as a business consultant or will my job primarily consist of sales?
- Will I be paid a salary or will I be paid on a commission basis? Will the company expect me to pay upfront and be reimbursed later for work-related expenses such as airfare to the training program?
- When I do a Google search for this company, what are people saying about it? To get you started in your research you can read a May, 2006 Inc. article titled "Inc. 500 Company Fends Off Lawsuits, Customer Complaints" at **www.inc.com/criticalnews/articles/200605/ipa.html**.

## 5.1.4 Small Firms

Small consulting firms are generally considered to be those that employ fewer than 100 people. According to the U.S. Bureau of Labor Statistics, over 90% of consulting businesses have fewer than 20 workers, and the majority of these employ fewer than five people.

A recent U.S. Bureau of Labor Statistics report on "Management, Scientific, and Technical Consulting Services" found that "despite the prevalence of small firms and self-employed workers, large firms tend to dominate the industry." More than half the jobs are found in the four percent of consulting firms with 20 or more employees. While less than one percent of consulting firms have over 100 employees, those firms provide over 22% of the industry's jobs.

Although smaller firms offer fewer jobs in total, they are a viable and desirable choice for many individuals looking to pursue a career in business consulting. Small firms offer business consultants with little experience an excellent opportunity to get a foot in the door. They also offer opportunities to consultants who don't hold an MBA, but who have expertise in a particular specialty because small firms tend to be more specialized in their services. For example, a majority of firms in the technical consulting industry are small.

> **TIP:** Although the term "boutique firm" is often used to refer to small consulting companies, the term actually applies to companies that specialize in particular types of consulting projects. While most small firms are also boutique firms, a few large firms are also boutique firms.

Although salaries are not as lucrative in small firms as large, there are a number of advantages to working in a small firm including: more contact with clients, more in-depth participation in consulting projects, and more opportunities to work locally. With a small firm, you may be able to get hands-on experience with all stages of a consulting project long before you might acquire such experience at a larger firm.

In addition, in a small firm you are more likely to be involved with and learn about other aspects of running a consulting business, including marketing. Some consultants also feel there is a stronger sense of teamwork in a smaller office, along with less red tape and office politics.

On the downside, as well as generally lower salaries and fewer perks, there may be less job security because the firm has fewer clients and may be affected by local market conditions. In addition, consultants who want experience with a broad range of consulting projects in a variety of specializations are unlikely to gain that experience with a small firm.

There are many small consulting firms in every city across North America. You can find consultants that belong to the Institute of Management Consultants USA by visiting **www.imcusa.org** (click on "Find a Consultant" under the "About IMC USA" drop down menu, then do a search for your city). The Canadian Association of Management Consultants also has a member directory which you can search at **www.cmc-canada.ca**.

To find other small consulting firms, consult your Yellow Pages or local Chamber of Commerce for firms in your area. Many listed may be small independent consulting firms that are looking for a fresh perspective and someone to grow with the company.

However, you should be aware that, while a few of the small consulting firms you may find in the Yellow Pages hire consultants, many are likely to be one or two person firms struggling to find enough consulting work for the principals. This is certainly not true of all local consulting companies, but it is true of enough of them that it is usually not worth investing too much time making cold calls to companies you find in the Yellow Pages. Instead, use the job-hunting techniques described in section 5.3.

## 5.2 Corporate Jobs

### 5.2.1 Internal Consulting

Many large corporations with ongoing consulting work have consultants on staff, believing it enhances their ability to address situations and complete projects in a cost-effective manner.

Consultants who work on staff for corporations and other large organizations are known as *internal consultants*. Internal Consultants work within the corporate structure to resolve business and technical issues confronting the organization. According to the Association of Internal Management Consultants (**www.aimc.org**):

> "Internal Consultants are found in government agencies, educational institutions and non-profit organizations as well as in business and industry. Their services are focused on improving the quality, effectiveness and bottom-line performance of their organizations."

An internal consultant has the opportunity to intimately learn the business practices and corporate culture of their employer. Some internal consultants are generalists who work on a variety of types of projects for their employer, ranging from planning to organizational development and reengineering. Other internal consultants specialize in one particular area such as human resources or information technology. The consultant's clients may be the company's various departments, divisions, or branch offices.

**TIP:** The job title business analyst is widely-used to describe positions in the financial and information technology industries. According to the online encyclopedia Wikipedia, "Business analysts help identify business problems and propose solutions... The BA typically performs a liaison function between the business side of an enterprise and the information technology department or external service providers."

If you are interested in learning more about the role of an internal consultant, an excellent overview is available in a free online book published by the United Nations International Labour Organization.

Titled *Internal Management Consulting: Building In-house Competencies for Sustainable Improvements*, by Joseph Prokopenko, Hari Johri, and Chris Cooper, it covers everything from management of assignments to fee charging mechanisms and marketing of internal consulting services. It also discusses:

> "The basics of internal consulting – its major concepts, roles, evolution, the position of the internal consulting groups (ICG) within parent organizations, the main features of internal consulting jobs, possible clients and consultant-client relationships, comparisons between internal and external consulting, when they compete and when they complement each other, and the advantages and disadvantages of both consulting approaches."

**TIP:** If you want to approach a company to create a job for you this publication can help you explain the benefits of having an internal consultant on staff. See section 5.3.4 for advice on how to create a job.

### 5.2.2 Types of Corporate Employers

Employers of internal consultants include large corporations, non-profit organizations, and government departments and agencies.

There are a number of places to do your homework about organizations you want to work for, whether you are looking for prospective employers or conducting research before an interview. Your public library will have numerous directories with lists of companies, government departments, and non-profit organizations. You can also find lists of organizations online. Of course, you should also visit the websites of each company or organization you are interested in for further information.

## Corporations

Perhaps the best place to start looking for large corporations is Hoovers (**www.hoovers.com**), where you can search for a specific company, or click on "Companies" or "Industries" to search by industries. Another valuable site for researching large U.S. companies is CNNMoney.com which has links to the Fortune 500, Fortune 1000 companies in your state, and top employers at **http://money.cnn.com/magazines/fortune/fortune500**.

To find large Canadian corporations check out *The Globe & Mail's Report on Business* list of "The Top 1000" at **www.theglobeandmail.com/report-on-business/rob-magazine/top-1000**.

## Government

Business consultants are hired by federal, state, provincial and local governments. According to the U.S. Bureau of Labor Statistics "The majority of those working for the Federal Government are in the U.S. Department of Defense." However, there are opportunities in many other departments as well.

To find links to U.S. government departments, go to the U.S. Government's official web portal at **www.usa.gov**. You can find an alphabetical list of agencies and links to federal, state, and local governments and departments. Links to Canadian federal, provincial, and territorial government departments and agencies can be found at **http://canada.gc.ca/othergov-autregouv/prov-eng.html**.

## Non-Profit Organizations

For a searchable database of more than 1.5 million IRS-recognized non-profit organizations in the United States visit **www.guidestar.org**

then click on "Advanced Search" to search by your city or state. CharityVillage has a similar database of Canadian non-profit organizations at **www.charityvillage.com** (click on "Volunteer Listings" under drop down menu in search bar).

# 5.3 How to Find Job Openings

There are a variety of ways to find job openings. This section covers both traditional and non-traditional ways to find job openings, including how to create your own job.

## 5.3.1 On-Campus Recruitment

Many employers of business consultants participate in on-campus recruitment, holding interviews on college or university campuses to look for new employees. On-campus recruitment is an excellent way for undergraduate and MBA students to find a summer internship or an entry-level consulting job.

Many firms do not restrict the interviews to those currently attending the institution; they also welcome alumni with work experience to participate in on-campus recruitment.

> **TIP:** On-campus interviews offer you access to open positions and a chance to pick the brains of those currently working in the industry. You can get valuable information (and possibly find a great job) by attending these interviews and any seminars or other events that accompany the interviews.

Depending on the employer and the college, on-campus interviews may run in the fall or the spring, or both. Invariably, there will be a registration process for interviews, which can include deadlines for the submission of resumes and academic transcripts prior to the visit.

The interviews generally have to cover a lot in a short time. They may be around 20 – 30 minutes, with one to three representatives of the employer. If a recruiter is interested, you will be asked to attend a follow-up interview or final round of interviews. These could be held on campus, a location near campus, or the firm's local office.

### Preparing for On-Campus Recruitment

Being prepared for on-campus recruitment means more than just showing up. Here are a few suggestions to make the most of this opportunity:

- Attend any events that your campus career center organizes to help students prepare for on-campus recruitment.
- Bring at least two copies of your resume along with any relevant certificates or letters of recommendation.
- Prepare ahead of time by researching each firm you're interviewing with. Most colleges' career centers will have this information on hand, but it can also be obtained from the corporate web site.

  **TIP:** ZA Consulting, a firm that actively participates in on-campus interviews, suggests bringing evidence of the research you've done on the firm to demonstrate both initiative and professionalism. It also gives you something to refer to during the interview.

- Chances are your competition for the positions will have an education similar to yours. Therefore, standing out from the crowd requires some planning and creativity. Identify your unique skills that are transferable to business consulting, and be prepared to tell the employer about specific examples of times you used those skills in your schoolwork or extracurricular activities. See section 5.5 for more interview preparation advice.

Your college may coordinate on-campus recruitment through the campus career center or Monster College (**http://college.monster.com**). Contact your campus career center or visit the career center's website to learn more.

## 5.3.2 Advertised Positions

"Checking the job ads" is the traditional way to look for job openings. However, it can also be the least effective way for most consultants to find a job. That's because for every good entry-level position that's advertised, there may be a hundred or more applicants. Nevertheless, if you want to do a complete job search, or if you have specialized skills, an Ivy league MBA, or extensive work experience, you could find your next job advertised online.

## Company Websites

Many large firms and corporations post information on their websites about how to apply to work for them. In addition to lists of current job openings, they may have any of the following:

- online application form
- explanation of what they're looking for in employees
- description of their work environment
- profiles of current employees
- information about career paths at their company
- advice on how to prepare for an interview, including examples of the types of consulting cases you might be asked to discuss with the interviewer.

Large companies get many applications from those seeking consulting positions, but don't overlook smaller firms' sites. They also look for fresh talent.

Even if a company website does not have jobs posted, most provide information on how to pursue employment with the company. If there is no link for "careers" on the home page, click on the link for information about the company. That will usually take you to a page that includes a link to job postings. Section 5.2 of this guide includes websites for some major employers.

## Job Websites

While print media such as newspapers and business magazines continue to provide a reliable source of information about who's hiring and current openings, the Internet has taken over much of this role.

### Posting Your Resume at Job Sites

While the traditional relationship has been one in which companies post openings in hope of finding someone that fits a broad and general set of criteria, today's consultants and other job seekers have often become the "posters," submitting resumes to Internet job sites, and HR recruiters have become the "seekers."

Recruiting this way gives firms and corporations a better understanding of the skills and individuality of a person. The resume posted is not tailored to meet a specific set of qualifications and skills; it's on the web as a personal and professional reflection of how you want the world to see you, not what you were instructed to be.

The result is that an increasing number of firms are using this method to attract new talent and fill specific consulting needs. There are many widely used websites that you can post a resume on for no cost or little cost, and they're proving to be an excellent source of permanent and contract positions for experienced consultants and those whose skills are in demand.

Before deciding to join Demarche Consulting in Seattle, Washington, consultant Bill Speck posted his resume on both HotJobs.com and Monster.com.

> "I had several interviews with good firms as the result of posting my resume online. In fact, it was the manager of a company that contacted me through HotJobs that passed my resume onto Demarche. Online posting is really emerging as a consultant's primary means of finding work in business."

Today, most newspapers run job ads on their website as well as in the paper. For example, you can find the *Wall Street Journal*'s job ads for consultants at **http://jobs.wsj.com/Careers/Jobsearch**. Or start your job search on the home page of the WSJ's Careers section at **http://online.wsj.com/public/page/news-career-jobs.html**.

Job-seekers can now find positions advertised at a variety of other job sites, the most popular of which are:

- *Monster*
  **www.monster.com**

- *CareerBuilder*
  **www.careerbuilder.com**

- *Yahoo! Careers*
  **http://careers.yahoo.com**

- *Workopolis*
  **www.workopolis.com**

Also check the following sites which search thousands of job boards, online classifieds, and company websites for the position you specify:

- *Indeed*
  **www.indeed.com**

- *SimplyHired*
  **www.simplyhired.com**

At any given time you can find hundreds of consulting positions advertised on Internet job sites. However, most of these are actually sales jobs as described in section 5.1.3.

**TIP:** If you do a search at a job board without specifying a location and find the identical "consulting" position advertised in dozens of cities, it may be a sales position.

Most actual consulting positions advertised on the large job boards are those that are difficult to fill, primarily senior positions or those requiring special skills or knowledge. For example, information technology consulting positions are likely to be advertised on the job boards.

When searching the job boards, use a variety of search terms to see if you can find suitable positions. Try the following terms, and use the "advanced search" function if possible to return the best results. Also try the terms "consulting" and "analyst" to get additional results.

- management consultant

- business consultant

- internal consultant
- associate consultant
- business analyst
- research analyst
- terms related to your specialization such as "human resources," "strategic planning" or "organizational development"

On many boards, the search term "management consultant" returns the best results. For example, here's an excerpt from an ad found during a recent keyword search for "management consulting" at HotJobs:

> MANAGEMENT CONSULTANT
> As a key member of a management team focused on productivity/ process improvement and culture change consulting for medium-sized to Fortune 500 companies, you will ... determine root causes of company's issues including quality, operational efficiencies, material utilization, labor costs and implement permanent solutions.

**TIP:** Make sure you check out the Vault Consulting Job Board at **www.vault.com/jobs/jobboard/searchform.jsp**. (Search for "Consulting" under the Industry heading.) It brings up only consulting jobs, so you don't have to weed through some of the irrelevant postings you might find at major job boards.

## Recruiters

Recruiters are hired by companies to find candidates to fill jobs the company has open. The term "recruiter" is used to describe both a company that does recruiting and an individual who does recruitment.

Unlike on-campus recruitment (described in section 5.3.1), recruiters are not employed by the company doing the hiring. Instead, they work for a firm that specializes in recruitment and provide services to a variety of client companies. Other terms used to describe companies or individuals who provide recruiting services include:

- employment agency
- executive search consultant

- headhunter
- staffing agency
- search firm

Generally, companies hire recruiters to find candidates for positions that are highly specialized or difficult to fill. As a result, they are not normally used to fill entry-level consulting positions. However, if you have at least five years of experience or a technical or financial background, you may find recruiters a possible source of opportunities.

You can find local recruiters online or in the Yellow Pages (look under "employment") then visit their websites to find current job opportunities. You may also encounter recruiters when responding to job ads you find in the newspaper or job boards. You can also try the following sites which list a variety of consulting positions which recruiters are seeking candidates for.

- *Management Recruiters International*
  (Choose "Find a Recruiter" then choose "Consulting - IT" or "Consulting - non IT")
  **www.mrinetwork.com**

- *Find A Recruiter*
  (Choose "Consulting Services")
  **www.findarecruiter.com**

**TIP:** Beware of firms that expect you to pay a fee. Recruiters should be paid by the employer, not the job-hunter. For example, the firm Bernard Haldane & Associates (now called BH Careers International) has faced legal action in several U.S. states on the grounds of misleading job seekers, primarily unemployed executives and professionals who paid fees ranging from $5,000 to $16,000. A press release from the State of Minnesota Office of the Attorney General announcing a 2004 lawsuit against the company says:

> "Bernard Haldane represents to job seekers that it has exclusive access to a 'hidden job market' with thousands of employment opportunities not available to the general public; that its fees ... will likely be reimbursed by the hir-

> ing company; and that consumers who use its services obtain a job within 90 to 120 days. The lawsuit alleges that these representations, and others, are false, deceptive, and misleading."

If you are a senior consultant who can benefit from recruiters, you can find links to a selection of helpful articles on working with recruiters at **www.rileyguide.com/firms.html**.

## 5.3.3 Unadvertised Positions

According to an article on "hidden jobs" on the CNNMoney website, "eighty percent of available jobs are never advertised." You can view the article here: **http://money.cnn.com/2009/06/09/news/economy/hidden_jobs**.

Even among the types of employers that usually do advertise for consultants, smaller companies are unlikely to spend hundreds of dollars to post jobs at a site such as Monster.com. So how do these employers find employees? The two primary ways are through referrals and direct contact from job-seekers.

### Referrals

Many employers find employees through referrals, or word of mouth. When a business owner needs a new employee, they will typically ask friends, business associates, and current employees if they know anyone who might be suitable for the job.

Studies have consistently found this is how more than half of management and professional positions are filled. The classic study in this area was done in 1974 by sociologist Mark Granovetter, now with Stanford University. (You may have read about this research in Malcolm Gladwell's bestseller, *The Tipping Point*.) In Granovetter's study, titled *Getting a Job: A Study of Contacts and Careers*, he reported that 56% of survey participants found their job through a personal contact. While it was a small survey sample of 282 men in one community, similar results have been found in follow-up studies.

For example, a 2002 Global Career Transition Study by DBM (formerly Drake Beam Morin) of 6,917 DBM clients who changed careers that year reported that 54% worldwide and 61% in the United States found re-employment through networking. According to the report, "Networking is still the number one way job seekers, worldwide, are finding new employment opportunities." Likewise, the U.S. Department of Labor's 2005 *Occupational Outlook Handbook* reports that "over half of all employees get their jobs through networking."

What is perhaps most significant for job-seekers is the fact that most positions obtained through word of mouth are found through acquaintances instead of through friends or family. Granovetter's study found that 84% of the respondents who found a job through personal contacts learned about the opportunity from someone they saw only "occasionally" or "rarely." That's because you likely know many of the same people that your close friends know, whereas acquaintances are likely to know other people and hear about different opportunities.

While tapping into the contacts you already have and doing some informal networking is a great way to start looking for work, it is a good idea to also take action in expanding your network of contacts through meeting and interacting with people in the industry. You can arrange information interviews as discussed in section 4.4.2. In addition, you should attend social and business events where you will have the opportunity to meet contacts including meetings of local professional associations, trade shows, conferences, and other events.

In section 7.3.4 you will find practical advice on how to network to find consulting clients. You can use the advice in that part of the guide to help you meet and connect with people who can hire you – or recommend you to someone who can hire you – for a full-time job.

> **TIP:** Even if you're not currently employed as a consultant, have some personal business cards made up. Your name, phone number, email and website on a professionally designed card will create a polished impression and make it easy for people to pass on information about you. See section 7.2.1 for advice on designing and distributing business cards.

## Direct Contact

Even if you don't know anyone connected to a particular company, it may still be possible to get a job there by contacting the company directly. About 10% of the participants in Granovetter's study were hired after applying directly to an employer.

It happens rarely, but sometimes a manager will have just decided that they need a new person when they happen to receive a phone call or email from someone who looks like they might be an ideal candidate for the job. Many employers would rather find someone this way than invest all the time and effort in advertising the job, screening resumes, and interviewing numerous candidates.

If you decide to make "cold" contact with employers (as opposed to the "warm" contacts that come through networking), it's a good idea to focus on specific types of employers, such as large firms, small firms, or corporations in a particular industry. This will allow you to target your job search most effectively since it takes time to track down hiring managers' names, tailor your resume, and prepare personalized cover letters explaining why you want to work with that particular organization.

You may be able to track down information online or by calling the organization and asking to speak with the person who hires entry-level consultants. That individual's title will vary depending on the type of organization. It might be *Managing Principal* in the case of a small firm, *Recruiting Coordinator* in the case of a large firm, or the head of a department in the case of a corporate employer.

Your initial call to a consulting firm might be as simple as:

> "Hi, my name is __________. I'm calling with interest in putting my consulting skills to work with your firm. Can you tell me if there are any entry-level openings at the moment?"

If the person on the other end of the line isn't able to provide information about openings with the firm and how they hire, ask if you can be put through to someone who does have knowledge of the hiring practices and current openings.

Here are some tips to keep in mind when contacting employers by phone:

- Ask to speak to the person in charge of hiring. Do your best to find out their name ahead of time so you can ask for them specifically.

- If the person you're trying to call isn't in, find out the best time to call back, rather than just leaving your name and number.
- When you get in touch with the person in charge of hiring, introduce yourself and, if you have been referred by someone else, mention that person's name as well.
- Ask for a meeting at a specific time, e.g., "Would Wednesday afternoon or perhaps Thursday morning work better for you?"
- If there are no openings at the current time, ask if you can call back in the future to see if any positions have opened up.

## 5.3.4 Create a New Job

If the job you want doesn't exist, you may be able to create it, either with your current employer or a new one.

### Create a Job with Your Current Employer

One option is to create a job for yourself with your current employer. If you can suggest a way to offer business consulting services to your employer that adds more to their processes than they're paying you then they may jump at the chance. It's up to you to convince them how you will add value beyond what they're paying you.

For example, you might offer to examine various company processes such as human resources issues or information technology problems, or offer to create an e-business component they previously had not thought of. Hiring an outside consultant to look at and improve these areas of the business might cost more than hiring you to work on these projects at your present salary, saving the company money. And you will gain valuable experience with a possibly more sympathetic client whose business processes you already know well.

Here is the story of how one woman created her own business consulting job, adapted from the *FabJob Guide to Become an Etiquette Consultant*.

> Business etiquette consultant Jacqueline Whitmore is the author of Business Class: Etiquette Essentials for Success at Work and founder of the Protocol School of Palm Beach (**www.etiquetteexpert.com**), a

business etiquette consulting firm whose clients include Citibank, Ernst & Young, Bloomingdale's, State Farm, Sprint, and Office Depot.

Before starting her own consulting company, Jacqueline created her own job at The Breakers, a world-famous resort in Palm Beach. As an employee of the resort, she took the initiative to complete an etiquette training program then approached her boss to make her the first "protocol officer" for The Breakers, a position in which she served as an internal consultant advising hotel personnel on dealing with VIPs.

## Create a Job with a New Employer

If you want to create a job with a company that you don't currently work for, it will take more effort, but it is possible if you can show that you will give the employer more value than you cost. To do this, you need to know what you can do for an employer that will outweigh the costs to the employer of hiring you.

Here are some examples of things employers see as "costs" when they hire a new employee:

- Your salary
- Your benefits
- Resources you'll need to do your job (e.g. computer, supplies)
- Time of other staff members to train you
- Time of your supervisor to oversee your work

As you can see, you will need to demonstrate to an employer that you would bring them more value than simply covering the cost of your salary. As a business consultant, you are uniquely qualified to show how your work as an internal consultant could create value for an employer. Typically, that means work that increases a company's profits, whether through generating more sales, reducing the company's costs, or other means.

For an entry-level consulting position with a small consulting firm, you may be able to bring value in other ways as well. For example, a principal at a consulting firm may see value in having you free up your boss's time to do more important work. You might even be able to convince a busy self-employed business consultant to hire you as her assistant if you can convince her that, with your help, she could do more of the tasks she enjoys and fewer of the tasks she doesn't enjoy, while being able to take on more clients and earn more money.

### Working Interviews

One way to prove your value to an employer is with a "working interview." Working interiew is a term that is sometimes used to describe a temporary paid position that may lead to full-time employment if the worker does a satisfactory job.

However, when you are looking at creating a new position, you can have a "working interview" by volunteering to spend a day or more doing the job you would be hired for. Here's how one applicant pitched an author of this book in an email application for a marketing position:

> "If you are uncertain of my qualifications or fit within your organization I am willing to provide a week of my time for a working interview during which I would carry out the day to day functions of the position on a volunteer basis."

In this case, the applicant was not asked to volunteer her services for a week, but the initiative she took in making the offer helped her land the job. Even a single day spent in a working interview could help you land a corporate consulting position.

## Who to Contact

To decide which companies to apply to, read the business pages of daily newspapers and watch the TV news to find out what companies in your area need, so you can determine how you can fill that need. Look for small growing companies which are likely to need help but are unlikely to be inundated with unsolicited job applications. (Large or well-known companies may receive thousands of resumes.)

To create a job for yourself, you will need to deal directly with someone who has the authority to hire new people. This does not mean contacting the human resources department of a large company, unless that is the department you want to work with. The human resources department fills positions that already exist. If you want to create a new position, you will need to speak with the appropriate department manager or, in the case of a smaller company, the owner of the company.

You will need to meet with this person and learn what their needs are in order to figure out how you can create value for them. It's best if you can establish a relationship with someone through networking. However, you may even be able to create a job through cold calling. For example, here is the type of message you might leave on someone's voicemail:

> Hello <name of employer>, this is Annie Analyst. I am an experienced business analyst, and would like to meet with you to discuss how I could help <insert name of company> increase profits by cutting costs. Please call me at <insert your phone number> so we can schedule a time to meet.

If the company is looking to increase profits, as many companies are, this call is more likely to get returned than a call simply asking if there are any job openings. (See section 7.3.2 for more advice about cold-calling, including how to ask for a meeting when you get someone on the phone.) You may need to be persistent and make a lot of calls, but if what you are offering is something that will bring a company more value than it costs, you can create a job.

For many people, creating a job is simply too much work. After reading how much self-employed business consultants can earn, you may think: "If I'm going to ask people to hire me, why don't I do it for contracts worth hundreds or thousands of dollars a day instead of asking for a job worth thousands of dollars a month?" While there's a certain amount of job security in a full-time job, many people who are attracted to business consulting prefer self-employment. If that's you, you'll find good advice on starting your own consulting business and getting clients in Chapters 6 and 7.

## 5.4 Job-Hunting Materials

### 5.4.1 How to Prepare a Resume

Even if you have not yet held a full-time job as a business consultant, you can write a powerful resume to help you land a consulting position. Exactly what you will include on your own resume depends on the job you are applying for as well as your previous experience.

This section offers advice on writing your resume and includes links to sample resumes for consultants. If you are a recent graduate or have changed careers within the past few years, you likely are already familiar with the basic types of resumes, so you may want to skip that part. If you have not looked for a job for many years, it's recommended that you read the entire section.

## Types of Resumes

There are three common resume formats: chronological, functional, and combination.

### Chronological Resume

The chronological resume is the most commonly used format. It lists work experience in reverse order, starting with the most recent. Employers prefer chronological resumes because the format makes it easy for them to quickly weed out candidates whose previous experience doesn't precisely match what they're looking for.

A 2005 HotJobs.com survey found that 84 percent of recruiters prefer chronological resumes so it's a good choice for those with a solid work history in consulting. However, if you are new to consulting, a functional or combination resume will likely be a better choice for you.

### Functional Resume

Instead of listing your experience chronologically, the functional resume organizes your experience to highlight your skills and accomplishments. In a functional resume you create headings for each consulting skill you want to demonstrate (such as problem-solving or leadership), and summarize your previous experiences and accomplishments using those skills.

The functional resume is a good choice for career changers because it emphasizes your relevant skills rather than specific jobs you have held. However, because this format is often used by applicants who have gaps or weaknesses in their work history, some employers view functional resumes with suspicion.

### Combination Resume

The combination resume (also known as a *hybrid* resume) combines elements of both the chronological and functional resumes. It includes a section with headings of relevant consulting skills and summaries of your accomplishments in those areas. This section is followed with a summary of previous jobs similar to what you might include in a chronological resume.

This resume is a good choice for new consultants because it highlights your skills while giving employers the chronological work history that most want to see on a resume.

## Resume Dos and Don'ts

You can see examples of these dos and don'ts in the sample resumes that follow.

- Do put your contact information (name, address, telephone, fax, e-mail) at the top of your resume. Or you can put contact information at the bottom if your resume is a single page.
- Do include an objective or summary statement that is relevant to the position you are applying for. Use language that speaks to the employer's needs and the value you will bring them; don't just state what you want. For example, Richard Valiquette, a consultant specializing in sales and owner of Creative Coaching Solutions in Calgary, Alberta, has this objective on his resume: "To contribute to the success of your team and increase revenue growth for your organization."
- Do show that you have the consulting skills described earlier in this book. Include accomplishments and experiences that demonstrate your skills in areas such as analytical problem-solving, leadership, project management, making presentations, working with clients, and other skills used in consulting.
- Do include relevant volunteer experience, such as serving on boards of charitable organizations or consulting work for businesses owned by friends and family members. See section 4.4 of this book for ways to get volunteer consulting experience.
- Don't just list your responsibilities. Instead, use action verbs to describe what you achieved in each position, such as: initiated,

launched, activated, designed, implemented, expanded, increased, etc. Wherever possible, quantify your achievements.

- Do tailor your resume by using the same wording as the employer. For example, if their job ad says they are looking for someone with "expert presentation skills," state that in your resume: i.e. not "excellent" but "expert." Your resume may be scanned electronically for specific keywords. So if the ad asks for experience in "business analysis," use that exact wording.
- Don't include extraneous information. Some employers make a decision about a resume within seconds, so a resume containing too much irrelevant information could be rejected before the employer has finished reading it. Avoid mentioning personal information such as your age, marital status, or unusual hobbies.
- Do include degrees and relevant continuing education such as business seminars you have attended. Include your GPA if you're a recent grad and it's over 3.3.
- Do include any professional affiliations and certifications. This includes membership in consulting associations (listed in section 8.3 of this book).
- Do include relevant accomplishments including awards, scholarships, prizes, and any other recognition of your business expertise such as articles you have written or that have been written about you.
- Don't include references on your resume unless asked to do so. It will be assumed that they are available on request, so you don't need to write that either. One option you may want to try is to include quotes from your references in the form of testimonials.
- Do make your resume's length appropriate for the amount of experience you have. You may have read that your resume should be a maximum of two pages. However, many consultants have extensive business experience; in that case, it's fine to have a resume longer than two pages.

**TIP:** In a few circumstances, such as if you are applying for a senior position (e.g. vice-president) or overseas, you may be asked to submit a curriculum vitae, also known as a CV. This is a much more detailed overview of your experience.

- Do choose an attractive paper stock, lay it out nicely, and make sure there are no typos. You are applying for a job where professional presentation matters. If you are sending your resume by email, do use the specific format the employer has asked for. Don't send email attachments unless the employer requests them, or they may be deleted.

On the pages that follow you will find several sample resumes for consultants with different specializations and levels of experience. The samples also show different resume formats.

The perfect resume is of course the one that gets you called in for an interview, and it will be different for each job and each individual. It's wise to ask someone (ideally someone who hires consultants) to review your resume. However, there are many different opinions on what makes a perfect resume, so in the end it's best to use your own judgment, and tailor it to the position you are applying for.

## Sample Achievements

Richard Valiquette, owner of Creative Coaching Solutions in Calgary, Alberta (**creativecoaching@shaw.ca**) is a consultant specializing in sales. Here are some achievements he includes on his resume.

### Achievements

As a key member of many sales teams, my competitive spirit and focus on creating results have led me to achieve exceptional sales results on a personal level and exceed team targets as a manager.

- Increased sales productivity 150% in 90 days: Epcor Call Center
- Nominated for the Platinum Award for achieving the highest revenue growth within all channels: Direct Energy
- Won The Directors Cup Sales Award for top sales seven consecutive times: Direct Energy Essential Services
- Exceeded sales targets achieving 130% for three consecutive years: TELUS Communications

## Sample Resume #1
*(Experienced Consultant)*

### Chris Consultant
4321 Solution Street
Sunnyday, CA 91111
Phone: (123) 555-1212
chris@chrisconsultant.com

### Objective

To use my education and experience in corporate finance to assist corporations with being competitive in today's tight-margin, high-tech market.

### Skills Summary

- Excellent organizational skills and a high level of accuracy.
- Good numeracy, written, verbal and interpersonal skills.
- Work effectively with others to generate a positive and productive work environment.
- Able to adjust schedules according to operational needs.
- Work well under pressure and meet deadlines.
- Able to hold sensitive information in confidence.
- Proficient in office procedures and use of office equipment.
- Experienced and proficient with MS Office.

### Employment History

**Sr. Business Analyst, CA Business Systems**
**2004 – Present**

Responsible for all aspects of new-business finance. Develop yearly business projections and short-term financial goals. Team lead on company's largest acquisition to date. Promotion to Sr. Business Analyst in 2007. Currently leading a team of 25 financial analysts. Frequently participate in forming key partnerships with Fortune 500 clients.

**Financial Planner, AB Financial**
**2002 – 2005**

Responsible for maintaining the personal finances of over 20 clients. Help develop low-risk and high-risk portfolios, using stock market, mutual fund and realty investment strategies. Advise on tax-saving strategies, and retirement investments. Deliver seminars on benefits of investing with the company to prospective clients. Was key player in creating company-wide, client-tracking software.

**Small Business Financial Advisor, Home Business Inc.,**
**1999 – 2002**

Advise clients on all financial aspects of starting a home-based business. Conduct feasibility and market studies. Development of short-term, long-term financial goals. Assist clients with procurement of small business loans through various financial institutions.

## Education

**Master of Business Administration**
Wharton School, University of Pennsylvania, 1998-1999

**Bachelor of Arts (History)**
Michigan State University, 1993-1997

## Computer Skills

Proficient in AccPac, Simply Accounting, Microsoft Word, Microsoft Excel, Microsoft Access, and Microsoft PowerPoint.

## Memberships / Volunteer Activities

- Vice-President of Alumni Association, Michigan State University
- Member, Sunnyday Chamber of Commerce
- Professional Member, Institute of Management Consultants USA
- Convenor of Little League Baseball Tournament for last 5 years

# Sample Resume #2
*(Career-Changer)*

**CHRIS CONSULTANT**
4321 Solution Street
Sunnyday, CA 91111
Phone: (123) 555-1212
chris@chrisconsultant.com

**SUMMARY**

A problem-solving leader who consistently delivers revenue generating and cost saving solutions for organizations.

**CONSULTING EXPERIENCE**

Successfully led teams in all stages of consulting projects for a variety of organizations including small businesses, non-profit associations, and the XYZ Corporation. For each project:

- Met with clients to conduct needs analyses and determine each project's scope, deadline, team, and budget.
- Carried out qualitative and quantitative information-gathering techniques including document review, case study analysis, interviews, or conducting surveys.
- Used appropriate problem-solving techniques such as Risk Analysis and SWOT Analyis to identify possible solutions.
- Presented recommendations and carried out training programs to assist organizations in implementing recommended solutions.

Sample projects include developing an electronic communications policy for a corporation to address concerns about employee privacy, and preparing a strategic plan to increase donations through a non-profit organization's website. (Online donations have increased 87% since implementation.) Details of these and other project successes available on request.

**SKILLS**

- Skills include project management, analytical problem-solving, team leadership, sales, business writing, making presentations
- Proficient in a variety of computer programs including Microsoft Office, MS Project, and PowerPoint
- Conversant in Spanish

*"I have worked closely with Chris on a number of major communication projects and found her to be knowledgeable, professional, and extremely resourceful. She readily accepts a challenge and uses her intelligence and abilities to solve problems creatively."*

– Jane Jones, Vice-President Communications, XYZ Co.

*"Chris was our company's top team leader. Her teams consistently achieved their goals ahead of schedule and under budget."*

– Ed Employer, President, ABC Company

**EMPLOYMENT AND VOLUNTEER HISTORY**

- Owner-Consultant, CC Communications Consulting, 2011 to present
- Communications Manager, XYZ Corporation, 2006-2011
- Operations Coordinator, ABC Company, 2002-2005
- Humane Society, Communications Committee, 2010-2012 Chaired the committee in 2011

**EDUCATION**

- Enrolled in courses on project management and leadership at University of Sunnyday Business Studies Department
- Completed seminar on strategic planning offered by American Management Association, 2011

**MEMBERSHIPS**

- Member, International Association of Professional Business Consultants
- Member of City of Sunnyday Chamber of Commerce, Executive Women International, and Toastmasters

**TIP:** As Sample Resume #2 shows, you can create an impressive resume even without a business degree or previous paid experience as a professional consultant. This sample includes experience and credentials you may be able to acquire relatively quickly using the techniques described in Chapters 3 and 4 of this book – such as consulting experience obtained through volunteer work, continuing education courses, and joining a consulting association. This resume also shows how a career changer can emphasize relevant project experience from previous jobs.

## Sample Resume #3
*(Internal Consultant)*

### Chris Consultant
*Available to solve operational problems.*

**Professional Strengths**
A track record of cost-effective operational improvements in the furniture manufacturing industry. Relate well to all levels of staff and management, drawing out ideas and developing buy-in. Take the initiative when a problem emerges. Project management and business consulting expertise applied in a practical setting.

**Career Highlights**
- Replaced aging equipment with the latest, automated wood finishing equipment; worked with shop floor manager to integrate it into the assembly system, seamlessly; with minimal downtime and complete staff support, saving the company $90,000/yr in wastage
- Re-deployed staff to a new office furnishing production line, scheduled retraining
- Instituted a fail-safe, delivery tracking system, improving delivery performance from 77% to 100%

**Work History**

| | |
|---|---|
| 2008 - Present | Assistant to VP Operations, Highland Furnishings, functional role is floating trouble shooter, with autonomy to research challenges, recommend and action changes. |
| 2005 - 2008 | Supervisor, Woodworking Department, Highland Furnishings |
| 2003 - 2005 | Woodcutter, operating all equipment in the department, Highland Furnishings |

**Education**

| | |
|---|---|
| 2010 | Certificate in Project Management from USA Distance Learning |
| 2007 | Certificate in computerized furniture design |
| 2004 | Graduated from Brockville Technical School with diploma in wood finishing, Honor Roll |

**4321 Solution Street • Sunnyday, California 91111**
**Phone (123) 555-1212 • chris@chrisconsultant.com**

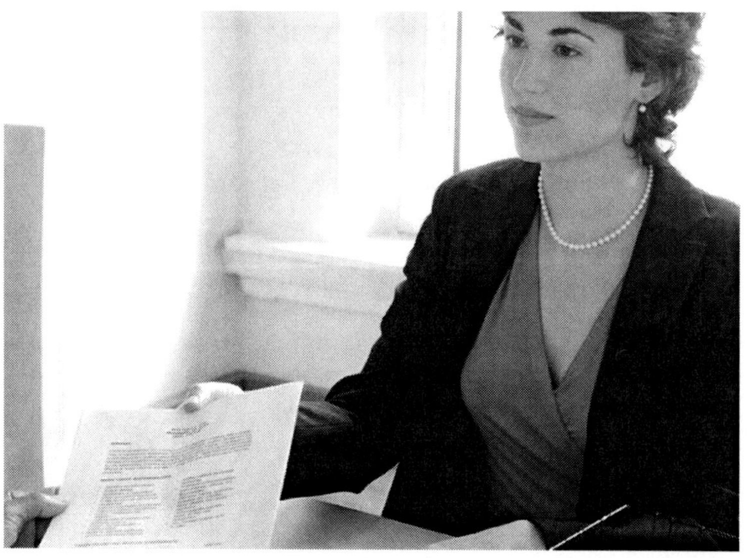

## More Sample Resumes

See the following samples online for more ideas for your own resume:

- *Sample Resume: Entry Level Management Consultant*
  **www.careerknowhow.com/resumes/samples/manageconsult.htm**

- *Sample Resume: Executive Consultant*
  **www.kawconsulting.com/Sampe%20Resume.htm**

- *Sample Resume: Business Development Executive*
  **www.jobbankusa.com/resumewrite/ResumeTemplates/business_development_executive_resume_template.html**

- *Sample Resume: MBA Graduate*
  **http://bit.ly/LJQtsaCOPY0**

## 5.4.2 How to Prepare a Cover Letter

When you apply for a consulting position, your cover letter probably will be scrutinized. The reason is simple: many firms use the cover letter as an opportunity to assess the candidate's writing skills and ability to craft the right message to draw in the reader. And as writing skills are an important part of success in consulting, this is a logical source of information. So make sure you spend time crafting a top-notch cover letter.

Your cover letter is also the first place you display the confidence that is going to be important in your business consulting success. You want to emphasize your interest in the profession and ability to perform well in it. You want to show some personality and position yourself ahead of other applicants.

This section summarizes the cover letter format used by many business consultants. It is followed by a sample cover letter and web addresses of other sample cover letters for consultants.

> **TIP:** Keep your cover letter to one page. Because employers may make quick judgments, a short and memorable letter can be more effective than a long one.

### Salutation

Use the research methods described in this chapter so that you can insert the real name of the person receiving the letter.

### Introduction

State the position you're applying for, and a short phrase explaining why you are a good fit.

### Experience and Skills

This paragraph should focus on the relevant experience you have in consulting or any other jobs that have applicable transferable skills. If the firm where you're applying has a particular niche, focus on skills relevant to this specialty.

### Interest and Knowledge

You can use this paragraph to show off your knowledge of the business as well as your interest in the profession but keep the focus on this particular firm.

### Closing

In this part of the letter you want to leave the employer with a positive impression and convince them to take the time to read your resume. In one or two brief paragraphs you can summarize your experience, refer to your resume, thank the potential new employer for their time, and explain how you will follow up. Because business consultants are expected to show leadership and take initiative, don't conclude by saying you hope to hear from the employer. Instead, let them know when you will contact them to follow up.

### Sample Cover Letters

Sample cover letters for a junior consultant and an internal consultant appear on the next two pages. The second letter is written in a more conversational style. This approach can be especially effective if the company culture is informal. Below are web addresses of online cover letter samples for graduating students and a senior consultant.

- *Sample Cover Letter: Executive Consultant*
  **www.kawconsulting.com/Cover%20Letter%20Sample%20-%20webb%204-15-06.htm**

- *Sample Cover Letter: Graduating Student Applying to a Consulting Firm*
  **http://jobsearch.about.com/od/coverlettersamples/a/coverconsulting.htm**

- *Sample Cover Letter from McKinsey and Company: Graduating Student (International)*
  **www.mckinsey.com/locations/prague/downloads/Cover%20letter.pdf**

## 5.5 Job Interviews

Your preliminary work has paid off: The employer wants to meet with you for an interview. But before you break out the champagne to celebrate, you'll have more work to do. Although you might be able to impress the interviewer and get a job offer during your initial meeting, in most cases you will need to jump through a few more hoops before being offered the position.

## Sample Cover Letter #1

*(Formal Letter to a Consulting Firm)*

Chris A. Consultant
5678 Main Street
Prosperity, NY 12321
(987) 654-3210
chris@chrisconsultant.com

October 1, 2012

ABC Consulting, Inc.
99 Corporate Drive
Successville, NY 12345

Attention: John Q. Analyst, Managing Partner

I am writing to apply for the position of Junior Business Consultant as advertised in last week's Analyst Journal.

As Research Associate for XYZ International Consulting, I was responsible for the daily research and analysis of over two dozen active clients, including such Fortune 500 companies as Best Tech, Inc. and United Medical Industries. Based on my proven track record for performance, I was able to secure my position as Junior Business Consultant with XYZ inside of six months.

I am particularly interested in the high-tech market segment to which ABC Consulting caters, and I believe that my proven ability to fast-track research and data accumulation will be of a great benefit to your daily operations.

Enclosed is my resume for your review. As you can see, my education and experience in the field promises a mutually beneficial and successful arrangement as Junior Business Consultant with ABC.

My thanks in advance for your consideration. I will phone you next week to follow up. In the meantime, if you have any questions you are welcome to contact me at (123) 555-1212. I look forward to speaking with you.

Sincerely,
Chris A. Consultant

## Sample Cover Letter #2

*(Less Formal Letter to a Corporate Employer)*

Chris Consultant
5678 Main Street
Prosperity, NY 12321
(987) 654-3210
chris@chrisconsultant.com

October 15, 2012

Re: Your Oct. 15 advertisement for internal operational consultant

Dear Mrs. Brownley,

You are looking for an internal consultant to improve operational efficiencies at Ivanhoe Furniture and I offer a remarkably good fit for that job.

I have advanced to that role in Highland Wood Furnishings and now function as a roving troubleshooter. Working with management and staff, we have implemented some outstanding improvements with results going straight to the bottom line.

Even factoring in the cost of new equipment and training and the downtime of conversion, management here agrees that I have been the prime mover in saving Highland over half a million dollars and thousands of person hours in the last five years.

You will be particularly interested to know that all this was accomplished with zero labor unrest. In fact, the repeatedly heard suggestion of floor staff reflects the confidence they have in my recommendations and implementation programs. When anything goes wrong, they joke, "We've got a problem. Bring in Chris!"

I would like to apply my experience and people-friendly approach to an organization the size of Ivanhoe, which I have long admired. Thank you for taking the time to review my resume. I will call you next week and hope we can chat about this exciting opportunity.

Regards,
Chris Consultant

For most consulting positions, there are at least two rounds of interviews. The first is typically a "fit" interview in which the employer is looking to see if you have the experience and personal qualities the firm is looking for. Your first round of interviews could range from two separate half-hour interviews with different members of the firm, to a lengthy panel interview. The second interview is typically a "case" interview in which you will be given problems to solve. After that, you may be called in for meetings with additional people you would be working with to ensure you would fit well with the team.

The exact number of interviews will depend on how senior the position is (more senior positions usually require meeting with more people), as well as the organization. Large firms and corporations typically require more interviews than small consulting firms.

In a small firm, the principal (the firm's owner) frequently chairs the interview process and makes the final hiring decision. As a result, the hiring process is usually fairly direct: one or two interviews and you're done. In many instances, a candidate can get acquainted with the principal right from the beginning, whereas with a larger employer you may not meet some of the key players until after the first interview.

This section covers both fit and case interviews, and offers advice on preparing for the interview and following up afterwards.

## 5.5.1 How to Prepare for an Interview

Preparation is key to ensuring that prospective employers see you as someone who is a fit with their company. You can get ready for the interview by conducting further research, dressing professionally, and coming prepared with everything you might need during the interview.

### Researching the Company

Once you've scheduled the interview, it's time to learn more about the employer so that you can ask relevant questions and speak to their particular needs during the interview. Chances are, most of what you learn will not become a topic of conversation during the interview. However, the employer will be listening for evidence that you are thoroughly familiar with their company. In a recent survey of the 1,000 largest companies in the U.S. by the staffing company Accountemps, 47% of the executives polled said that the single largest mistake an interviewee can make is to display "little or no knowledge of the company" for which they were applying.

Your first stop for company information should be the company's website. Also check out websites such as Hoovers (**www.hoovers.com**) for company overviews and histories, key people, financial information, and industry news and trends.

It's also a good idea to catch up on current events which might have a bearing on the company with which you're interviewing, as well as on the business world in general. Sites like CNNMoney.com (**http://money.cnn.com**) and CNN.com are both good resources for doing a quick brush up on the morning's world and business news. Finally, review the consulting resources mentioned throughout this book so that you can be up on industry news, particularly anything related to the employer's niche.

> **TIP:** Don't forget that interviewers can research you online just as easily as you can research them. Do a Google search of your name to see what comes up.

## How to Dress

Work attire for business consulting generally follows the same guidelines as that of any other corporate job. While some firms may be more casual or flexible with their expectations, it's a good idea to walk into your interview looking like somebody who works there. After all, the impression you're striving for is of somebody who fits in.

In a recent article on CanadianLiving.com, Roz Usheroff, a communication and image specialist, instructs, "Absolutely research the company you are going to interview with. Know their dress culture." The single easiest way to ensure that your entrance attracts the kind of attention you're looking for ('Who's the new guy?' not 'Who's *that*?') is to investigate the formalized dress code of the company you're interviewing for beforehand. There are a number of ways that this information can be found.

## Basic Business Wardrobe Options

Marjorie Brody, Certified Management Consultant and founder of Brody Personal Development (**www.brodypro.com**) recommends the following basic business wardrobe options:

**Women:**

- Black or gray suit
- Dark burgundy or navy suit
- Contrasting jacket and skirt
- Two-piece dress
- Several white, off-white blouses
- Solid color blouse; may be pastel
- One pair gold, one pair silver earrings
- Scarves that pick up colors from the suits
- Black pumps; navy or taupe pumps
- Neutral or taupe hosiery
- Black leather handbag
- All weather coat
- Black, brown, or burgundy briefcase

**Men:**

- Solid-color navy and gray suits (one each color)
- Five pairs black socks, two pairs navy socks
- Pinstriped navy suit, same in gray
- Four burgundy/red print or striped silk ties
- Two patterned silk ties
- Charcoal-gray suit
- Two navy/mauve ties
- Navy sport coat with gray trousers
- One black leather belt
- Six white cotton shirts
- A blue or pinstriped shirt
- Leather briefcase
- One pair black slip-on shoes, one pair black lace-up shoes

Do you know somebody who works there, or somebody who knows somebody? Ask them about the dress code. For the more assertive, there's always the option of taking a quick trip to the company's parking lot as employees arrive or depart for work to get a first-hand look. Just remember to make it a quick trip; no loitering or anything conspicuous. Avoid visiting the office before your interview if the parking lot is controlled by security, requires an appointment to be on the property, or presents other obstacles which could put you in an uncomfortable predicament.

If you don't have an opportunity to learn about the dress code or observe people who work at the company, then dress in standard corporate attire.

For women, a matching pants suit or jacket and skirt in navy, dark grey, brown or black coupled with a tailored blouse in an appropriate neutral color is a great place to start. For men, a two piece suit in navy or dark grey with a white or neutral shirt and a simple (i.e. not loud or overly trendy) tie represents a classic corporate-minded outfit. Much has been made of the tie's necessity in an interview setting these days, but in this instance, it should be considered essential.

In the final analysis, it's always best to use simple good judgment when weighing the options between one outfit and another, with a nod to erring on the side of the more conservative. This also applies to any jewelry, cosmetics or other accessories which might prove distracting or risk being considered flashy. And of course, be sure to follow basic "good office neighbor" hygiene in the form of groomed hair, clean nails, polished shoes, and the like. Remember, when you're being judged on whether or not you'll fit in, every detail counts, no matter how small.

If you're just getting started in consulting and need to build your business wardrobe, the list on the previous page can help you plan ahead.

## What to Bring

In the interest of projecting a confident demeanor when arriving for an interview, you want to appear as unencumbered as possible. However, while it would be nice to stroll in with nothing but your personality to guide you along, the fact of the matter is that it's important to be prepared to provide some manner of documentation or proof of your skills and experience if asked. The basics of what to bring to a corporate interview include:

- Several extra resumes
- An updated list of personal references
- Any letters of recommendation
- Copies of certificates or transcripts
- Copies of any career-related awards you may have received
- A dozen or more personal business cards
- A calculator
- Your daytimer or PDA (but make sure your BlackBerry, cell phone, or anything else that could ring is turned off during the interview)
- Some basic writing supplies (two new black or blue ink pens, a sharpened pencil or two, and one each of memo and legal-size notepads)

The writing supplies may become particularly handy for a consulting interview in the off chance that you are asked to take an employment test prior to your formal case interview. While pen and paper will most likely be provided, it would be important to look (and be) prepared.

Organize all of these documents and supplies in some manner of a hard or soft shell briefcase in black, brown, or some other neutral color. Be sure to know where everything is for easy, fumble-free access before you arrive.

### Visual Aids

In addition to the items listed above, one way to differentiate yourself from other applicants is by producing a visual aid or two which illustrate a particular achievement or statistic relevant to your work experience. For example, if you were responsible for increased productivity in your area, a graph showing the numbers could be valuable. Were you responsible for a particularly large project involving many distinct phases and requiring numerous employees or departments? A flow chart outlining the project from start to finish emphasizing your role in coordinating the different facets would be particularly impressive.

When employing visual aids, make sure that the presentational value is on par with the achievement. Don't try to render the finer points of a multi-million dollar international project on a handwritten cue card. Simple, easy to read, laser or inkjet printed items on white stock is ideal. However, you don't need to invest in an extravagant presentation which you may not have an opportunity to present.

Above all, don't force the introduction of these visual aids into the interview process. If the opportunity to illustrate a relevant point comes up, ask for permission to present the visual, and summarize its significance in brief. Don't try to command the floor just to prove a point, and be prepared to not present it at all if no easy segue arises.

### Resources for Answering Interview Questions

If you haven't been on a job interview for a while, or if you could use some assistance with answering questions during a job interview, the following resources offer good sample questions and answers:

- *Job Interview Questions and Answers*
  **http://jobsearch.about.com/od/interviewquestionsanswers/a/interviewquest.htm**
- *Job Interview Questions Database*
  **www.quintcareers.com/interview_question_database**
- *Monster.com Interview Questions*
  **http://career-advice.monster.com/job-interview/interview-questions/jobs.aspx**
- *Ten Tough Interview Questions and Ten Great Answers*
  **www.collegegrad.com/jobsearch/16-14.shtml**

## 5.5.2 Interview Questions

Much has been written elsewhere on the best way to approach interview questions. The scope of this section is not to attempt to provide an exhaustive list of all possible questions and answers, but rather to put you in the frame of mind where you can easily identify or tailor the nature of the question or answer to serve both your concerns and the concerns of the employer.

### Answering Questions

During a fit interview, questions will primarily focus on your background. It may include a review of your resume, a brief overview of your personal and work experience, and a line of questions geared towards getting a better sense of who you are as a person and a potential employee. In addition to traditional questions such as "Tell me about yourself," or "Why do you want to work for our company?" you are likely to be asked "behavioral questions" about specific past behaviors. The purpose of behavioral questions is so the employer can attempt to predict how you are likely to behave in the future.

"Tell me about a time when you experienced conflict at work," is an example of a behavioral question. The interviewer will not be satisfied with a hypothetical answer about what you "would" do in a conflict situation. They want to hear about an actual time you experienced conflict. The purpose is not to see if you have ever had a conflict (they expect you have); the purpose is to see how well you resolve difficult situations and, if something did not work out in the past, what you learned from it.

For a consulting position, you can expect to hear behavioral questions such as: "Describe your most successful project so far. What did you do to make it a success?" and "Describe a project where something went wrong. How did you solve the problem?" When confronted with these types of questions, describe the situation, say what you did, relate the outcome, and finish with what you learned from it.

Remember that the interviewer is not just evaluating *what* you say, they are also evaluating *how* you say it to see if you have the personal traits they are looking for in a consultant. You should therefore speak confidently, communicate clearly, and assert leadership. In other words, answer as a successful business consultant. A question as seemingly innocent as, "Why is blue the world's favorite color?" could well be looking for you to challenge certain assumptions. After all, what data asserts that blue is the world's favorite color?

However, be mindful of "over-answering" or giving too much information in response to a question, particularly if it pertains to a fairly basic or incidental facet of business consulting, at least in the preliminary interview. The time to present a strong case full of factual assumptions and reasoned projections will come later in the formal case interview (see Case Interviews, section 5.5.3).

### How to Answer "What Is Your Biggest Weakness?"

If you think a good answer is you're "a perfectionist who won't quit until the job's done right," think again. The interviewer has probably heard the same thing from countless other applicants and doesn't believe it's a weakness any more than you do.

According to Vicky Oliver, author of *301 Smart Answers to Tough Interview Questions*, the worst thing you can do is give your interviewer a "canned" answer, such as saying you are a workaholic. Applicants who give such a typical answer may be perceived as dishonest or unoriginal.

Oliver is one of 40 career experts and hiring managers who gave one of the authors of this book their best tips for handling the weakness question. So what is a good answer? "Confessing that you're 'impatient' is a small weakness that often goes hand in hand with high performance," says Oliver.

But present it with a positive spin. Carole Martin, author of Boost Your Interview IQ, offers this possible answer: "I know I could improve my patience when working with people who don't work at the same pace as I do. What I have found is that by helping members of the team who are having problems, I can move the project forward instead of being frustrated and doing nothing." You can find more advice to help you answer this question at **www.FabJob.com/tips211.html**.

### Asking Questions

While seemingly obvious, it is worth restating that you should do as much as possible in the way of research on the consulting firm's basic philosophies, business practices, history, clientele, etc. This way you can ask specific questions which show that you've done your homework, that you know who they are and what they do, and that you are ready to join the fold.

The flip side of this coin is that you should not ask any questions which have been addressed in the employment ad, on the company's web site, or are otherwise readily answered or common knowledge about the firm. Research is what a business consultant does, so make sure you've done yours, and show that you are knowledgeable about their industry as well as their particular company.

For example, you might ask a question such as:

> "I noticed on your website that your company is planning to expand into the overseas widget market this year. With the government's announcement last week of a new widget tariff, what impact do you expect that to have on your plans for overseas expansion?"

Finally, ask questions to get a good sense of the firm's operations and your specific duties. Make sure that while you're busy proving that you're a good fit for the company, you're also satisfying yourself that the company is a good fit for you.

## 5.5.3 Case Interviews

As a business consultant, it is understood that you will need to possess the wide range of critical and analytical skills necessary to address any given client's needs. A case interview is the method used by a potential employer to assess these skills, an exercise in "thinking on your feet" which tests your ability to provide answers and form educated responses in real time.

For those embarking on their first round of business consulting interviews, the Ohio State University Career Connection describes the case interview process as:

Hypothetical — but often very concrete and practical — problems or situations encountered in your field. Regardless of the type of case, the employer is interested in knowing how you analyze information to deduce an answer.

While you may be asked some case questions in the first interview, it is the second interview that is more likely to focus on a series of written questions or verbal examinations involving scenarios, or case studies, meant to challenge your consulting abilities. This interview may take place with a major partner in the firm present, and the process can run anywhere from 45 minutes to an hour or more.

This section discusses what types of questions to expect during a typical case interview, as well as some practical considerations to keep in mind during your preparation.

## Case Questions

There are as many ways to group case questions, as there are case questions. Regardless, you can count on being faced with questions that fall into one (and very likely all) of these categories:

- Brain Teasers
- Market Sizing
- Business Strategy
- Contemporary Business

Within these categories are questions that range from simple, thought-provoking puzzles to tough analytical questions simulating real on-the-job scenarios. The important thing to remember, as expressed by the consulting firm McKinsey & Company, is to demonstrate logical, analytical thinking:

> "In most instances there is no right answer to the problem. It is critical that you demonstrate your ability to think in a structured way and that you reach a reasoned conclusion that is supported by the evidence."

The following are some examples of the types of questions you may be asked during your case interview.

## Brain Teasers

Don't be surprised if your case interview begins with one or more simplistic (though not necessarily easy) "brain teaser" questions akin to riddles or trivia. These questions aren't meant to stop you in your tracks over the right answer so much as they are a warm up of sorts to engage your analytical thinking.

Examples of the sorts of questions you may be asked include:

- Why are there 5,280 feet to a mile?
- A dark room contains a candle, a lantern, and a fireplace. One of these must be lit before you can know that the other two are there. What do you light first?
- A man's age is half of a perfect square, two times a perfect square, and one-eighth of a perfect square. Reversing the digits of his age is also a perfect square. How old is the man?

## Market Sizing

A market sizing question asks you to estimate a rough figure based on a set of assumptions for a given social, economic or geographic group. Remember, often your ability to explain the reasoning and logic behind your answer will prove more important than coming up with a "right" answer. You will most likely not be provided with all of facts necessary to easily address the question, so while you may be free to ask for more information, be prepared to make many of these assumptions on your own. Be sure to brush up on your math skills beforehand, as you will almost certainly not be allowed the use of a calculator.

Some examples of market sizing questions:

- What is the average morning work commute time in New York City?
- Which state employs the largest number of park rangers?
- How many gallons of decaffeinated coffee are consumed in the U.S. every year?

## Business Strategy

With broad applications and far-reaching variables involving a particular business or sector with which you may very well be unfamiliar, the business strategy question forces you to examine the sorts of all encompassing issues you will face on a regular basis as a working business consultant. These questions are often long, involved scenarios which focus on your ability to employ forward thinking and strategy, with topics such as mergers and acquisitions, market changes, or the effects of new technology on a given business.

Kinds of theoretical scenarios you may be presented with:

- A large pizza restaurant chain known primarily for its speedy delivery has just acquired a competitor. This competitor, while highly regarded for quality food, offers more dining room seating, but does not offer delivery. Will a name change to the acquired restaurants and the introduction of delivery service boost or reduce the chain's sales?
- Should automobile manufacturers offer rebates for safe drivers?
- A U.S. manufacturer of cellular phone accessories is considering expanding their line to include items for a new phone which, while a considerable success in Japan and Europe, has yet to be approved in the United States due to carrier compatibility issues. How long should the company wait before they commit resources to production?

## Contemporary Business

Contemporary business questions examine your command of current events in topics such as global business, technology and domestic issues. Your ability to provide meaningful insight is an indicator of your interest in a variety of topical subjects, and shows a potential employer that you are actively engaged in the examination of how business lives and breathes.

While these sorts of questions are necessarily subject to tomorrow's headlines, current examples might be:

- Will the Apple iPod remain the industry innovator in portable MP3 players?
- Is China poised to usurp the U.S. as the dominant economic world power?
- Which alternative automobile fuel source stands to be most widely adopted: Bio-diesel, electric, or hydrogen cell?

Obviously, the key to success with contemporary business questions is to stay apprised of news which may affect the business world, be prepared to present a position on these topics, and support your argument with a factual foundation.

## Case Interview Resources

- *Bain & Company*
  **www.joinbain.com/apply-to-bain/interview-preparation**

- *Boston Consulting Group*
  **www.bcg.com/join_bcg/interview_prep/default.aspx**

- *CaseQuestions.com*
  **www.casequestions.com**

- *Massachusetts Institute of Technology (MIT)*
  **http://bit.ly/Np4Ktg**

- *McKinsey & Company*
  **www.mckinsey.com/Careers/Apply/Interview_tips**

- *Novantas*
  **www.novantas.com/careers_cases.shtml**

- *Oliver Wyman*
  **www.oliverwyman.com/careers/19.htm**

## 5.5.4 Following Up

Even though the act of getting your foot in the door and surviving the rigors of a formal case interview can and should feel like the major obstacle towards securing your new position, it's important to remember that many firms can interview dozens of applicants before making their decision. With this in mind, it's important to grab one more opportunity to make yourself stand out from the crowd and restate your interest in their firm.

The most practical and effective way to do this is with a quick follow up phone call, or a thoughtful note or card (like the one on the next page) thanking your interviewer for their time and consideration. Be sure to address everyone involved in the interview process by name, as it's important to leave as many people as possible with a good impression of you.

You can also use this opportunity to elaborate on any questions or concerns which came up in the interview that you now feel were not addressed adequately or confidently on your part. Keep this portion brief, as too much may be seen as a sign of ill confidence, or that perhaps you feel like the interview didn't go well. Finally, end the call or note with your intention to follow up in a week or so to see if a decision has been made, and make sure to do so.

Try to make the call or send the card or note the day after your interview, as decisions can be made quickly, and you can never be certain whether you are their first interview or last. Hand-delivering the note or card is fine, so long as you don't press the issue of seeing a busy Senior Partner face to face in the middle of a busy work day. You may have to leave it at the front desk if an appointment to enter the building is required; if this is the case, it's a good idea to place it in care of the lead interviewer's assistant or secretary, as many executives rarely have the time to rifle through their mail in the course of a day.

Of note, generally speaking, a gesture as important as your follow-up note should not be left to the informalities of an email, as you run the risk of relegating your future with the firm to the whims of their network "spam" program.

## Sample Thank-You Letter

Chris A. Consultant
5678 Main Street
Prosperity, NY 12321
(987) 654-3210
chris@chrisconsultant.com

July 2, 2012

Mr. John Q. Analyst
Managing Partner
ABC Consulting, Inc.
99 Corporate Drive
Successville, NY 12345

Dear John,

Thank you for the taking to time to discuss my potential employment as Junior Business Consultant yesterday.

After meeting with you and Mary Partner, I feel more confident than ever that my experience and skills as a business consultant are a great match for both ABC Consulting and your clients, and it is my sincere hope that we are able to work together.

Should you require anything else of me in the way of further information or references, please do not hesitate to contact me at your convenience. I will follow up with you next week via phone to see if any progress has been made in your decision.

Again, thank you for your consideration, and I look forward to hearing from you soon.

Sincerely,

Chris A. Consultant

## 5.6 The Job Offer

You've been offered the job. Take a moment to congratulate yourself on how all your efforts have paid off, then focus on the final stage in accepting a business consulting job: Ensuring that their offer meets with both your expectations and aspirations. After all, you may very soon find yourself seated at one of the firm's desks for many hours a week, so it's wise to take some time to evaluate any last minute pros and cons before making your final commitment.

### 5.6.1 Negotiating Salary

What if their proposed salary offer falls short of your expectations? A survey by CareerBuilder.com found that 58% of the executives surveyed leave room for negotiations when proposing a new hire's salary. Of course, in order to negotiate for more, you'll have to present a strong case for why your particular set of skills and experience might warrant a higher salary than what's currently on the table.

Should you choose to take this approach, spend as much time as you can rehearsing your case, then make an appointment with the interviewer either in person, or by phone. Make sure to arrange for the appointment within two days of their formal offer, as this will ensure that you convey your continued interest in the position.

Before you begin negotiations, make sure that you're on top of current industry salary ranges in your geographic location. You may be able to learn typical salary ranges for your position by networking with other consultants, if you are fortunate in having a network of industry professionals who are generous in sharing information. However, many professionals are guarded with salary information, so you may need to rely instead on online resources.

For example, you can find average salaries for consulting jobs based on years of experience and geographic area at PayScale.com. The direct link is **www.payscale.com/research/US/Job=Management_Consultant/Salary**. Average earnings for consultants working in various industries can be found at the Bureau of Labor Statistics website at **www.bls.gov/ooh/Business-and-Financial/Management-analysts.htm#earnings**. While the information is not broken down in detail, it does offer a possible starting point for salary negotiations.

For a fee, you can find current salary information including the results of management and strategy consulting salary surveys, at Vault.com. You can preview the information that's available at **www.vault.com/wps/portal/usa/salaries** (go to the Consulting Salary Reports). At the time of publication, the fee for job-seekers ranged from $14.95 per month for a three month subscription to $9.95 per month for a one year subscription.

Once you arrive at a figure based on your research, consider preparing your counter offer based on the slightly higher end of what you would be willing to accept. So long as your talents warrant consideration at this higher pay scale, there's a good chance the employer will propose a salary somewhere between their initial offer and yours, if not accept your offer outright.

If this is your first business consulting position, remember that what the position might lack in a hefty paycheck, it will make up for in valuable experience working in the field and you'll be in a much better position to negotiate a raise in the near future.

## 5.6.2 Deciding Whether to Take the Job

No amount of money or prestige will make it any easier to show up for work when you have grave reservations about the job or your work environment. Above and beyond the general nervousness and unease associated with the big interview, ask yourself:

- Did you feel at home in their office?
- Did the employees you noticed appear happy, or stressed?
- Will you likely be overwhelmed by the workload, or perhaps underwhelmed?
- How will the hours affect commitments to your family, social life, or important hobbies?
- Will there be room for advancement on the scale that you'd like to see your career progress?

All of the seemingly unquantifiable factors of this nature play a large part in painting the bigger picture that is the job worth taking and keeping. For many great questions you should ask yourself when considering a job offer, check out **www.forbes.com/2006/03/01/careers-joboffers-salary-cx_sr_0302bizbasics.html**.

But what if your talents lie in the pursuit of something a bit more independent-minded or entrepreneurial? Perhaps your particular work experience or skills lend themselves to handling a wider range of clients or markets than a job at an established firm would likely take advantage of? Is your expertise in a field very specialized or in demand? In our next chapter, we examine the ways and means of getting yourself out and into the field on your own with "Starting Your Own Consulting Business".

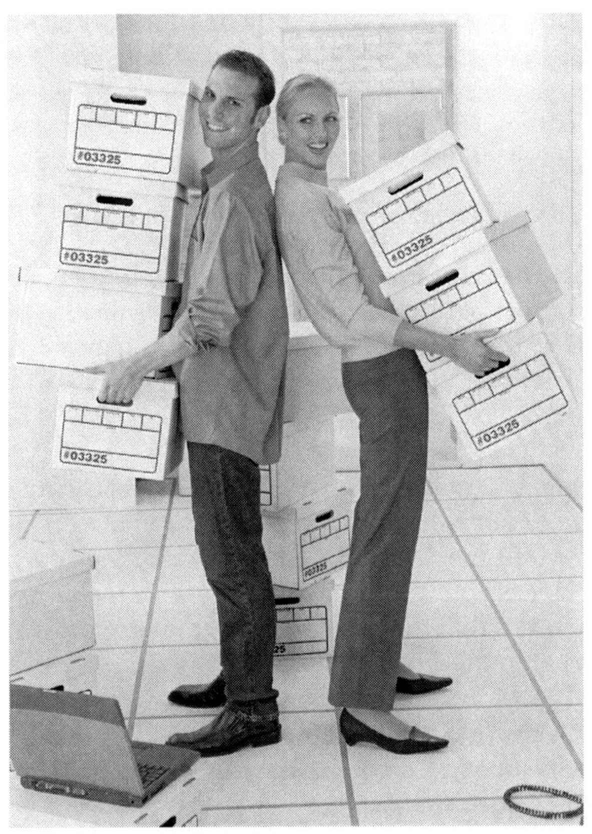


# 6. Starting Your Own Consulting Business

For many business consultants the decision to start their own business seems like a no-brainer. With all the apparent benefits a consulting business offers in comparison to other alternatives – including low start-up costs, greater autonomy, and the potential for significantly higher income – it may appear that becoming an independent consultant is only a logical choice.

Starting your own consulting business is also an emotionally appealing choice. You might envision:

- Working from home and having more time to spend with your family

- Having the freedom to work only on projects that are socially responsible and challenge you intellectually
- Being able to work the hours you want so you have time for the pursuits you enjoy
- Having the financial means to achieve your other life goals

You may rightly feel that predictions about the number of new business failures don't apply to you because you are not starting from the same place as other entrepreneurs. Because of your business expertise, you may have greater confidence, connections, and access to the resources you will need to get started.

However, before you make the leap to independent consulting, it is wise to do the type of analysis and planning that you would recommend for a client. Beyond the decision to start a consulting practice, there are many other choices you will face. To assist you in making those choices, it is recommended that you use decision-making tools such as those described earlier in this book.

**TIP:** You can find information about a variety of decision-making tools such as Cost-Benefit Analysis and Six Thinking Hats at **www.mindtools.com**.

## Starting Full-Time or Part-Time

If you are currently employed, some of the questions you may need to consider are:

- Should I quit my job and start my consulting business on a full-time basis?
- Should I remain at my current job and start a consulting business on the side?
- Would my employer let me keep my job on a part-time basis so I could be available to meet with clients during business hours and have a secure source of income while I'm getting my business off the ground?

- If I leave my job to start my own consulting business can I rely on my current employer to become one of my clients?

While some of your choices will depend on external factors such as whether or not your employer allows employees to moonlight, other choices will be yours to make. Again, some of these decisions may seem like no-brainers.

For example, Tag Goulet, one of the authors of this book, was able to increase her income 500% by moving from a full-time job with a major corporation into an external consulting role with the same company. However, if your consulting contract with your employer has a limited term, as hers did, you will need to consider how you'll land other consulting clients and sustain your income in the future.

## Other Start-Up Decisions

Whether or not you are currently employed, there are many other decisions you will face when starting your consulting business. For example:

- Should I have a consulting specialization or offer general business consulting services?
- Should I incorporate?
- Should I work with one or more partners?
- Where should I set up my office?
- What should I name my company?
- What systems do I need to set up (e.g. for invoicing)?
- How much should I invest in start-up costs?
- Should I hire support staff?
- What types of insurance should I get?
- What fees should I charge?

This chapter is designed to help you make these and other decisions you will face in starting your business. (The next chapter will help you decide how to market your business to attract clients.) It begins with creating a business plan and continues with an overview of other factors you'll need to consider in starting your own business. Chapters 6 and 7 also offer strategies, tips, and advice for optimizing your chances of success in the early stages, and insight into how to make your business successful in the long term.

**TIP:** If you are a small business consultant, some of the information on starting a business may be basic. However, you may nevertheless pick up some good ideas that you can use in your own business or with your clients.

Throughout the chapter you will also find many helpful resources for further information. If you could use more help with all areas of starting a business, the following are excellent sources of information:

- *Small Business Administration*
  The SBA offers help with business start-ups and has a variety of programs and services for the small business owner. There is at least one SBA office in every state in the United States. Call the Answer Desk at 1-800-U-ASK-SBA (827-5722) or visit **www.sba.gov**.

- *SCORE*
  A non-profit organization, SCORE has over 10,000 volunteers who provide counseling and mentoring to new business start-ups. They also offer business tips on their website. Call 1-800-634-0245 or visit **www.score.org**.

- *Canada Business Network*
  You will find a wide range of information at this site, including a step-by-step guide to walk you through starting your new business. Visit **www.canadabusiness.ca/eng**.

- *Nolo.com*
  Nolo is a publisher of plain English legal information. Their website also offers free advice on a variety of other small business matters. At their website at **www.nolo.com** and click on the "Business Formation: LLCs & Corporations" link under the "Get Informed" drop down menu.

# 6.1 Getting Started

## 6.1.1 Creating a Business Plan

Business planning involves putting in writing all the plans you have for your business. If you will be seeking financing for your business, the lender will expect to see a business plan that shows you have a viable business idea with an excellent chance for success. Even if you don't need financing (most consulting businesses don't), putting ideas on paper will give you the "road map" of where you want to go with your business and how you are going to get there.

A business plan can also help you avoid costly surprises. If you are considering whether to leave a secure job to start your own consulting business, a business plan can help you determine the resources you will need to start your business and decide when the timing is best to get started. It will help you determine if you have enough funds set aside to support yourself while you get the business up and running.

If you make the effort to draw up a good plan now, you can be confident that it will pay off in the future. You may find over the course of your research that your thoughts change about how you will set up your business. For example, you may have been planning to specialize in consulting for companies in a specific industry, but during your research you might identify a growing trend that would make it profitable for you to offer your services to other industries as well.

After reading this chapter, and the next one on finding clients, you will be able to start creating your own business plan. It is a document you will probably read repeatedly as you start to operate your business. In the meantime, this section will give you an introduction to business planning, walk you through key components of a business plan, and conclude with a variety of resources to help you create your own business plan, including links to further information, business planning software, and free business plan templates.

**TIP:** If your business plan is going to be shown to anyone, such as potential investors, make sure you proofread it carefully.

While the format of a business plan can vary, one good approach is to divide the body of your business plan into the following sections:

- A description of your business
- Your marketing plan
- Your financial plan
- Your management plan

In addition, your plan should include the following items:

- A cover sheet
- A table of contents
- An executive summary
- Financial projections
- Supporting documents

## Description of Your Business

A description of your business is just that—a description of the business you plan to start and operate. The key is to include information about your business so that everyone who reads your business plan will know you're on to something viable.

You'll need to state in this section that, as a business consultant, you'll be operating a service business. Get specific about the services you'll provide. If you will have a consulting specialization, state that in your description. Also indicate if you plan to offer additional services such as executive coaching or employee training.

The description of your business should also explain what the legal structure of your business be. Will you have a sole proprietorship, for instance, or incorporate? You'll find more information about legal structures in section 6.1.2.

In this section you can also discuss the consulting industry generally, touch on points you will address in other parts of the business plan, and include details about how your business will operate.

For example, you could describe your business hours. Do you plan to be available during regular business hours? If you are working at another full-time or part-time job, when will you be available to meet with clients? You could also identify the planned location of your business, and why it's conducive to your business.

You can conclude the description of your business by clearly identifying your goals and objectives such as sales targets. Support them with information you've acquired about being a business consultant. It's here that you're explaining exactly why you're starting this business and what you hope to accomplish with it.

Your own company description will be unique to your consulting business. You'll find business plan models you can follow in the resources listed at the end of this section.

### Should You Specialize?

Most professionals market themselves as specialists. For example, unless a doctor is a general practitioner, he or she will specialize as a pediatrician, cardiologist, plastic surgeon, etc. Similarly, lawyers specialize in criminal law, intellectual property, immigration, etc. Likewise, most business consultants choose to specialize.

Many consultants feel it is easier to get started in the business as a specialist rather than a generalist because you have narrowed down the options of who your potential clients may be and these potential clients will perceive you as an expert in the areas they wish to improve upon.

Lonnie Pacelli (**www.leadingonedge.com**), consults in project management and leadership development, and is author of several books including *The Project Management Advisor*. He says there is increased pressure for consultants to differentiate and focus.

> *"There are lots of consultants out there covering just about every function in every industry. Being a management consultant just doesn't cut it. You've got to create a specific focus (e.g. project management) and have some differentiating factors which make you unique (e.g. publishing a book)."*
>
> — Lonnie Pacelli, President
> Leading on the Edge International

However, depending on your particular consulting business, it may be better for you to be the equivalent of a general practitioner. Ruth Ann Karty of Taking Care of Business Consulting Services in rural Clarkfield, Minnesota, chose to keep her practice in the country because she enjoys the lifestyle. She says:

> *"It's difficult to be a specialist if you're consulting in a rural area. It's just too small. You have to be a generalist and be open to helping small and medium-size businesses with all their needs."*
>
> — Ruth Ann Karty
> Taking Care of Business Consulting Services

You can find information about consulting specializations in section 2.1. When choosing a specialization, in addition to considering which areas you have experience in and are most enthusiastic about, you will need to consider which areas are most in demand.

Also watch for emerging trends which can help you recognize opportunities for your consulting business. For example, the rise of e-commerce created a need for e-business consulting. Likewise, increasing globalization created opportunities for consultants who could help North American companies venture into emerging markets. The resources in section 4.3 can help you keep on top of business trends.

## Your Marketing Plan

Following are key elements of a typical marketing plan. You will find additional information to help you plan your marketing in Chapter 7 of this book.

### Your Clients

The most important elements of a good marketing plan are defining your market and knowing your customers. Knowing your customers is important because it allows you to tailor your services to accommodate those clients.

You don't want to limit yourself to a market that is too narrow—that can limit the scope of your business once it's underway. For example, you'll have many more prospective clients if you target "medical offices" rather than "chiropractors." And targeting all "professional service providers" will give you an even larger market. Quantify your market and use your marketing plan to paint a picture of a wide and ready market that needs your consulting services.

### Competition

All businesses compete for customers, market share, and publicity. So it's smart to know who your competitors are and exactly what they're doing. To provide services that are different and better than those of your rivals, you need to evaluate your competitors' services, how they're promoting them, who's buying them, and other information.

### Pricing

You'll learn more about setting fees later in this chapter, but know that you should address this issue, at least briefly, in your business plan. This section should consider factors such as competitive pricing, costs of labor and materials, and overhead.

### Your Market Strategy

You'll need to think about how you'll advertise and promote your business. Have a budget in mind, or at least set percentages of your income that you'll invest back into marketing the business.

## Your Financial Plan

Financial management is crucial to running a successful business. Your business plan should describe both your startup costs and your operating costs. The startup budget includes all the costs necessary to get your business up and running. Operating costs are ongoing expenses, such as advertising, utilities, rent and so forth.

Remember to include the following items in your budgets. Notice that some expenses overlap on the startup and operating budgets. More information about expenses is provided in section 6.2.1.

### Start-up Budget

Legal and professional fees, licenses, equipment, supplies, stationery, marketing expenses.

### Operating Budget

Make a budget for your first three to six months of operation, including expenses such as: personnel (even if it's only your own salary), rent, insurance, marketing expenses, legal and accounting fees, supplies, utilities, printing, postage and courier, membership dues, subscriptions, and taxes.

Your financial management plan also should address the accounting system you plan to use. Many small business owners conduct their own accounting, using software such as Quicken (**www.quicken.com**) or QuickBooks (**www.quickbooks.com**), while others hire someone to set up a system.

## Your Management Plan

No matter how large your business is, managing it requires organization and leadership. Your management plan will therefore address issues such as:

- Your background and business experience, and how they will be beneficial to your consulting business
- The members of your management team (even if you'll be the only member)
- Assistance you expect to receive (financial help, advice, or other forms of aid)
- Plans for hiring employees, either now or in the future
- The duties for which you and any employee or employees will be responsible
- A general overview of how your business will be run

## The Extras

In addition to these major areas, your business plan should include the extras mentioned earlier:

### A Cover Sheet

This identifies your business and explains the purpose of the business plan. Be sure to include your name, the name of the business, and the name of any partners, if applicable. Also include your address, phone number, email address, and other relevant information.

### Table of Contents

This goes just under your cover sheet and tells what's included in your business plan. Use major headings and subheadings to identify the contents. Although it's the first thing to appear in the plan, it should be the last thing you write. That way you already have all the content and page numbers in place.

### Executive Summary

Basically, this is a thumbnail sketch of your business plan. It should summarize everything you've included in the main body of the plan.

### Financial Projections

This is an estimate of how much money you'll need to start your business, and how much you expect to earn. Remember to support your projections with explanations.

### Supporting Documents

If you will be seeking start-up funding, you'll be expected to include financial information. This may include your personal (and business, if applicable) tax returns for the past three years, a personal financial statement (get a form from your bank) and a copy of a lease agreement if you will rent office space.

## Resources

There are a number of excellent resources available to help you write your business plan. The following are among the best:

- *SCORE*
  Offers an outstanding free business plan template, available in Word or PDF formats. They also offer an online workshop on how to "Develop a Business Plan" and many other resources. Visit the home page at **www.score.org** and click on "Templates & Tools" or go directly to **www.score.org/resources/tab-a**.

- *American Express OPEN Forum*
  The OPEN Forum (**www.openforum.com**) provides a number of articles, resources and crash courses for small business owners. "How to Write a Business Plan" by Guy Kawasaki highlights the eight most important characteristics of successful business plans. You can read the article at **www.openforum.com/idea-hub/topics/the-world/article/how-to-write-a-business-plan-1**.

- *Small Business Administration: Writing A Business Plan*
  The Small Business Administration has links to sample business plans, a business plan workshop, an interactive business planner and more. Go to **www.sba.gov/category/navigation-structure/starting-managing-business/starting-business/how-write-business-plan**.

- *Canada Business Network: Business Planning*
  The Canadian Government's Business Network offers detailed information about every step of business planning. Go to **www.canadabusiness.ca/eng/page/2865**.

- *Business Plan Pro Software*
  If you want help creating a professional business plan, another option is to buy business planning software from Palo-Alto Software. The standard version of Business Plan Pro is available for $99.95; the premier version is $160. Both are available at **www.paloalto.com/common/products/bpdesc.cfm?affiliate= fabjob**. Business Plan Pro offers a step-by-step guide to creating a business plan, as well as 500 samples. To see a free sample of a business plan for a consulting company go directly to **www.paloalto.com/products/solutions/education/sample_plans**.

## 6.1.2 Choosing a Business Legal Structure

Like all entrepreneurs, business consultants are faced with the decision of how to legally structure their business operation. You may be familiar with the different forms of legal structures, Sole Proprietorship, Partnership, Corporation or Limited Liability Company, but it's worthwhile to review them briefly so that you can consider your options. In this section we will look at the advantages and disadvantages of each for businesses.

### Sole Proprietorship

A sole proprietorship is any business operated by one single individual without any formal structure or registration requirements. A sole proprietorship is the simplest and least expensive business legal structure when you are starting out. It is also the easiest because it requires less paperwork and you can report your business income on your personal tax return. One drawback to this type of business is that you are personally liable for any debts of the business.

Without going through any formal processes, you can begin your consulting business simply by getting the word out that you're in business. With this said, however, there are usually business licenses and permits required by local municipalities in order for you to conduct business. The costs of these licenses are usually minimal, but be sure to check with your local municipal licensing office.

**Business Licensing**

Wherever you decide to locate your business, you should first check with your local municipal and state governments to see what licensing requirements you need to meet. Check local zoning laws at city hall if you decide to work from home to be sure that you're zoned to allow home-based businesses.

The U.S. Small Business Administration has helpful information about state and federal licensing requirements. Visit **www.sba.gov**. Under "Starting & Managing a Business", click on "Licenses & Permits."

In addition to information about how to obtain licenses and permits based on your zip code, this page provides a list of links with licensing requirements for each state.

For information about licensing and regulations for small business owners in Canada, check out the Canadian Government's Canada Business Network site at **www.canadabusiness.ca**. Click on "English," then click on "Permits and Licenses" to begin a search based on your location.

Karin Kolodziejski of Metaskills Consulting (**www.metaskills.com**), chose to run her consulting business as a sole proprietorship because she did not feel that an incorporated business offered her much advantage over an unincorporated business.

> *"When I first started my consulting business, I ran it as a sole proprietorship for the first two years. Then after two years I incorporated the business, and kept it this way for another two years then switched it back to a sole proprietorship and continue to run my business this way. Why I did this was that I simply didn't feel that the paperwork involved in running an incorporated business was worth the tax advantages given an incorporated business."*
>
> — Karin Kolodziejski
> Metaskills Consulting

Here are some of the advantages and disadvantages of starting your consulting practice under the sole proprietorship model.

## Advantages

- Easy to start
- Low start-up costs
- Flexible and informal
- Business losses can often be deducted from personal income for tax purposes

### Disadvantages

- Unlimited personal liability: the sole proprietor can be held personally responsible for debts and judgments placed against the business. This means that all personal income and assets, not just those of the business, can be seized to recoup losses or pay damages.
- All business income earned must be reported and is taxed as personal income.
- More difficult to raise capital for the business

## Incorporation

Incorporation of a business means that a separate, legal corporate entity has been created for the purpose of conducting business. Like an individual, corporations can be taxed, sued, can enter contractual agreements and are liable for their debts. Corporations are characterized by shareholders, a board of directors and various company officers. As such, ownership interests can be freely transferred.

Creating a corporation requires filing of numerous documents to legalize your consulting business, as well as formally naming a president, shareholders, and director(s), all of whom can be a single person as set out in the company charter. As the rules and forms required for incorporation vary from state to state and province to province, it's best to consult your local business licensing office or a local lawyer specializing in incorporation.

While it is probably best to seek legal expertise when incorporating, if you have the expertise and knowledge, you can incorporate your own business or use one of the many online resources that specialize in these matters. Here are a few websites offering such services, often for only a couple of hundred dollars:

- *BizFilings*
  **www.bizfilings.com**
- *The Company Corporation*
  **www.incorporate.com**

- *Companies Incorporated*
  **www.companiesinc.com**

- *Intuit—My Corporation.com*
  **www.mycorporation.com**

- *Form-a-Corp, Inc.*
  **www.form-a-corp.com**

Although some business consultants do not see the necessity for incorporation, others like Pat Curley of St. Lawrence Business Consultants Ltd. see it as a must for anyone entering independent consulting:

> *"I incorporated my consulting business right away. I wanted to protect myself and my personal assets from liability. I strongly recommend incorporating."*
>
> — Pat Curley
> St. Lawrence Business Consultants Ltd.

Here is a list of some of the advantages and disadvantages to incorporating your consulting firm.

### Advantages

- Protect personal assets and income from liability by separating your business income and assets from your personal.
- Corporations get greater tax breaks and incentives
- Ownership can be sold or transferred if the owner wishes to retire or leave the business
- Banks and other lending institutions tend to have more faith in incorporated businesses so raising capital is easier

### Disadvantages

- Increased start-up costs
- Substantial increase in paperwork
- Your business losses cannot be offset against your personal income
- Corporations are more closely regulated

An *S Corporation* is similar to the corporation in most ways, but with some tax advantages. The corporation can pass its earnings and profits on as dividends to the shareholder(s). However, as an employee of the corporation you do have to pay yourself a wage that meets the government's reasonable standards of compensation just as if you were paying someone else to do your job.

## Partnerships

Another business structure that some consultants choose over sole proprietorship or incorporation is the partnership. A partnership is precisely as its name implies, a business venture entered into by two or more people with the intent to carry on business and earn profits. Partnerships can be beneficial for consultants as the workload and finances can be shared, and partners with differing areas of expertise can increase business opportunities.

You must register your partnership with a corporate registry. This does not mean that you must incorporate, only that you are making a formal declaration of entering into business with another person or persons. Be sure to consult your local business registry and a lawyer specializing in business registry. The primary purpose for doing this is for each partner to protect himself or herself concerning issues such as sharing profits, liability and dissolving the partnership equitably.

Below are some of the potential advantages and disadvantages to partnerships:

### Advantages

- More initial equity for start-up costs
- Broader areas of expertise can lead to increased opportunities
- Lower start-up costs than incorporation
- Some tax advantages

### Disadvantages

- All partners are equally liable for the other's mistakes with the same liability as a sole proprietorship

- Profits and losses must be shared
- The business must be dissolved and reorganized when a partner leaves

Beyond any legal issues, before going into business with a partner you should spend many hours talking about how you will work together, including:

- What each of you will be responsible for
- How you will make decisions on a day-to-day basis
- What percentage of the business each of you will own
- How you see the business developing in the future
- What you expect from each other

During your discussions you can learn if there are any areas where you need to compromise. For example, one of you may want to start your business as a part-time job, while the other wants to work full-time and eventually build a business that will employ a dozen or more people. You can avoid future misunderstandings by putting the points you have agreed on into a written "partnership agreement" that covers any possibility you can think of (including one of you leaving the business at some point in the future).

## Limited Liability Company (LLC)

A Limited Liability Company is a newer type of business legal structure in the U.S. It is a combination of a sole proprietorship (where there is only one member of the LLC) or partnership and a corporation, and is considered to have some of the best attributes of each, including limited personal liability.

An LLC business structure gives you the benefits of a partnership or S corporation while providing personal asset protection like a corporation. Similar to incorporating, there will be substantial paperwork involved in establishing this business structure. LLCs have flexible tax options, but are usually taxed like a partnership.

Here are some of the advantages and disadvantages of LLCs:

**Advantages**

- Limited liability similar to a corporation
- Tax advantages similar to a corporation
- Can be started with one (except in Massachusetts) or more members like a sole proprietorship or partnership

**Disadvantages**

- More costly to start than a sole proprietorship or partnership
- Consensus among members may become an issue
- LLC dissolves if any member leaves

In the end, choosing a business legal structure for your consulting practice is a personal choice, and the advantages and disadvantages should be considered thoroughly. Many consultants begin their independent venture as a sole proprietorship because of the low costs, and incorporate as the business grows and the engagements become larger and more complex. For more information about business structures take a look at the resources available at FindLaw.com. The direct link is **http://smallbusiness.findlaw.com/incorporation-and-legal-structures**.

For some additional government resources to help you decide which structure to choose in the U.S., try the Small Business Administration (**www.sba.gov/category/navigation-structure/starting-managing-business/starting-business/establishing-business/incorporating-registering-you-0**). In Canada, visit the Canada Business Services for Entrepreneurs site at **www.canadabusiness.ca**. Click on "English," then on "Starting a Business," scroll down and click on "Getting Started" and choose "Forms of Business Organization."

## 6.1.3 Choosing a Business Name

Like most entrepreneurial endeavors, independent business consultants have the choice of either using their own name as part of the business name or choosing a relevant yet "catchy" name for the business. But there are a few things to consider when deciding how to present and market your consulting practice.

Using your own name for the business, which most often includes your surname such as Smith Consulting, is an excellent way to establish yourself as a leader in the field and get your name out at the same time. The drawback to using your surname as part of your business identity, particularly when starting out, is that it may be unfamiliar to those searching for consulting services, prompting these potential clients to go with larger, more established consultants.

On the other hand, if you have already made inroads into the business community and established an excellent reputation, using your own name in your business may pay off. Former associates and clients will recognize and associate your name and company with quality and subsequently turn to you when in need of consulting services.

Likewise, if you have achieved fame and respect in another arena, clients are likely to be attracted to your new consulting business if you name it after yourself. An excellent example of this is former New York City mayor Rudolph W. Guiliani, honored by *Consulting Magazine* as "Consultant of the Year" in 2002, whose consulting firm is named "Guiliani Partners LLC" (**www.giulianipartners.com**).

Of course, the other option is to choose a business name with characteristics that appeal more to you as an individual, or that you think may appeal to your potential clients. Perception can play a major part in landing clients as a business consultant. So take this into consideration when deciding on your business name.

Founder and president of St. Lawrence Business Consultants Ltd., Pat Curley, in Buffalo, New York, used a "broader" business name instead of his surname with a strategic purpose in mind: "I decided to use a business name because I wanted to give the perception of a larger company, but I also chose this type of name in anticipation of the growth of my business."

One trend in recent years for naming businesses has been to employ the use of acronyms; think of IBM (International Business Machines). Acronyms offer an easy way for potential clients to remember your name, and an easy way to incorporate your name into your business and still appear as a larger company at the same time, such as JS Consulting (Jane Smith Consulting).

Although choosing a business name for your consulting practice is entirely up to you, there is one essential consideration: your business name should not resemble the name of another similar business offering similar services. For one thing, prospective clients may confuse the other business with yours and go with your competitor's services instead of yours. In addition, if you do use a name too similar to another business that was in business first they will have grounds for legal action against you.

Before officially registering your business name, you must conduct formal fictitious names and trademark searches. (The fictitious names database is where non-trademarked business names are listed.) A trademark database lists all registered and trademarked business names. In the U.S., the essential place to start is with the U.S. Patent and Trademark Office. You can hire a company to do a name search for you, or conduct a free search yourself at the PTO's website at **www.uspto.gov/main/trademarks.htm**.

In Canada, the default database for name searches is the Newly Upgraded Automated Name Search (NUANS) at **www.nuans.com**. There is a $20 charge for each NUANS search. You can also hire a company such as Arvic Search Services (**www.arvic.com**) or **www.biznamesearch.com** to help you with name searches, trademarks and incorporating your business for a fee. Check online for "corporate registry services" to find other companies.

## 6.1.4 Choosing Your Location

For business consultants, choosing a business location is not as complicated or as pressing as it is for retailers where location means everything. Business consultants have the luxury of setting up shop wherever they choose. There are, however, some factors you may wish to consider when deciding where to do business.

### Your Business Connections

This factor in choosing a business location is obvious: the more people you know in the business world, the better your chances of getting engagements. While you might choose to start your consulting practice in a new city where you have always wanted to live, it will likely take longer to get your business off the ground than if you choose to work in the city where you have the greatest number of established business and personal connections.

For many, the greatest number of connections will be in the city where they currently work. But perhaps you have moved many miles away from your home town to attend school or take a job. You may now want to consider moving back to your home town, to where people know you best. You'll be returning with credentials, experience and a vision. Make some calls and search the Internet to determine whether where you want to work has the ability to sustain your practice.

## Urban or Rural

Choosing to start your consulting in either a city center or rural environment is another factor to consider. In urban areas, there is more money to be made from bigger clients, as well as more prospects per square mile. However, competition for these clients will come from big players in the industry, as well as numerous other independent consultants. Depending on where you live, you may have the option of working with both rural and urban clients. For example, if you live close to a major city, you could solicit jobs in the city and commute.

## Home Office or Office Space

Much like choosing a business name, your choice of office location may depend on client perception. However, if you don't intend to invite clients to your office, and there often is no need to do so in consulting, then a home office is the most economical place for you to establish your business. Many consultants choose to keep their office in their home for the long term.

Before you can decide where to house your business, you have to determine what functions you need your office to serve. Take into consideration the services you provide and what tasks you will need to do in your office. Consider whether you will meet with clients at your office. Many consultants don't, and always travel to the client's home or place of business. You will also need to consider if you have enough space to store documents and other materials, and space for future employees or partners to work.

### Home Office

This is the cheapest and easiest office location. And don't forget the short commute time. If you have the space in your home to set up a dedicated office that will allow you to run your business, then you should probably consider this option.

You'll need to check your local zoning laws, as some areas don't allow you to run a business from your home, while others have no such restrictions. There are other areas that allow you to run a business as long as no clients come to your home. Contact your local government for more information before you proceed.

Working from your home offers the additional benefits of easier setup, claiming a home office deduction on your taxes (if you meet the criteria), and generally more time with family. Cons include the inevitable distraction from family and neighbors, working too much, failing to separate work and personal life, feeling isolated, and lack of space.

### Office Space

If you decide to rent space, start by determining what your requirements are. You can use the checklist on the next page as a starting point.

If you want the appearance of a professional office space, but cost is an issue, consider shared office space in a business center or executive suite. These facilities are typically furnished offices that provide you with receptionist and mail services. They may also offer photocopiers, fax machines, Internet access, and conference rooms that you can use for client meetings. Check the Yellow Pages under "office space" or do a Google search for your city and "shared office space," "business center" or "executive suite."

# 6.2 Financial Matters

## 6.2.1 Start-up and Operating Expenses

Although your clients will reimburse you for expenses that can be directly attributed to the projects you do for them (see section 6.2.6), you will have a number of business expenses that you won't be able to bill to your clients. Fortunately, a consulting business is a relatively inexpensive business to start.

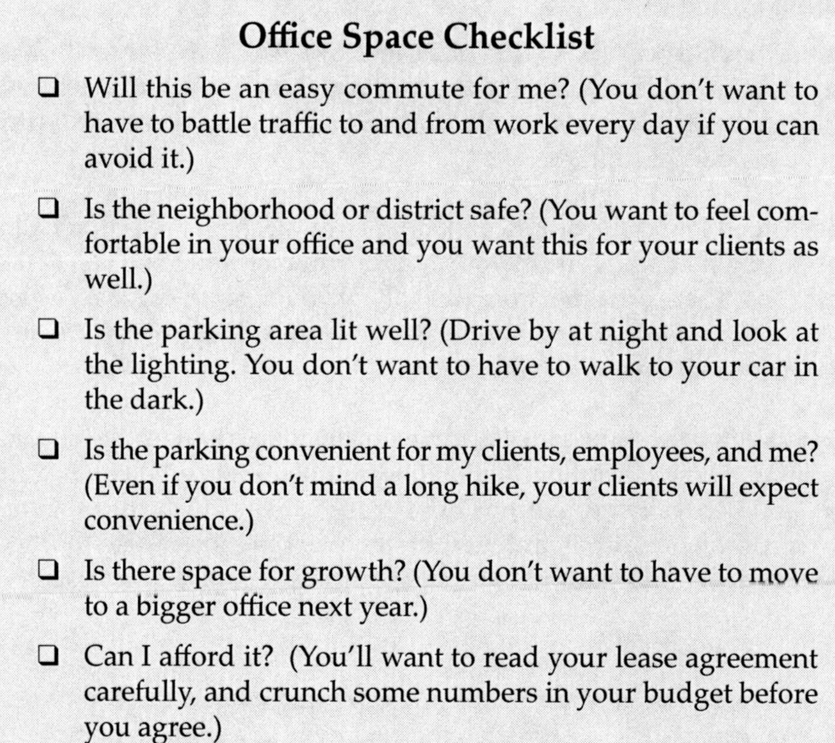

### Office Space Checklist

- ❑ Will this be an easy commute for me? (You don't want to have to battle traffic to and from work every day if you can avoid it.)
- ❑ Is the neighborhood or district safe? (You want to feel comfortable in your office and you want this for your clients as well.)
- ❑ Is the parking area lit well? (Drive by at night and look at the lighting. You don't want to have to walk to your car in the dark.)
- ❑ Is the parking convenient for my clients, employees, and me? (Even if you don't mind a long hike, your clients will expect convenience.)
- ❑ Is there space for growth? (You don't want to have to move to a bigger office next year.)
- ❑ Can I afford it? (You'll want to read your lease agreement carefully, and crunch some numbers in your budget before you agree.)

Use the budget forms that appear on the next few pages to estimate your start-up expenses and your monthly operating expenses. Note that even if an item is listed, that doesn't mean you have to budget for it. You may not need it, or you may already have it. You should also consider if there are expenses not on this list that will apply to you.

Your monthly operating expenses include both fixed and variable costs. Fixed costs remain the same from month to month regardless of the amount of work you do (examples include rent and membership dues), while variable costs may vary from month to month (examples include travel and taxes). To estimate monthly variable costs, start by estimating a yearly total than divide that by 12 for a monthly average.

Creating a monthly budget will help you plan for your first year in business. After the first year, you can then build a budget for year two based on what you actually spent during your first year. Your monthly budget will also help you determine what costs you need to cover before you start making a profit.

Your own costs may vary widely from those of other consultants, depending on what you currently have and what you plan to do with your business. For example, your rent might range from $0 if you have a home office to $1,000 per month for leased office space.

### Start-Up Expenses

| | |
|---|---|
| Office furniture<br>(see checklist later in this section) | $________ |
| Computer | $________ |
| Printer/copier/fax/scanner<br>(separate or all-in-one) | $________ |
| Office software | $________ |
| Business phone line installation fee | $________ |
| Telephone | $________ |
| Office supplies | $________ |
| Stationery | $________ |
| Business cards | $________ |
| Printing<br>(brochures or other marketing materials) | $________ |
| Website setup costs<br>(design, domain name, etc.) | $________ |
| Business licenses/fees | $________ |
| Professional consulting<br>(lawyer, accountant) | $________ |
| Other<br>(list each item) | $________ |
| **TOTAL** | $________ |

## Monthly Operating Expenses

| | |
|---|---|
| Salaries | $__________ |
| Benefits | $__________ |
| Rent (or portion of mortgage) | $__________ |
| Office supplies<br>(see checklist later in this section) | $__________ |
| Telephone | $__________ |
| Internet service | $__________ |
| Postage and courier | $__________ |
| Travel expenses including mileage | $__________ |
| Insurance costs | $__________ |
| Membership dues | $__________ |
| Printing materials | $__________ |
| Marketing expenses | $__________ |
| Web hosting | $__________ |
| Magazine subscriptions and<br>professional literature | $__________ |
| Training and conferences | $__________ |
| Legal and accounting services | $__________ |
| Banking expenses | $__________ |
| Entertainment | $__________ |
| Taxes | $__________ |
| Other (list each item) | $__________ |
| **TOTAL** | $__________ |

Following are checklists of typical equipment and supplies. Most of the large retail office supply chains can set you up with everything you need for your office at a reasonable price.

- *Staples*
  **www.staples.com**
- *Office Depot*
  **www.officedepot.com**
- *OfficeMax*
  **www.officemax.com**

### Supplies and Small Equipment

- ❑ Accordion files
- ❑ Binders
- ❑ Brochures
- ❑ Business cards
- ❑ Business stationery
- ❑ Calculator
- ❑ Cell phone
- ❑ Day planner or PDA
- ❑ Envelopes (all sizes)
- ❑ File folders
- ❑ File labels
- ❑ Index cards
- ❑ Laser pointer and other supplies for making presentations
- ❑ Mailing labels

- ❑ Mailing envelopes
- ❑ Paper
- ❑ Paper clips
- ❑ Paper cutter
  (for trimming brochures, postcards, etc.)
- ❑ Pens, pencils, markers, and erasers
- ❑ Post-it notes
- ❑ Postage stamps
- ❑ Rubber bands
- ❑ Ruler
- ❑ Stapler and staples
- ❑ Tape

## Furniture and Equipment Checklist

- ❑ Bookcases for reference material
- ❑ Chair(s)
- ❑ Computer and software
- ❑ Printer/fax/copier/scanner
- ❑ Desk (one or more)
- ❑ Filing cabinet
- ❑ Lamps and lighting
- ❑ Storage shelves
- ❑ Work table
  (for putting together packets of material)

## 6.2.2 Start-up Financing

Although the start-up costs for consulting are minimal, you may want to secure a loan or investment to get through the early months, purchase some office equipment, or lease office space. The following may be possible sources of funding for you:

### Your Own Savings

Never forget that you might be your own best source of funding. To raise your own capital you might cash out stocks, bonds, life insurance, or a retirement account. Or you may have something of value that you could sell.

#### Credit Cards and Lines of Credit

These are great vehicles for "stop-gap money" — that is, money you need right away to pay for something that you know money is coming in for, such as printing materials for a client. But try not to use credit on a long-term basis. You'll end up paying costly interest that can really drag down your business.

### Family and Friends

One of the greatest resources for your start-up money may be people you know who believe in you and your ideas — your family and friends. They may help you with money when all other resources fail, they may agree to payback terms that aren't as strict as commercial lenders, and they are pulling for you, too. As with any other kind of loan, it is important to ensure that both parties understand and agree to the terms of the loan. Make sure you have a written document which states when and how you will pay the loan back.

### Partners

For some new business owners, finding a person who wants to partner with them, share the responsibility of their new business, and who will bring some money to invest, too, is the perfect solution. If you plan to partner with another business consultant, you can find some good advice in section 6.4.

A silent partner may simply be looking to make money by investing in your business. These investors work one of two ways: they want to see their initial money returned with a profit, or they want to own part of your business. You have to decide if you feel you will be able to meet the terms of the investor and if you want to share ownership of your business with another person.

## A Commercial Loan

Commercial loans are loans that you can get from a financial institution. These include traditional banks, credit unions, savings and loans and commercial finance companies. The terms of your loan will depend upon several things, including your credit score, your collateral, and your ability to pay back a loan. Be sure to compare interest rates and terms of lending to see which institution offers the best deals.

### Loans for Start-Ups

When you are starting your business, financial institutions will likely lend the money to you personally rather than to your business, as a result, they are much more interested in your personal financial status than your business plan. A business just starting up won't count as collateral, so you'll probably need to guarantee the loan with personal assets like your house or your car.

They will look at how much money you need every month to pay your bills, what kind of resources or assets you have, what kind of debt you are in, and how you will repay this debt while you are putting your total effort into opening your business.

### Loans for Established Businesses

Once your business is established, if you want a commercial loan in order to expand – for example to open consulting offices in other cities – the financial institution may be willing to lend the money to your business rather than to you personally.

In that case, the lending institution will insist on seeing a formal business plan that demonstrates clearly-defined financial and business goals. You will also need to prepare a loan proposal, which includes a credit application, and provide information about your business including the following:

- The type of loan you're applying for
- Amount you are requesting
- What you will use for collateral
- How the money will be used
- Information about your business, its name, legal structure, tax numbers, existing loans, taxes owed, assets
- Details about the business owners or principals: name, mortgages, source of other income

### Government Resources

In the United States, the Small Business Administration (SBA) does not actually lend you the money to start your new business. However, they do guarantee loans through commercial lenders. For information and answers to financial questions, visit **www.sba.gov** and click on "Loans & Grants."

In Canada, the Business Development (BDC) bank offers business owners support and long-term funding. BDC offers start-up financing up to $100,000 that can be repaid over a period of up to 6 years. For information about the BDC's services and other helpful business information, visit **www.bdc.ca/en**.

## 6.2.3 Taxes

As you know, businesses are responsible for many different types of taxes and you need to know your responsibilities when you operate your own consulting firm. While most consultants work with a tax advisor or accountant, you can also refer to a number of resources.

The Internal Revenue Service (IRS) has a number of informative documents online that you can read to become better informed about your tax obligations as a small business owner. Visit the IRS—Small Business and Self-Employed One-Stop Resource site at **www.irs.gov/businesses/small** and check out the IRS Tax Guide for Small Business at **www.irs.gov/pub/irs-pdf/p334.pdf**.

For Canadian residents, the Canada Revenue Agency provides basic tax information for new business owners including how to register for the Goods and Services Tax (GST), for which all businesses with earnings over $30,000 CDN must register. Find information for Small Business and Self-Employed Individuals at **www.cra-arc.gc.ca/tx/bsnss/menu-eng.html**.

It is also important to be informed about your tax obligations at the state and local level. Tax laws and requirements vary state by state and province by province. Also make sure you find out exactly what you are responsible for in your own city. For U.S. state tax information visit BankRate.com. The direct link is **www.bankrate.com/finance/taxes/check-taxes-in-your-state.aspx**. In Canada, the CRA has links to provincial tax information for small business at **www.cra-arc.gc.ca/tx/bsnss/prv_lnks-eng.html**.

You will also need to understand payroll taxes if you plan to hire employees, and each new employee needs to fill out paperwork when they are hired. In the U.S. this will be the W-4 and I-9 forms. In Canada, employees complete both a T-4 and a Canada Pension form.

Check with your state or province's labor office to make sure you are clear about all the forms employees must fill out to work for you. Visit the IRS or CRA sites for additional information on the legalities of payroll taxes and information on where to get blank copies of the forms your employees will need to fill out. For U.S. forms do a search at **www.irs.gov/formspubs**. For Canadian forms visit **www.cra-arc.gc.ca/formspubs**.

## 6.2.4 Insurance

Insurance can help protect the investment you make in your company from unforeseen circumstances or disaster. Types of insurance for the small business owner are listed in this section. Contact your insurance broker to determine what types of coverage are right for you.

You may also want to check out the National Association for the Self-Employed (**www.nase.org**) which offers reasonably priced insurance plans for self-employed people. Some insurers offer specific insurance for home businesses. Insure.com has a valuable article that discusses how to shop for home-based insurance at **www.insure.com/articles/businessinsurance/home-business-insurance.html**.

## Liability Insurance

This insurance (also known as *Errors and Omissions Insurance*) protects you against loss if you are sued for alleged negligence. It could pay judgments against you (up to the policy limits) along with any legal fees you incur defending yourself. For example, if you neglect to distribute a new company policy document to the company's employees, thinking that management was responsible for doing this and the company experiences financial losses as a result, you might find this type of insurance valuable.

## Property Insurance

This insurance covers losses to your personal property from damage or theft. If your business will be located in your home, you're most likely already covered with homeowner's insurance. However, it's a good idea to update your plan to provide coverage for office equipment and other items that aren't included in a standard plan.

If your business will be located in a building other than your home, you may need an additional policy. If you rent space, you'll need property insurance only on the equipment you have in your office — the owner of the building normally would pay for insurance on the property.

## Life and Disability Insurance

If you provide a portion of your family's income, then you need to carry life insurance and disability insurance to make certain they are cared for if something happens to you. If you become sick or otherwise disabled for an extended period, your business could be in jeopardy. Disability insurance would provide at least a portion of your income while you're not able to be working.

## Business Interruption Insurance

This insurance covers your bills and lost profit while you are out of operation for a covered loss, such as a fire. Just because the business is shut down doesn't mean the bills stop coming. This type of insurance covers ongoing expenses such as rent or taxes until your business gets up and running again.

### Car Insurance

Be sure to ask your broker about your auto insurance if you'll be using your personal vehicle on company business.

### Health Insurance

If you live in the United States and aren't covered under a spouse's health plan, you'll need to consider your health insurance options. You can compare health insurance quotes at **www.ehealthinsurance.com** which offers plans from over 150 insurance companies nationwide.

> **TIP:** Some insurance companies offer discount pricing for members of particular organizations. When you are looking for organizations to join, whether your local Chamber of Commerce or a national association, check to see if discounted health insurance is one of the member benefits.

Canadians have most of their health care expenses covered by the Canadian government. For expenses that are not covered (such as dental care, eyeglasses, prescription drugs, etc.) self-employed professionals may get tax benefits from setting up their own private health care plan. Puhl Employee Benefits (**www.puhlemployeebenefits.com**) is an example of the type of financial planning company that can help you set up your own private health care plan.

### More Information

The Small Business Administration has an excellent risk management guide for small businesses available online at **www.buzgate.org/8.0/pdf/ft_risk.pdf**.

## 6.2.5 Setting Your Fees

One of the biggest challenges for novice business consultants is determining how much to charge clients and how to present the bill. In a November 2006 article at Forbes.com, journalist Mary Crane wrote:

> "New entrepreneur consultants tend to undercharge for their services. This mistake is understandable. ... it's difficult to know the going rate because most consultants vigilantly guard their prices."

However, through the research and interviews conducted in the process of writing this book, we found a number of consultants willing to share their fees and the process used for setting those fees. We have distilled their advice into a step-by-step formula you can use for setting fees. This section also offers insights on factors you may want to consider in setting your own fees.

As mentioned in the introduction, independent business consultants can earn $35 to $400 or more per hour. Factors affecting the fees you may charge include:

- Your income requirements (this includes how much you want to be paid, your business expenses, and how much profit you want your company to earn)
- Your reputation
- Your specialization (Forbes.com reports that strategy consultants usually charge the highest fees, followed by operations, human resources, and IT consultants)
- Your client and their budget (large corporations typically pay more than small businesses or non-profit organizations)
- Your relationship with the client
- Your competitors' fees if you will be competing for projects
- Your geographic location (urban-based consultants interviewed for this book usually charge more than rural-based consultants, while Forbes says those in large cities on the East or West coasts typically charge "up to 25% higher than ... their Midwestern and Southern counterparts")

As you can see, some of these factors involve market conditions, while others, such as your income requirements, are entirely under your control. Some consultants can charge higher fees because they refuse to respond to RFPs or compete for projects, choosing instead to convince targeted clients of the value they can bring them. (Marketing to clients is covered in the next chapter.)

Business Consultants can structure their fees in a variety of ways. The most common ways for consultants to charge for their services are one or more of the following:

- Hourly rate
- Daily rate
- Per project fee
- Monthly retainer
- Based on performance

This section of the book provides information about each of these types of fee structures, followed by advice on charging for expenses, invoicing, and getting paid.

## Hourly Rate

Charging by the hour is a common fee structure for business consultants. For example, a recent study of engineering consultants by IEEE-USA found that 73% charged on an hourly basis. While any consultant may choose to charge an hourly rate, particularly for a short engagement, hourly rates are ideal for beginning consultants. The Forbes.com article reported that "customers are more comfortable working on an hourly basis with new consultants."

So how do you determine your hourly rate? While you could simply pick an hourly rate you would like to charge (such as $100 per hour), or an annual salary you would like to earn (such as $100,000) divided by the number of working hours in a year to determine your hourly rate, most consultants take a more systematic approach in setting their fees.

To ensure that your costs are covered and that your business can prosper, it's recommended that you do some number-crunching using the formula below. Try it with different figures (such as different annual incomes) to help you settle on an appropriate hourly fee to charge.

1. Decide how much you want for your annual salary.
2. Estimate your number of working hours per year.
3. Estimate how many of those hours will generate revenue.
4. Determine your overhead costs.
5. Decide how much profit you want to earn.
6. Calculate your hourly rate.

## Step 1: Decide Your Annual Salary

To get started, choose a figure you would like to earn as your annual salary. For the purpose of illustrating how this formula works, we'll assume you want to earn an annual salary of $80,000.

## Step 2: Estimate How Many Hours You'll Work

While you may be planning to work "full-time," that means different things to different consultants. Some consider full-time to be eight hours a day, five days a week, with two weeks off for vacation. If so, you will work:

40 hours per week x 50 weeks = 2,000 hours per year

Your own hours per year will likely vary from this amount. If you are like many entrepreneurs, you may find yourself working more than 40 hours per week. For example, you may work 10 hours per day or six days per week. On the other hand, you may want more vacation time or you may want to consult on a part-time basis. Plug your own estimated hours into this formula.

## Step 3: Estimate Your Paid Hours

The next step is to estimate the percentage of your working time that will be spent on revenue-generating activities. This is a key consideration that is sometimes overlooked by entrepreneurs. However, the reality is that you will not be spending 100% of your working hours on revenue-generating activities. Instead, you will need to assume that some of your time will be spent on other activities. Here are a few examples:

- Administrative work
- Attending networking events
- Preliminary consultations (many consultants provide the first meeting to prospective clients for free)
- Other marketing activities
- Submitting proposals that don't result in work
- Learning (reading, taking courses, etc.)
- Down time (sick days or time off)

In an article at the *Wall Street Journal*'s CareerJournal.com, author Stephen Fishman wrote, "you'll probably spend at least 25% to 35% of your time on tasks such as bookkeeping and billing, marketing your services, upgrading your skills and doing other things you can't bill to clients." Kennedy Information, which publishes *Consulting Magazine*, estimates consultants spend 58% to 62% of their time working directly for their clients, which means 38% to 42% of the typical consultant's time is not billable to a client.

Because your first year in business is likely to involve additional work to get the business off the ground, it's wise to estimate a higher percentage of time spent on such tasks in your first year than you might estimate for subsequent years. For the purpose of our example, we will assume that 40% of your time will be spent on tasks that don't generate revenue, so 60% of your hours will be paid.

60% of 2,000 hours = 1,200 paid hours per year

### Step 4: Determine Your Overhead Costs

As mentioned, your clients will reimburse you for expenses that can be directly attributed to the projects you do for them (see section 6.2.6). But you will have a number of overhead expenses that you won't be able to bill to your clients. Overhead is all the non-labor expenses needed to run your business. Some examples include: rent, utilities, insurance, office equipment, and membership fees.

Overhead costs can vary tremendously from one consulting business to another. For example, a home-based business is likely to have considerably lower expenses than a consulting firm with office space and an administrative assistant. Use the total amount that you came up with in section 6.2.1. For example, if you estimated that your monthly operating costs will be $4,000:

$4,000 per month = $48,000 per year

### Step 5: Decide How Much Profit You Want

Profit is generally expressed as a percentage of your total costs (your salary plus expenses). How much profit would you like your consulting business to earn? Unless you want to start a non-profit organization, the answer should certainly be more than 0%. Exactly how much more is entirely up to you.

There's no standard for how much profit you should be earning. Most recommendations we found ranged from 10% to 25% annual profit. Because you may have higher costs in your first year, you may want to aim lower than you might in subsequent years. So for the purpose of our example, we'll assume you want to earn a profit of 10%. Here's how you would calculate that based on our previous figures:

$80,000 salary + $48,000 expenses = $128,000 total costs

$128,000 x .10 = $12,800 profit

### Step 6: Calculate Your Hourly Rate

Once you have figured out the other numbers, you can easily come up with an estimated hourly rate, which you would then round up or down to come up with a fee that appears professional. Here's the hourly rate calculated from the numbers used throughout this example:

$80,000 salary + $48,000 expenses + $12,800 profit = $140,800

$140,800 divided by 1,200 hours = $117.33 per hour
(which you might round to $120 per hour)

To see what you would need to charge in order to earn a larger salary, work fewer hours, spend more on overhead, or make a larger profit, you can plug other numbers into the formula.

For example, if you want to work the same number of hours, but earn $100,000 per year instead of $80,000, spend $5,000 per month on overhead instead of $4,000, and earn a profit of 15% instead of 10%, here's how you would calculate your hourly rate:

$100,000 salary + $60,000 expenses + $24,000 profit = $184,000

$184,000 divided by 1,200 hours = $153.33 per hour
(which you might round to $150 per hour)

Likewise, if the figure you come up with doesn't seem reasonable for your market (e.g. you want to consult to non-profit organizations in a small town), and you are willing to work more hours, earn a lower annual income, spend less on overhead, or make a smaller profit, you can plug in figures that will reduce your hourly rate. Generally, a competitive hourly rate for business consultants in urban areas ranges from $100-$150. Experienced consultants can charge more and consultants working in rural areas typically charge less.

### Keeping Track of Your Hours

Below is a sample showing how you can keep track of your hours so you can bill your clients accordingly.

**Sample Time Tracking Record**

| Task | Date | Time | Hours |
|---|---|---|---|
| Meeting with management team | 08/02/12 | 09:00-10:30 | 1.5 |
| Preparation of presentation | 08/14/12 | 15:00-17:00 | 2.0 |
| Delivery of questionnaire to staff | 08/15/12 | 09:30-12:00 | 2.5 |
| Preparation of final analysis | 08/20/12 | 19:00-23:00 | 4.0 |

## Daily Rate

Many business consultants offer a daily rate (also known as a *per diem*) instead of, or in addition to, their hourly rate.

There are two systems most used by consultants to come up with a daily rate. The first, and most commonly used, is to simply multiply your hourly rate by eight. This is based on the assumption that you work eight hours per day on average.

So if your hourly rate is $150, you can quickly calculate your daily rate as follows:

$150 per hour x 8 hours = $1,200 daily rate

Although you will bill your clients your daily rate for each eight hours you work, you can still have flexibility in your schedule. For example, you might put in 12 hours one day and four hours the next, and charge for two days.

The other system for calculating your daily rate is to give clients a discount from your hourly rate as this may encourage clients to hire you for a period of days, rather than hours. We found such discounts ranging from 4% to 20%.

Here's how you would calculate a 5% discount off the $150 per hour rate:

$150 per hour x 8 hours x .95 = $1,140 daily rate

## Per Project

Consultants also have the option of charging a per project fee (may also be referred to as a *fixed fee* or *flat rate*). Many clients like per project fees because they know the maximum amount they will pay for a particular project. This fee structure may also work well with clients who balk at what they consider to be a high hourly fee. Clients who resist paying a consultant hundreds of dollars per hour may happily pay thousands of dollars for a consulting project that solves a problem for them.

You can use this fee structure for both short-term and long-term projects. One option when charging a per project fee is to charge a fixed fee for a specific deliverable, such as charging $3,000 to do a SWOT Analysis. To come up with a fees for a particular project you can either base it on how many hours it would take you to complete the project or you could base it on the value of the project to the client. For example, if your hourly rate is $100, but it only takes you 15 hours to do a particular project, you could charge more than $1,500.

Another option is to calculate a fee based on each particular project. In that case, you would meet with the client and conduct a needs analysis to calculate the number of hours it would take you to complete the project. You could then multiply the estimated number of hours by your hourly rate to come up with a total project fee, or else give the client a discount off your hourly rate. For example, if you calculate that it would take you 50 hours to complete the project and your fee is $100 per hour, your project fee might be $5,000 or a discounted amount such as $4,500.

> **TIP:** As an alternative to giving an exact fee, you can provide a range that the fee will fall within.

A per project fee structure works well for experienced consultants who can estimate how much time each particular project will take. The IEEE-USA study of engineering consultants found that 17% charge on a per project basis. According to the Forbes.com article, "Typically... high-level consultants like strategic planners or management coaches will charge per project."

For less experienced consultants, the difficulty with per project fees is estimating how long it will take you to complete a project. Beginning consultants may underestimate the number of hours a project will take, or they may neglect to include in the contract everything the client is required to provide. For example, if you require current market data in order to carry out the project and are expecting the client to provide that data to you, make sure that is stated in your contract (see section 6.3 for a sample contract). If they aren't able to provide the data and you haven't stated in your contract that market research is not included in the project fee, you may have to carry out the research yourself for no additional fee.

> **TIP:** Unless you are confident in your ability to calculate how much time each project will take, you may want to avoid a per project fee until you have more experience with that type of project.

If the project scope hasn't changed, it is unprofessional to try to renegotiate the project fee after the project has started because you neglected to account for all aspects of the project or miscalculated how many hours it would take you. Not only are clients unlikely to comply, they may question your expertise and it could keep them from hiring you for future projects. Instead, it may be better to chalk it up as a learning experience, work overtime if necessary to do the job as promised, and revise your fee for the next project.

However, if the project involves scope creep, where it expands beyond what was originally agreed upon, then it is reasonable to expect the client to pay a higher project fee. Make sure you have a clause in your contract to address what happens if the project expands beyond what was agreed upon. Then as soon as you are asked to do additional work or it becomes apparent that additional work will be necessary, meet with your client to inform them about the situation and let them know the additional cost if they decide to proceed with the additional work.

In order to quote an accurate project fee you'll need to know the exact scope of the project. That's where it becomes essential to do a needs analyis as described in section 2.2.1. Many consultants offer a free initial consultation. However, unless the project is a small one, that initial meeting will not be sufficient to gather all the information you need to accurately quote a project fee.

> **TIP:** Many consultants invest hours of unpaid time preparing proposals, however, you do not have to do so. Instead, you might charge a project fee to prepare a proposal. (See section 7.4 for advice on preparing proposals.)

## Monthly Retainer

A monthly retainer is a fee that clients pay you on a monthly basis. In return, you agree to be available for a particular number of hours of work each month. You are paid the retainer whether or not the client needs you for the full number of hours, and if you work more than the agreed number of hours you can bill for a higher fee.

Steady work like this is a triumph for a business consultant, as it's income that can be relied upon every month. It's also good for the client, because it ensures they have an expert who knows their company available to them every month on an ongoing basis, usually for a lower cost than it would cost the company to hire a full-time employee.

A retainer arrangement may be made for any period of time acceptable to both the client and the consultant. For example, you might work on retainer for a period of three months, six months, a year, or longer. If a retainer arrangement is renewed, it might be for the same fee or you might renegotiate the fee or number of hours.

To calculate the fee you can multiply your hourly rate by the number of hours you agree to be available to the client. However, many consultants will offer a discount, such as 10% off their hourly rate, to encourage clients to agree to a retainer. According to Entrepreneur.com, "the average income when a consultant is paid on a retainer basis is $3,500 per month."

## Pay for Performance

Some clients, particularly those with limited budgets, may offer to pay you based on your performance. You might be offered a commission, a percentage of future revenue, or a fee based on the results you create for them. For example, if you are a marketing consultant, a small business might offer to pay you a flat fee for each new client it gets as a result of your marketing consulting. Some new companies will offer consultants shares in the company in lieu of payment.

Some business consultants charge clients a percentage fee when they are hired either to save companies money, or help companies earn money. For example, you may be hired to help streamline a company's processes, with the ultimate goal of making them more efficient and more profitable. Another scenario might be that you are hired as an advertising consultant and charged with the task of boosting sales. In either of these scenarios, you will be paid an agreed percentage of the dollar amount saved or earned. According to Pat Curley, a good take-home percentage for a business consultant is 3% of the project.

Pay for performance could give you the opportunity to make a great deal of money well above what you could make under other fee arrangements. However, there is also the risk that you will earn nothing. For example, if you're paid in shares and the company goes out of business, the shares will be worthless. In her consulting blog at **www.ConsultantJournal.com**, Vancouver marketing consultant Andréa Coutu, MBA, writes the following (reprinted with permission):

> *"Consulting fees based on performance pose several risks. For example, the company's performance in other areas may affect the area in which you are measured. It may take months or more to see the results of the work, meaning that the consultant will not see any revenue for a long period, effectively giving the company an interest-free loan. The company may not cooperate with you in implementing your full recommendations, compromising your ability to reach the potential you projected. Moreover, you may have a hard time checking to see whether the client has manipulated results. Can you be sure that your results are being reported accurately? Most importantly, you shift the focus from high quality planning to short-term gains. If you essentially*

*become a partner by sharing in the client's risk, you lose your objectivity. At the very least, seek a base rate plus performance pay or share of ownership. Sticking to contingency and performance-based fees opens a can of worms."*

— Andréa Coutu, MBA
**www.ConsultantJournal.com**

The bottom line in charging a percentage is to make sure that you are confident that you can accomplish the client's goals, and that it will actually result in revenue for you. It's also wise to ensure you have the financial resources to support yourself through the engagement.

**TIP:** If you're working on a percentage or pay for performance basis, you can ask the client to pay you a token per diem.

## 6.2.6 Charging for Expenses

Project expenses are a fact of life for business consultants, and clients are more often than not willing to reimburse their problem-solver for expenses above and beyond a consulting fee.

Expenses can be subjective and will vary from client to client. Generally, however, clients are willing to reimburse for items and activities that are perceived as being necessary to performing and completing the project. Below is a list of expenses that most clients will cover as part of doing business.

**TIP:** To ensure there are no misunderstandings, your contract with each client should specify what types of expenses will be billed to the client. (Section 6.3 has a sample contract.)

### Travel

Travel is a typical expense that most clients are willing to cover. Travel expenses include both mileage incurred on business, and sometimes commuting costs, as well as any airfare, train, or long-distance travel in your personal automobile. Most clients have a standard percentage that they offer employees for mileage and will likely extend this to the business consultants they hire.

## Accommodations

Anytime the client requires you to travel overnight or out of town is an expense that should be covered by the client. This includes if you have to travel from your home town and stay in the client's town in order to perform the engagement. If you are required to make the hotel arrangements, be sure to be reasonable about your choice, but also be sure that the hotel has the facilities you require to conduct business, such as fax and Internet capabilities.

## Parking

It is reasonable to request that parking fees be reimbursed, as these expenses can run $300 or more per month in busy city centers. This includes parking fees incurred at airports or hotels.

## Meeting and Meal Expenses

There may be occasions when your client requires you to meet with or entertain one of their clients who is fundamental to their business and the meeting is necessary in order to carry out the engagement. Any expenses incurred for meals can be charged back to your client.

## Equipment and Facilities Expenses

If you need to rent or purchase any hardware such as a projector or specific software, this can generally be charged back to the client. However, the client will expect that, as a professional business consultant, you have made some investment into your business for such items as a computer and the necessary software for doing your job. If you are expected to rent off-site meeting rooms or other facilities, this is clearly an expense that is the responsibility of the client.

## Printing and Supplies Expenses

You will usually be expected to cover minor printing costs, such as making copies of final reports, as part of your consulting fee. The same is true for incidental office supplies used in carrying out the consulting project. If you will need a significant amount of printing or supplies for the project, for example if you need printed questionnaires for thousands of employees, you may be able to use the client's copying facilities. However, you should confirm this during your initial consultation, and add printing and supplies as separate items to be expensed if necessary.

## Paying Service Providers

Service providers are individuals and companies that provide services you may need for your consulting projects. For example, you may need to hire a market research firm to organize a focus group.

If you plan to hire service providers, you have several options. One option is to pay the service provider's fee, then submit the invoice to your client along with other agreed upon expenses. In this case, you would need to specify in your contract that this service would be billed in addition to your consulting fee.

Another option is to have the service provider bill your client directly. That way you won't risk being in the position where you have to pay the service provider's bill before you have been paid by the client. However, this creates additional administrative work for the client, and you may prefer not to have the client establish a relationship directly with your supplier.

> **TIP:** It is not unheard of for a client to drop a consultant they perceive as the "middle man" and deal directly with service providers on future projects. Unless you absolutely trust your service provider not to compete for consulting business with you, you may not want to take that risk

Possibly the best option is to partner with the service provider (see section 6.4.1 for advice on how to establish a partnership) and offer their services under the umbrella of your consulting company. In that case the service provider is working for you rather than your client and would invoice your company. You in turn would invoice the client for the service as part of your consulting fee. Although you might be out of pocket for a while until you are paid by the client, this option can ultimately be more profitable for you. When giving the client a quote for your services, you could include the services at a price marked up to cover your overhead. For example, if the service provider charges you $1,000, you might charge the client a fee of $1,500 for that particular service.

### Miscellaneous Expenses

There usually are a number of small expenses that are required in the course of doing business, and despite each individual expense being minimal they can add up to a hefty amount. These expenses include items such as: courier expenses, postage, and long-distance charges.

When deciding what to charge your client as an expense, it is important not to "nickel-and-dime" a client. Nothing strains a relationship quicker than a client feeling as if they are being presented with petty charges. It may be prudent to build some of these expenses, such as postage and telephone calls, into your overall fee structure. This way, these charges won't appear on your invoice.

You will need to keep receipts for everything that you hope to be reimbursed for. If obtaining a receipt is not possible, be sure to write down all pertinent information such as day, time, cost, location, etc.

### What Not to Expense

As a reminder, here are a few items you should not try to bill your client for as an expense.

- Liquor
- Dry cleaning
- Local travel if you live in the same town as your client, although the client may offer you mileage
- Hotel upgrades (stick with the basics)
- Personal entertainment
- Anything that you believe you should cover as part of doing business as a consultant

## 6.2.7 Getting Paid

To keep your business financially healthy, you will need to ensure that you are paid in a timely manner. The first step is to ensure you have a contract that states when you will be paid. See section 6.3 for a sample contract. This section provides a detailed overview of when and how to invoice your clients.

## When to Ask for Payment

Many organizations have a policy of paying invoices after 30 days, although some stretch that to 45 days, 60 days, 90 days or even longer. As a small business owner, you may not be in the position where you can wait a month or longer to be paid after a project ends. You can therefore ask for a deposit and interim payments.

### Deposits

It's acceptable to ask the client for a deposit (advance payment) to be paid before you begin working. The deposit helps you cover your overhead costs until subsequent payments come in. For a short-term project you might require a deposit of 50% and payment upon completion of the assignment.

For long-term projects, for example if you have a year-long contract where the fee is on a monthly retainer basis, you could ask to be paid up front for either the first month alone, or both the first and last month. For example, if the monthly retainer is $2,500, you could ask for a deposit of either $2,500 or $5,000 before beginning work.

### Interim Payments

Even if you collect a deposit, you don't have to wait until the end of the project to collect the rest of your fee. The general rule for invoicing frequency is to do it often. Clients prefer to pay out small amounts at several intervals rather than one large, lump sum; it's easier on their accounting books and will provide you with a steady cash flow throughout the engagement.

You could invoice the client at the end of each phase of a consulting project, upon completion of specific project milestones, or based on elapsed time. For example, if you're actively engaged in a year-long project, invoicing on a bi-weekly or monthly basis is an appropriate frequency for both parties.

> *"If an engagement is going to take 24 months, you are going to want to get paid in the interim. So even though you've agreed on a per engagement fee, you must establish a monthly payment with the client that takes into consideration how much travel you'll be doing, how much a subordinate can do for you, and any third-parties you might need to hire. For example, if a 2-year*

*engagement is going to net $240,000, build in a provision that you're paid $10,000 a month for 24 months."*

— Pat Curley
St. Lawrence Business Consultants Ltd.

On the other hand, if the engagement is only for a few weeks or a month, it's appropriate to submit the invoice for the balance of your fee promptly upon completion of the project. If you're ever in doubt about the frequency of invoicing, simply address the issue with the client; they will appreciate knowing what to expect, and you will be fully aware of how to approach the process and can adjust your accounting accordingly, based on cash owed.

## How to Invoice

There are two basic types of invoices used by business consultants, itemized and non-itemized. An itemized invoice contains a breakdown of what is being charged for, and a non-itemized simply presents a bill for agreed-upon services performed. In most cases it is better to present an itemized invoice, but in cases when there is an agreed single fee for a short-term engagement, including expenses, a non-itemized invoice is acceptable. The items that should be included in an invoice are listed below, followed by a sample invoice. Remember to keep both a hard copy and an electronic copy of each invoice for your records.

### Your Business Name

Make sure the client has no doubt about whom the invoice is from. For a professional appearance, print the invoice on letterhead.

### Invoice Number

Invoice numbers are like check numbers, they allow you to keep track of what invoices have been issued and what is still outstanding (see the *Sample Invoice Tracking* document below). There are several different numbering systems that can be used. You can use several-digit numbers or incorporate letters to distinguish the type of project or the city, state or province in which the project took place. Many consultants prefer to use a numbering system that incorporates several digits in anticipation of growth of the business, and your client gets the impression that you have many clients and more business with an invoice number that reads 100-000-001, rather than just 001. Your tracking number can appear anywhere you like on the invoice.

### Client Name and Contact Information

Be sure that your invoice identifies the company (full legal business name) you did the consulting work for and includes the name of your contact at the company. For your reference, include the company address and other contact information.

### Invoice Date

This date will be the date that the invoice is submitted. The project dates will appear in the body of the invoice.

### Purchase Order Number

Some organizations use purchase order (PO) numbers to manage expenses. If a client uses purchase orders, they will either give you a paper copy or your contact person at the company will tell you the purchase order number.

### Reason for Invoice

This is a brief summary of the services provided to the client. It usually has the prefix Re: and allows busy people to glance at the invoice and know what the invoice is for. For example: "Re: Consulting services for improvement of quality assurance division." Including only "Re: Consulting Services" may suffice, but a large company may be employing more than one consultant at a time, so use your judgment.

### Services Provided

Under this heading you will be more specific about what services you provided to the client. If the payment structure was per engagement plus expenses, then this section should reiterate, or point to, what was agreed upon as the scope of services to be provided, as laid out in the letter of engagement. For example:

Consulting services, as per the letter of engagement......$4,000

If, however, you are charging by the hour, the services section of the invoice will have to be more specific. For example:

Initial meeting (2 hours @ $100/hr) ............................ $200.00
Team meeting (3 hours @ $100/hr) ............................ $300.00
Preparation of employee questionnaire
(5.5 hours @ $100/hr) .................................................. $550.00

### Expenses

If expenses have not been built into your consulting fee and will be paid individually, they should be itemized much like Services as shown below. Whenever possible, attach receipts for expenses to your invoice.

Meeting with client
(Round trip 100 miles @ $0.30/mile) .......................... $30.00
Airport parking............................................................ $15.00
Hotel and meals for conference................................. $380.00

### Total Amount Payable

Despite the fact that any good business person will double-check the numbers, do not make the client do the calculation, but provide a visible and accurate grand total. Be sure to denote if payment is to be made in U.S. or Canadian dollars.

### Terms of Payment

An invoice should state when payment is due, for example: "Payment due upon receipt" or "Payable within 30 days."

Closely related to the above is the inclusion of a single line, either included with payment date or by itself, that stipulates additional charges are applicable if payment is not received by a certain date. For example: "2% interest per month on overdue accounts"

### Where to Send Payment

Even if the invoice is printed on your letterhead, it's a good idea to place a "Payable to:" line on your invoice that includes your business name and address.

## Business or Tax Information

An important item to remember to include on an invoice is any business or tax number. In the U.S., if you're a registered business you'll be provided a Federal ID number. In Canada, businesses are required to charge the Good and Services Tax (GST). So be sure to include this number, as you'll be required to charge your clients this tax. To get this number, contact your local government tax office. See section 6.2.3 for more about taxes.

## Designing an Invoice

There are several ways to create an invoice. It can be done using a template in any of the numerous software packages designated for the home office, or it can be made from scratch using Microsoft Word or Excel. Use what you're comfortable with, but ensure it is as clear and concise as possible.

On the next few pages are a Sample Invoice and a Sample Invoice Tracking Document.

### Sample Invoice Tracking Document

| Invoice # | Client/ Address/ Phone | Date Billed | Sent to... | Amount | Date Payment Rec'd |
|---|---|---|---|---|---|
| 100-000-001 | BT Financial<br>345 Banks Rd.<br>Orlando, FL<br>555-555-5555 | June 20, 2012 | Billing Dept. | $3,879.98 | July 2, 2012 |
| 100-000-002 | HR Recruiting<br>452 Long Rd.<br>St. Louis, MO<br>555-666-1234 | Sept. 2, 2012 | Tammy Smith (Accounts Receivable) | $4,791.83 | Sept. 15, 2012 |
| | | | | | |
| | | | | | |

## Sample Invoice

*On Business Consultant's Letterhead*

**Date:** *[date]*

| **Invoice #** | 100-000-001 |
|---|---|
| **Federal Tax #** | 54321 |

**Client:** Client's Name
Company
Address

**Attention:** Name and Title of Contact Person

**Re:** Consulting Services as per the *[date]* letter of engagement. To investigate and deliver a recommended solution for the improvement of the manufacture of widgets.

| **Services and Expenses** | |
|---|---|
| **Item** | **Price** |
| Consulting Fee (as per agreement) | $4,000.00 |
| Meeting With Client<br>(round trip 100 miles @ $0.30/mile) | $30.00 |
| Airport Parking | $15.00 |
| Hotel and Meals for Conference | $380.00 |
| Less Deposit (paid *[date]*) | ($2,000.00) |
| **Balance Due:** | **$2,425.00** |

**Terms**

Payment is due within 30 days. Interest of 2% per month is charged for overdue accounts.

Please make check payable to: I.M. Aconsultant
XYZ Business Consulting Services
Somewhere, Somestate

Thank you for your business.

### Submitting an Invoice and Following Up

There are a variety of ways to submit an invoice to a client. You can deliver it by email, fax, mail, or courier, or present it in person. The key is to determine what works best for you and your client.

It is also important to establish where to send the invoice itself. For example, a large company may require the billing or accounting department to receive all invoices, whereas the owner of a smaller company may take a hands-on approach and oversee all of the expenses. Check with your client contact to find out where to send it.

If a client doesn't pay within the time requested on the invoice, then send another invoice, noting that payment is expected within a shorter time, perhaps five or ten days. This gives your client a reminder to quickly make the overdue payment. If a bill is not paid within 60 days, you will need to contact the client again. You can do this by phoning or writing. If you send a letter, you can make arrangements with the courier or post office to get confirmation that your client actually received it. If you're dealing with a corporate client that is slow to pay, you may have to make more than one phone call. If you work with that client again, you may want to consider requiring a larger deposit or interim payments before proceeding with work.

## 6.3 Client Contracts

Contracts are vital to your business. A contract can help to protect you and ensure you get paid for your services. It can avoid misunderstandings by ensuring you and your client have the same expectations of the work to be done.

Your contract or agreement should spell out what services you will provide for the client, when you will provide them, as well as when and how you are to be paid. The contract should also include your company name and address, as well as the contact name, company name (if applicable) and address of your client.

On the pages that follow you will find two samples. You can adapt these contracts to fit your needs. The first is a sample engagement letter you might use for a small consulting project with an individual client. You could ask your clients to sign it at your initial meeting, or have them return it to you later.

The second is a services agreement which you could adapt for use with a corporate client. It covers a number of additional areas, such as a liability disclaimer.

## Sample Engagement Letter

*(On Your Letterhead)*

*[Insert name of Client]*
*[Insert address of Client]*

*[Insert date]*

Attention: *[Insert name of client]*

As promised, I have set out below a description of the services that *[insert your company name]* will provide to you.

I will provide the following services:

*[Insert description of the services, such as consultations with the client, reviewing documents, etc.]*

My fee for the services performed will be as follows:

*[Insert rates, when payment is due, etc.]*

If you agree that the foregoing fairly sets out your understanding of our agreement, please sign a copy of this letter in the space indicated below, and return it to me at *[insert your address, fax number or e-mail address]*.

Yours sincerely,

*[Insert your name]*

Agreed and Accepted:

________________________________

*[Insert name of client]*

________________________________

Date

## Sample Services Agreement

THIS AGREEMENT is made this [date] day of [month], 20__.

BETWEEN
*[insert name of your client]* (the "Client"); and *[insert your name or your company's name]* (the "Consultant"), collectively referred to as the "Parties."

### 1.1 Services

The Consultant shall provide the following services ("Services") to the Client in accordance with the terms and conditions of this Agreement:

*[Insert a description of the services here]*

### 1.2 Delivery of the Services

**Start date:** The Consultant shall commence the provision of the Services on *[insert date here]*.

**Completion date:** The Consultant shall complete the Services by *[insert date here]* ("Completion Date").

**Key dates:** The Consultant agrees to provide the following parts of the Services by the specific dates set out below:

*[Insert dates here if you have agreed to specific milestones]*

### 1.3 Fees

As consideration for the provision of the Services by the Consultant, the fees for the provision of the Services are *[insert fees here]* ("Fees"). The Client shall pay for the Consultant's out-of-pocket expenses including [insert here] and other expenses as agreed by the Parties.

### 1.4 Payment

The Client agrees to pay the Fees to the Consultant on the following dates: *[e.g. 50% deposit payable before work begins; also specify whether the price will be paid in one payment, in installments or upon completion of specific milestones].*

The Consultant shall invoice the Client for the Services that it has provided to the Client *[monthly/weekly/after the Completion Date]*. The Client shall pay such invoices *[upon receipt/within 30 days of receipt]* from the Consultant.

Any charges payable under this Agreement are exclusive of any applicable taxes or other fees charged by a government body and such shall be payable by the Client to the Consultant in addition to all other charges payable hereunder.

### 1.5 Warranty

The Consultant represents and warrants that it will perform the Services with reasonable skill and care.

### 1.6 Limitation of Liability

Subject to the Client's obligation to pay the Fees to the Consultant, either party's liability arising directly out of its obligations under this Agreement and every applicable part of it shall be limited in aggregate to the Fees. The Consultant assumes no liability due to the quality of items or services purchased for the Client.

### 1.7 Term and Termination

This Agreement shall be effective on the date hereof and shall continue until the completion date stated in section 1.2 unless terminated sooner. If the Client terminates this agreement for any reason before the scheduled completion date, the Client will reimburse the Consultant for all outstanding fees and out-of-pocket expenses.

### 1.8 Relationship of the Parties

The Parties acknowledge and agree that the Services performed by the Consultant, its employees, sub-contractors, or agents shall be as an independent contractor and that nothing in this Agreement shall be deemed to constitute a partnership, joint venture, or otherwise between the parties.

### 1.9 Confidentiality

Neither Party will disclose any information of the other which comes into its possession under or in relation to this Agreement and which is of a confidential nature.

### 1.10 Miscellaneous

The failure of either party to enforce its rights under this Agreement at any time for any period shall not be construed as a waiver of such rights.

If any part, term or provision of this Agreement is held to be illegal or unenforceable neither the validity or enforceability of the remainder of this Agreement shall be affected.

This Agreement constitutes the entire understanding between the Parties and supersedes all prior representations, negotiations or understandings.

Neither Party shall be liable for failure to perform any obligation under this Agreement if the failure is caused by any circumstances beyond its reasonable control, including but not limited to acts of god, war, or industrial dispute.

This Agreement shall be governed by the laws of the jurisdiction in which the Client is located.

Agreed by the Parties hereto:

Signed by: ______________________________

On behalf of: ______________________________
*[the Client]*

Signed by: ______________________________

On behalf of: ______________________________
*[the Consultant]*

**TIP:** Before using any contract, make sure you have it reviewed by your lawyer to ensure it protects you and meets your particular needs.

You might use them for a small project such as consulting with an individual for a few hours. Even with small projects, ask your lawyer about including additional clauses to protect you, such as a limitation of liability clause (see the sample services agreement for an example).

# 6.4 Working With Other People

## 6.4.1 Strategic Partners

Strategic partners are individuals and companies that you hire to provide additional services to your clients. The primary reason for developing strategic partnerships is that companies that hire business consultants have come to expect "turnkey" solutions. In other words, they expect the business consultant they hire to handle every aspect of the project, and don't want to have to hire five or six consultants with different specialties in order to get results.

The reality of today's complex business environment means that a single engagement may encompass technology, finance, human resources, and operations management to name a few. You may be hired as an expert in operations management, but your client will expect that you are responsible for all aspects of the project.

> *"What they (strategic partners) provide is the ability to be scalable, increase our size and respond to any project of any size fairly easily. For example, I'll never have a need for a CPA on staff, but having one as a partner is helpful because we can use this kind of expertise on an as needed basis."*
>
> — Linda Paralez, Ph.D.
> Demarche Consulting Group, Inc.

### Who to Partner With

Who to partner with is determined by your strengths, or perhaps more accurately your weaknesses. For example, if your specialty is in financial areas, you might want to develop a relationship with Human Resources and IT professionals, among others.

The bottom line with developing strategic partnerships is to ensure that you never have to turn down a job because you're concerned about a lack of knowledge in one area or another. This is precisely what these partnerships are for—to fill in knowledge gaps and allow you as a business consultant to take on challenges you might otherwise have declined.

Another consideration for choosing a partner is personal compatibility. Even if you're in desperate need for a human resources consultant to round out your team in order to take on an engagement, if you can't work with this person because of fundamental differences in business or ideologies it won't work. As you'll read later in this section, you can interview a potential partner in order to assess personal compatibility.

Even when you believe a potential partner has the right skills set and compatibility level for the job, a further consideration that can't be ignored is the geographic location of that person. If the potential partner has to travel a hundred miles on a daily basis, will he or she be there in peak condition to perform? There are solutions to this, such as relocation for the length of the engagement, but these ultimately represent added costs to the project. However, if it's the right person for the job, then any travel or expenses will be well worth the risk.

So that you don't get stuck in a situation where you can't take an engagement as the result of one of your partners not being available, it's a good idea to have a minimum of three partners in each of the categories that you require frequent help in.

Also, partnerships don't necessarily have to be in fields that you know you'll require immediate assistance with in order to complete a project. You should also consider strategic alliances with suppliers of products and services that your clients could use.

For example, business consultant Scott Braucht of Scott Braucht & Associates in Verona, Wisconsin, says: "I develop key relationships with advertisers and marketing people at media outlets. I get pre-negotiated contracts that give my clients discounted prices or no fee at all." By doing likewise you'll be able to offer your client the ability to advertise at what is usually a discounted price because of your alliance with an advertising specialist and you will be able to take on one more aspect of the client's project.

> *"Every consulting project leads to the need for additional resources, such as programmers, designers, project managers, even gophers. If you can be the one to connect the people with the need, your business will prosper."*
>
> — Marty M. Fahncke
> FawnKey & Associates

## Where to Find Strategic Partners

One of the most effective ways to find competent strategic partners is through local associations. Most, if not all, professions have associations at the national and local levels. Section 8.3 has a list of national associations; consult these associations for local organizations and professionals in your area.

## What to Ask Prospective Partners

When you are the one who has been awarded a consulting contract, as well as the primary consultant responsible for seeing that the project is carried out, it's in your best interest to scrutinize any individual you're considering taking on as a partner. One of the best ways to do this is to conduct an interview just as any human resources department would do during the hiring process. After all, the person you will be partnering with is in essence your employee, so it's important to conduct due diligence.

There are two primary aspects of the individual that you want to determine in an interview: professional and personal suitability. The questions asked during the professional portion of the interview would change based on the specialty of the potential partner. However, below are a few example questions to facilitate the process.

## Professional Questions

Since you already have, or should have, a copy of this individual's resume, you are looking to ask questions that elaborate on the person's experience, and not just have them reiterate what you already know. To accomplish this, you might ask questions such as:

- Provide an example of two major problems you resolved during your last project or place of business.

- What skills did you bring to your last project?
- What skills can you offer this project?
- How do you define or determine progress during an engagement?
- Tell me how you approach solving a problem.
- What are your business strengths?

## Personal Suitability Questions

These questions aim to determine if you will be able to develop a working relationship with the individual. The key is to assess both personality and work style, by asking questions such as:

- Describe your typical working day.
- Do you prefer to work alone or as part of a team?
- How do you organize your time?
- How would a friend describe you?
- How do you react to criticism?

## Get References

Before making a commitment with a partner, ask them for a list of references from recent consulting projects. And, most importantly, check these references. Following is a list of sample questions to help ensure that you partner with the right people:

- How would you describe the individual's leadership, managerial or supervisory skills?
- Is the individual a good communicator, both orally and in writing?
- Did this individual make a budget and stay within its parameters?
- How were the individual's interpersonal skills, specifically with management, subordinates and peers?

- Did the individual meet his or her deadlines and deal effectively with time constraints?
- Would you call this individual a sound decision-maker?
- How do you rate the individual's ability to plan short-term and long-term goals?
- Is the individual technically competent?
- Would you describe this person as someone with honesty and integrity?
- How well did the individual manage crisis, pressure or stress?
- How would you rate the individual's overall performance?
- Is there any reason why you would not hire this individual again?

### Advertising Your Partnerships

Eventually, it's a good idea to advertise and promote the strategic partnerships that you have with individuals and firms. You can do this by posting the names of these partners on your website and printing them in your marketing materials.

Before doing this, however, it makes good business sense to complete a consulting project or two with this person or company before promoting the partnership. This way, you'll avoid having to change promotional material, and maintain your reputation. Additionally, you'll need your partners' permission to post their information on your website or print it in your marketing materials. For more about marketing, see the next chapter.

**TIP:** Your partnerships can work both ways. Your strategic partners may hire you when they get consulting contracts, and include you on their website and marketing materials.

## 6.4.2 Support Staff

You may be working on your own when you first start your business, but at some point you could decide to hire people to work with you.

For example, you might hire an assistant or someone to help market your company. You might hire these people as employees, or you might sign them on as contractors.

## Employees versus Contractors

Legally, if you hire an employee, you will have to pay payroll taxes on that employee, and probably make unemployment and workers' compensation contributions to the appropriate government agency. On the other hand, you can train those employees the way you like, and you can require them to do their work at certain hours and at places you choose.

If you hire contractors, those people will have learned their job skills elsewhere. They can choose how and when to do the work. You mutually agree on what product will be delivered or what services will be performed, as well as where and when they will be performed. But you cannot require them to be at your office or anywhere else for a certain number of hours daily. It is often best to spell out what you expect and what the contractor is to do or deliver in an agreement.

Other differences between an employee and a contractor, which also apply to you as a consultant, are:

- **Employees work only for you.** Contractors may have other clients as well as you, and can work for any and all of them.
- **Employees are paid on a regular basis.** Contractors are paid per project.
- **Employees work for a certain number of hours.** Contractors set their own hours, as long as they get the job done. That can be great for them if they are really fast, or not so great for them if they are really slow. As long as the project is finished on time to specs, it's great for you. (On the other hand, if an employee is slow, you may end up paying more salary to get the job done in overtime, or even hiring temporary help to get things finished.)
- **Employees can be fired or quit.** Contractors can't be fired in the usual way while they are working under contract. You may decide to have them stop working on a project, but you will be obliged to pay them according to your contractual agreement un-

less you are able to renegotiate the contract or successfully sue them if you are unhappy with their work. (Of course that would only be in extreme cases; it is best to avoid lawsuits altogether!)

Even though you are not writing paychecks to contractors, but rather checks for contracting fees, there are still tax considerations. For more information about employment taxes, contact the IRS or Canada Revenue Agency.

Before you hire, check with your local department of labor to find out all the rules and regulations required as an employer. There may be other state and federal rules and regulations that may apply to you, including: health and safety regulations, Workers' Compensation, minimum wage and unemployment insurance. Before you hire someone as an employee, it's a good idea to get some additional information concerning regulations, taxes and so forth.

In addition to your local department of labor, visit the sites below for more information:

- *Canada Business Network*
  (Click on "English," then click on "Employees, Payroll and Taxes" under the "Starting Your Business" tab)
  **www.canadabusiness.ca**

- *U.S. Internal Revenue Service*
  (Click "Businesses with Employees," then click on "Independent Contractor or Employee" link)
  **www.irs.gov/businesses/small/index.html**

- *U.S. Department of Labor*
  **www.dol.gov/opa/aboutdol/lawsprog.htm**

## Finding Employees

So, how do you find an employee when you need one? There are several routes you can take, including running an ad in the classified section of your area newspaper, working with an employment service, or seeking help on an online site such as Monster.com.

If you need help for just a limited time, you might consider contacting a temporary employee service. These services provide employees on a temporary basis. You pay the service, and the service pays the employee. It also provides benefits to the employee and takes care of payroll, taxes and so forth. You'll likely need to pay more to the service than you'd pay to a permanent employee, but if you only need help for a limited amount of time, it's probably worth it.

### 6.4.3 Tips for Working with Contractors

You are ultimately responsible for how well strategic partners and other contractors do their jobs, so you will need to find people you can depend on to do the job right, by the agreed upon deadline, for the agreed-upon price.

To help you choose contractors, make appointments to meet either by phone or in person. Ask what services they provide, their rates, and their availability. You need to know that you can depend on the contractor, and that they will be willing to work overtime if necessary to keep their agreements with you. (Unfortunately, some busy contractors consider deadlines to be "suggestions" rather than requirements.)

As the consultant hired by the client it will be your job to supervise them and ensure they get the job done. Remember your name (not the contractor's) is on the line if you bring in a contractor and they don't come through in a timely or professional manner or within cost. So look for someone reliable, and have at least one back-up for each job.

Before working with a contractor, you should do an online search to see if there are any complaints about them. You can also try checking companies with the Better Business Bureau (BBB) at **http://lookup.bbb.org** but keep in mind that the BBB is not a government agency. It is a private organization that makes money from fees paid by many of the companies the BBB rates and, as an article by Leslie M. Marable in Money magazine and at CNN.com reported, BBBs "sometimes fail to give unsatisfactory ratings to companies plagued by a history of serious complaints."

You should ask the contractor for references from previous clients. Call those references to find out what services the contractor provided, and whether the clients were satisfied. To uncover any problems, ask the client what they would do differently if they were hiring the same contractor, and which parts of the services they were least satisfied with. Also check if the contractor holds liability insurance, which may protect both them and you if the contractor's work is not satisfactory.

If you choose a strategic partner for a specific client or project, get agreements (e.g. for costs, delivery dates, services to be provided) in writing. This helps ensure that the contractor will provide what you've agreed to.

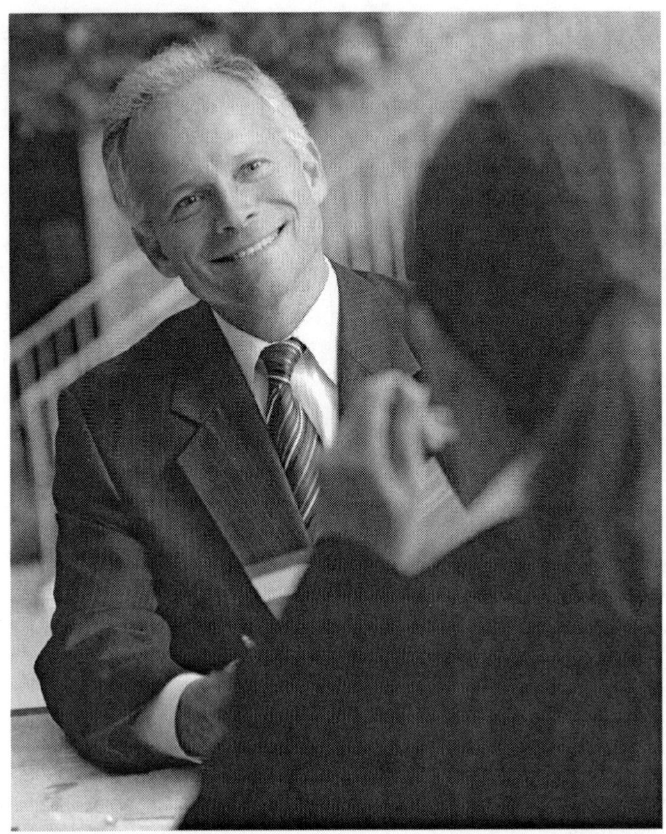

# 7. Getting Clients

Hiring a business consultant is a major undertaking for companies in terms of trust, time and money, so most go to great lengths to ensure they choose the right consultant for their business. In this chapter you will discover a variety of tools and techniques to help you effectively market yourself to prospective clients.

## 7.1 Choose Your Target Markets

Before you start trying to sell your services to prospective clients, you should decide which types of clients you want to consult for. These are your "target" markets. These are the groups of people and businesses that would be the best fit for your experience, contacts, skills and interests.

It is costly and time-consuming to try to market your business to "everyone" and the truth is that some people will be more interested than others in the services you have to offer. In fact, clients are more likely to hire you if they perceive you as an "expert" who specializes in what they need.

By identifying your target markets, you can focus your marketing efforts on the clients you most want to work with. In this section we'll consider possible target markets for business consultants, with tips on doing business with these markets and resources to help you find out more.

### 7.1.1 Small Businesses

Small business is the primary market for some independent business consultants. For example, Mara Osis, Principal of Amati Business Group (**www.amatibusinessgroup.com**), in Calgary, Alberta, says her company focuses exclusively on small business because entrepreneurs often find themselves overwhelmed or short on certain knowledge and skills.

> *"Small businesses need consultants for many areas of their business, from business coaching to marketing and financial issues. Many entrepreneurs go into business with a great idea and the right motivation, but lack specific skills. This is why small businesses rely on business consultants, and consultants on them."*
>
> — Mara Osis
> Amati Business Group

There is a variety of online resources available to help you target the needs of small business. The National Federation of Independent Business, for example, maintains an archive of polls from among its members that reflect a variety of trends and issues of importance to small business. Polls addressing topics such as the use (and misuse) of technology, business structure, legal issues, paperwork and record-keeping, taxes, and more are freely available on the NFIB website at **www.nfib.com/page/researchFoundation**, and can help you identify trends to which you can apply your specific area of expertise.

One poll on the NFIB website, for example, found that 84% of small business owners had consulted with three different types of professional counselors in the previous year and the likelihood of following a counselor's advice rose when the business owner paid for the advice. Clearly, small business owners think good advice is worth paying for. Although accountants and lawyers were the most frequently consulted, small business owners also sought advice from engineers; management, marketing and financial consultants; packaging, advertising and web designers; and a variety of other specialists.

Areas of concern for small businesses included advertising, marketing and promoting the business; human resources and personnel matters; legal issues; computers, software, websites and telecommunications; financial analysis and cash management; evaluation of business investments; government regulations other than taxes; and business layout and design. This poll suggests a wealth of opportunities for the independent business consultant.

> **TIP:** Individuals who earn a high level of income (such as successful authors, athletes, actors, and artists) are often in need of expert advice in various areas of business.

To find small businesses in your area, consult the local Chamber of Commerce and business sections of local newspapers. Many local Chambers publish lists of their business owner members which are available to other member businesses. For the U.S. Chamber of Commerce Directory visit **www.uschamber.com/chambers/directory**. For the Canadian Chamber of Commerce Network visit **www.chamber.ca/index.php/en/links/C57**.

If you decide to target small businesses, make sure you quickly weed out prospects who aren't willing to pay a consultant for business advice. Many small businesses have limited funds, some are run by entrepreneurs who are proud of their ability to do it all themselves, and others are owned by people who feel they are too busy to meet and work with a consultant.

Unless one of these businesses is facing an emergency situation, the owner may not be willing to spend the time or money to hire a consultant. While it may be clear to you how much more effectively such businesses could operate, or how much more profitable they could be, you may find this market a tough sell if you are dealing with prospects who don't see an immediate need for your services.

Even large firms that specialize in consulting to the small business market may find it a tough sell. International Profit Associates (IPA) has been accused of resorting to aggressive sales tactics in order to land clients. As of January, 2007, the Better Business Bureau of Chicago and Northern Illinois had received hundreds of complaints regarding "sales practice issues" with IPA, and reported that many of the complaints "allege high pressure sales tactics by its telemarketers."

While this market may be a tougher sell than other markets, if you have your heart set on working with small businesses, you can use the techniques described throughout this chapter to market your services. For example, you may be one of the successful independent consultants who is able to build a thriving practice by networking with small business owners.

> **TIP:** Some consultants who specialize in the small business market sell their advice to a wider audience by developing products that can be purchased such as books, reports, CDs, or teleseminars.

## 7.1.2 Large Corporations

As mentioned previously, many large corporations have made a conscious decision to focus on their core business and leave the rest to outside experts. This decision not only benefits corporations and their bottom lines, it can be good for business consultants.

The downside is that large corporations tend to hire large consulting firms, mainly because larger firms have more consultants on staff and thus a broader base of expertise for a wider variety of projects. However, larger consulting firms also cost more money to hire, which turns out to be an advantage for the small business consulting enterprise. As a specialist, if you target smaller, specific projects for large corporate clients, you will probably be able to complete them more cost-effectively than a bigger firm, and that makes you more competitive.

Many large corporations have become disenchanted with their relationships with the larger consulting firms. An article in *Fortune Magazine* noted that typical strategy consulting contracts had dropped from an average 6 to 18 months in the 1990s to about 90 days in recent years. Although many corporations still hire outside consultants regularly, either to supplement the existing talent pool or to take care of projects for which they have no expertise in-house, many large corporations are again looking to hire smaller individual consultants for short-term projects or as interim executives.

One way to target large corporate clients is by joining an independent consultants' network such as M Squared Consulting, Inc. ($M^2$), which can represent you to clients seeking a consultant. $M^2$ offers management level consulting services to corporate clients in areas like strategic planning, marketing, human resources, information technology and more. Their client list includes companies like Apple Computer, Gap Inc., Hewlett Packard, Visa International, and YMCA. For information on becoming a consultant visit **www.msquared.com/consulting_capabilities.php**.

Large companies often hire consultants after first posting Requests for Proposals (explored in detail in section 7.4.1) in newspapers or online ads, as well as on their own websites. This doesn't mean, however, that you can't offer an unsolicited proposal to a large corporation. Study their core business and use this information to generate ideas for offering your services outside the company's core operations.

You can find contact information for corporations through services such as Hoovers (**www.hoovers.com**), Hoover's Lead Builder (**www.hoovers.com/100007284-1.html**) and Lead411 (**www.lead411.com**). You can subscribe to Lead 411 for rates starting at $29.95 per month (a free trial is available). If you prefer to create your own contact lists, you can find a list of large corporations in directories at your local public library or online at the *Fortune* website at **http://money.cnn.com/magazines/fortune/fortune500** or *Report on Business*'s Top 1,000 list of Canadian companies at **www.theglobeandmail.com/report-on-business/rob-magazine/top-1000**.

### 7.1.3 Public Sector (Government)

Government opportunities are available at the national, state, and municipal levels. Like large corporations, government agencies often advertise consulting opportunities through requests for proposals.

By law, the public sector must offer any projects to the public for bidding, as per the Federal Acquisitions Regulations (FAR) in the United

States. So keep an eye on federal, state, and municipal sites where government agencies post RFPs. Again, the business sections of local and national daily newspapers are a valuable source for these notifications. Below are some websites that offer information and post projects for consultants and other experts interested in government contracts. The first two are government sites, while the latter two are examples of for-fee sites that will deliver government RFPs of interest to your email inbox as soon as they are posted.

- *Federal Business Opportunities*
  **https://www.fbo.gov**

- *Merx: Canadian Public Tenders*
  **www.merx.com**

- *GovernmentBids.com*
  **www.governmentbids.com**

- *BidNavigator (UK)*
  **www.bidnavigator.co.uk**

## 7.1.4 Nonprofit Organizations

Don't let the name fool you. Nonprofit organizations have money and paid employees; it's just not their mandate to make money. In many ways, working with a nonprofit is much like working with a large corporation, although their needs can be somewhat unique and usually revolve around their goals as a charitable organization.

If you have been involved with a nonprofit or charitable organization in the past, then that is probably a good place for you to start since they will appreciate that you are already familiar with the goals of the organization. Or you can search directories like the one at IdeaList.org (**www.idealist.org/if/as/Find**) to find nonprofits in your area. Most of the major nonprofit agencies list requests for proposals from time to time on their websites or in newspapers so it's a good idea to investigate those regularly if you're interested in working with a nonprofit.

Consulting for nonprofits is not always like consulting for profit-driven organizations. Although the consultant's role is essentially the same in both spheres, in a nonprofit environment the consultant's work will be scrutinized by a broader group of managers and a board of directors, each of whom is driven by his or her own passions and ideals with respect to the organization's goals and objectives. This can greatly increase both the time it takes to complete an engagement and the consultant's frustration as individual managers overseeing the project raise new issues.

In an article originally printed in *The Journal of Management Consulting* Harvey Bergholz, president of Jeslan Corporation which specializes in both nonprofit and for-profit consulting, points out the major differences between consulting for nonprofits and for-profits and offers advice on how to be successful as a consultant in a nonprofit setting. You can read this article at **www.jeslen.com/Not-For-Profit.pdf**.

The Georgia Center for Nonprofits has a list of the "Ten Characteristics of Excellent Nonprofit Consultants." One important characteristic for consultants working for nonprofits is sector experience and that includes "an awareness of the needs of organizations and support for the charitable missions of nonprofits." You can read the full text of this article on their website. The direct link is **www.gcn.org/Solve/Consulting/Insights/CharacteristicsofExcellentConsultants.aspx**.

You can get listed as a consultant at Idealist.org for free, or check out the National Council of Nonprofit Associations' "State Association Job Resources" page, which lists state associations as well as job openings with nonprofits around the country. Many state associations allow you to list your services in their directories as a consultant to nonprofit organizations. The Greater Chicago Nonprofit Gateway also maintains a list of national nonprofit organizations' job opportunities which can lead you to consulting prospects.

- *Idealist.org*
  $95 per year
  **www.idealist.org**

- *National Council of Nonprofit Associations*
  Click on "Nonprofit Jobs & Careers"
  **www.councilofnonprofits.org**

- *Greater Chicago Nonprofit Gateway*
  **http://gateway.northpark.edu**

You can also list yourself in a national marketplace directory like the one at the Association of Fundraising Professionals website at **www.afpnet.org**. Membership is required and costs $250 to join as a Professional Individual member.

## Your Unique Selling Proposition

*by Marg Archibald*

You have now chosen the optimal target market to pursue for business. Next, you want to separate yourself from the pack of other business consultants and be identifiable and memorable.

Decades ago, an advertising genius called Rosser Reeves, created just the concept to help you do that: the unique selling proposition. His label applied to the unique and memorable thing about a product – in this case you and your business – that will influence your customers to buy. This is the something that makes the right people – namely your chosen target market – believe that you are the right fit for them.

One brand of make-up chooses to make you look younger, another chooses to be kind to sensitive skin, a third presents itself in a container you would be proud to own. These are all unique selling propositions and they were chosen after extensive research into what customers want as well as what the competition is already offering.

### Creating Your USP

The USP you create for yourself will be based on the intersecting point between your strengths and the wants/needs of your target market. You are going to create one statement that captures the best reason for people to buy from you. Later, if you develop a slogan, it will be based on that USP statement.

A sheet of paper with a line down the middle will help you do this. Head the left column, "They want" and the right column, "I offer." You can see that the greater understanding you have of your target audience, the more effectively you can do this exercise.

To find out what your prospects want you should do some target market research. Ask the people who should be your clients. When you have gathered a list of what you believe would be their purchase priorities, create a short list of the ones that consistently seem most important. Then ask more prospective clients how they would rank the importance of those items in their purchase decision. Do not fall for the common misconception that purchase decisions are first and foremost based on price. Research indicates that even when buying accounting services, prospects ranked six other things as more important than price.

Now you are ready to document the "I offer" column. Start at the top with the specific knowledge and expertise you have, tasks you can do, your areas of expertise, the way you deliver service. As you work down the column, focus increasingly on the benefits that clients gain by contracting you. You are organized and disciplined. What does the client get? On time and on budget consulting. That's his benefit.

As you look at the things you offer, keep asking the question the client would ask: "What's in it for me?" The answer is the benefit you provide. Write that in the column.

When your list is thorough, look for matches between the columns. What have you got that they want? A powerful USP will resonate with your target market, create a feeling that you are a good consulting fit for them and virtually begin your sales process before you even meet them. Below are some sample USPs.

- Hands-on experience helping employers retain their best employees
- Track record of improving inventory management efficiencies
- Able to find any and all leaks to clients' bottom line
- Always on time. Always under budget.

Take time with this exercise. Do the research. Craft your USP and test it. Refine it. Your USP will be the foundation for your business development.

# 7.2 Marketing Tools

## 7.2.1 Printed Materials

Your printed materials include business cards, stationery (such as letterhead, envelopes, and mailing labels), and other marketing materials such as brochures.

If you have a computer with a high quality laser or ink jet printer, you may be able to inexpensively print professional looking materials from your own computer. Free templates for all the print materials you are likely to need in your business can be found online.

HP offers templates for a variety of programs at **www.hp.com/sbso/productivity/office**. For example, you can create a matching set of stationery (business cards, letterhead, envelopes) in Microsoft Word or a presentation in PowerPoint. The site includes free online classes and how-to guides to help you design your own marketing materials.

Another excellent resource is the Microsoft Office Online Templates Homepage at **http://office.microsoft.com/en-us/templates**. At this site you can search a database to find templates for:

- Business stationery (envelopes, faxes, labels, letters, memos, etc.)
- Marketing materials (brochures, flyers, newsletters, postcards, etc.)
- Meeting documents (agendas, minutes, presentations, slides, etc.)
- Other business documents (expense reports, invoices, receipts, time sheets, etc.)

As an alternative to printing materials yourself, and for materials that won't fit through your printer (such as folders), consider using a company that provides printing services. Your printed materials can be easily designed, paid for and delivered without leaving the house.

Here are links to some companies that provide printing services for small businesses:

- *FedEx Office*
  **www.fedex.com/us/officeprint/onlineprint**

- *Acecomp Plus – Printing Solutions*
  **www.acecomp.com/printing.asp**

- *The Paper Mill Store*
  **www.thepapermillstore.com**

- *VistaPrint*
  **www.vistaprint.com**

While the resources listed above can help with all your printing needs, here is some advice about two types of materials that are particularly important for marketing purposes – business cards and brochures.

## Business Cards

The first thing on your list of marketing tools is your business cards. This is one item that you can't do without as a business consultant.

The basic information to list on your business cards includes:

- Your name
- Your title (such as Principal or Senior Consultant)
- Your company name
- Your contact information (phone numbers, email address, fax number)
- Your web address

**TIP:** Business cards are considered a symbol of your status in many foreign countries, so if you are dealing with other cultures in your business, make certain that your title is printed boldly on your cards. If you work primarily with clients who speak another language consider having one side of your business cards printed in that language.

In addition, consider including the following items to promote you and your consulting services:

- Your degrees after your name (e.g. John Smith, MBA)
- Professional credentials (e.g. Member, American Marketing Association)
- Your specializations and services offered
- Your unique selling proposition
- Company logo
- Your mailing address

Your business card should be a reflection of you and your consulting business. Generally speaking, business cards for those in traditional industries such as business consulting should be simple in design. A safe bet is to avoid bright colors and use a standard black or dark type on a white background of good-quality paper.

Keep business cards the standard size, 2 x 3 ½ inches, and if possible, invest in a sturdy card that has a good weight and feel to it. If your budget is limited, a good source for high quality low-cost cards (currently $19.99 per 250 cards) is VistaPrint at **www.vistaprint.com**. Visit their site to see a wide variety of designs you can consider. You can browse designs by industry or you may find something suitable under their "Conservative" or "Lines" styles.

Always keep business cards on hand, as you never know who you might run into. Keeping your business cards in a case is more professional than keeping them scattered across the bottom of your briefcase or bag. It will also ensure that you only hand out pristine cards, and not a worn or stained card.

If you will be working with clients from other cultures, brush up on their customs for handling business cards. In presenting and accepting business cards, some countries believe you should study and review a card, others believe cards should be accepted and immediately put away. There may also be region-specific rules for presentation, such as which hand it is to be presented with.

## Brochures

Brochures give prospective clients an overview of what your business is about. Some consultants choose to develop very detailed brochures while others prefer a clean look with less detail. If you decide to create a brochure for your business, here are items to include:

- Your company name
- Contact information
- Your web address
- A description of your professional qualifications
- A description of the benefit of your services
- Information about the services you provide
- A photograph of you
- Testimonial quotes from satisfied clients

If you are printing only a few copies of your brochure, you may be able to find nice paper at your local office supply store or one of the websites listed earlier in this section, which you can run through your printer. If you have brochures professionally printed, the cost can range from a few hundred dollars (for one color on simple cardstock) to a few thousand dollars if you opt for color and glossy paper.

Many printers will have an in-house design department who can do the artwork for you, but make sure you have a hand in developing the text. You are the best-qualified person to describe what you can do for a client.

**TIP:** Be sure to spell-check and grammar check everything. Also check your phone number, e-mail address, and other contact information carefully to ensure clients can reach you.

While the challenge of designing an effective brochure is one thing, how to effectively distribute them is another. Brochures have an advantage over business cards in that they can sit in a waiting room and be picked up and read by the people waiting. Brochures can also be distributed by mail (see section 7.3.3), given out at events you're speaking at (see section 7.3.4), or handed out in conjunction with or instead of a business card.

## 7.2.2 Your Website

Your website can be an important tool for marketing your services. It gives your prospects an opportunity to learn more about you and your services at their convenience. It may also expose you to a potentially unlimited audience of those in need of your services.

### What to Include on Your Website

You can get a good sense of what to include on your own website by visiting sites of other successful consultants and consulting firms. (Many links are provided throughout this book.) For example, your website can include any of the following:

- Home page with links to navigate through your site
- "About Us" page so that your customers can learn more about you and your company. This should include your credentials and a photograph of you.
- A way to contact you, including at least your company name, telephone number and email address. This should ideally be on every page, but you can also have a "Contact Us" page with your business address and other contact information.
- Information about your consulting services and the benefits they offer to potential clients.
- Testimonial quotes from satisfied clients (see section 2.2.8 for tips on how to get testimonials).
- Helpful information you have written such as business articles, self-assessments, checklists, and other content that shows your expertise. Adding new content on a regular basis can keep people returning to your site.

To build up a contact list, you could offer a free email newsletter, and include a place at your website where visitors can subscribe.

## Designing Your Website

Software such as Microsoft Expression or Adobe Dreamweaver have made the creation of web pages possible for everyone. However, one problem with creating and maintaining a website on your own is that it can be time-consuming to build and to keep up-to-date.

If you don't have the time to spend on creating a polished website, you may prefer to have a professional web developer build and maintain your site. There is no shortage of web designers, so consult your local phone directory or search online for one in your area.

## Hosting and Domain Names

Once your web pages are prepared you will need to find an Internet service provider (ISP) server to host them. Many web designers are also in the business of hosting, as are those who register domain names. While the company you use to connect to the Internet may offer free web pages, you should use a hosting company that will allow you to use your own domain name, such as www.yourbusinessname.com.

When choosing a domain name it's best to use your business name or something closely resembling it. One popular site where you can search for and register your domain name is GoDaddy.com. They also offer inexpensive web hosting services. Visit **www.godaddy.com**.

## Promoting Your Site

No matter how much you spend on your website, if people don't know it exists, it won't help your business. Make certain you list your site on all your business forms, cards, and brochures.

Drive people to your site verbally, by mentioning to people, "That's a common problem. Have a look at the tip sheet about that at my website. There are things you can do yourself. Then we can come in and help with the big picture."

After you register your domain name be sure to get it listed on the major Internet search engines. The most powerful and popular search engine these days is Google. Be sure to read Google's prepared tips on how to make sure your site show up when people are searching and make your links more Google-friendly. Visit **www.google.com/support/webmasters** for information.

You can also submit your domain to Bravenet (**www.bravenet.com**), who will submit it to over a dozen search engines like Yahoo!, MSN and AOL for free.

## 7.2.3 Your Elevator Pitch

A well-crafted elevator pitch may be the single, most effective, and least expensive business development tool you can have. Your elevator pitch, like your business card, is a basic business marketing tool. But it can be particularly powerful in helping you generate sales.

The elevator pitch is a brief overview of your business and services that should take the same amount of time as a short elevator ride. You vividly and concisely outline a strong message, taking about 60 seconds to deliver a short speech about who you are and what you do. You need to be able to say in as few words as possible, but at the same time as clearly as possible, everything that will help the listener develop an immediate interest in you and your business.

Whether you are speaking to a group or to a single person, the principles of a good pitch are the same. It needs to be simple and memorable, and because we store memories based on the emotions attached to them, a pitch that generates feelings is going to be remembered. In business consulting, saying something memorable that offers proof you can save a business time or money is the strongest card you can play.

### Targeting Your Elevator Pitch

Your elevator pitch is always targeted, as closely as possible, to your audience. When you're pitching to a group you focus on what is common to the group; whether you're speaking to operations managers, business owners, or accountants.

In a group setting, your audience is probably less interested in you than a person you're having a one-on-one conversation with might be. Your elevator pitch is a chance to change that, make the group sit up and pay attention because you connect with what matters to them. The trick is to make them interested in what you have to say.

When you are speaking to one individual, two things change. You can tailor your pitch very specifically to that person, plus you can turn the speech into a dialogue in less than one minute since you already have the person's attention. Note that the core elevator pitch is the same, but how you fit it into a conversation changes.

## Group Elevator Pitch

You have 60 seconds to connect with the group and their priorities. You open with your name, title and company name. You briefly describe your business and an overview of your products/services. The key here is to be brief. You sketch out the things you do that would most interest this particular group.

You outline the kinds of clients you serve (ideally clients just like them), and tell a story proving how effective you are. This may include a quote from a happy client. You express interest in working for them or receiving referrals. You close with a memorable phrase, repeating your name and company. This is perfect when it is your turn to stand up at a luncheon and introduce yourself, although it is a bit too long in one-on-one situation.

An effective elevator pitch provides people with memorable words they can tell others and creates positive impressions that could lead to more word-of-mouth consulting engagements.

## One-On-One Elevator Pitch

People can tune you out in 10 seconds or less. An engaging, interactive, one-on-one elevator pitch gets the same information across that you would present to a group but involves the listener in dialogue sooner.

First, you need to find out more about the person you're speaking with. Use every bit of information you can glean about the person you're speaking to in order to make your pitch relevant. Your observations are providing you information from the time you approach each other. Keep the focus on the other person.

- Where might you have met before?
- Is he or she wearing a name tag? Does it list his or her company? Is that company one you could work with?
- What is his or her title?
- Who has he or she just been talking to? Have you picked up any additional information from that observation?
- How does the other person react to your name tag?
- How confident does he or she appear to be in this group?

When you initiate the conversation, you can open with: "Hello. I'm (your first and last name) with (your company name). I don't think we've met."

Then pause to get the other person's name and if possible any other info on what he or she does.

When the other person asks what you do, you can follow simple steps:

### Step 1: Connection

- "I work with people like you."
- "I work with businesses like yours."
- "I work in your industry."

If you know absolutely nothing about the other person, you can say, "I work with (business/organizations)."

### Step 2: Promise

"I solve/improve/maximize/resolve/optimize (whatever you do, very simply)."

### Step 3: Proof

"Clients say/my last client said/most people who use my services say…"

## Sample One-on-One Elevator Pitch

**Connection**

"I work with businesses like yours."

**Promise**

"I solve glitches in just-in-time inventory management."

**Proof**

"I'm just wrapping up a project that will save my client $100,000 this year."

**Probe**

"What system do you use at your company? How well is it working? Do you think there are any areas that need improving?"

**Close**

*(Strong Prospect)* "I'm interested in chatting with you further. I may be able to help out there and save you some money. I have an opening on Tuesday afternoon next week if you'd like to discuss this further."

*(Weak Prospect)* "I'm interesting in solving problems in (target) industry." Insert some chatting about the target industry and its problems, relate to his industry. Feel your way to gradually asking: "Do you know anyone with inventory issues? Could you suggest anyone in this room you think I should meet?"

### Step 4: Probe

Connect the proof back to the other person and how similar issues are handled at his or her company, or how much trouble the other person has with a particular issue: "Is that an issue at your firm?/Do you have that problem?/How do you handle that problem?"

### Step 5: Close

If this is a strong prospect, you probe further and gently work toward trying to set up a meeting. (See the sample above for an example of how to do this.)

If this is a weak prospect, you can ask if he or she knows of anyone that might be interested in your services. Consider that every single person you meet is a conduit to people that will be helpful even if they are not actual prospects: "You know these people. What is your sense of who in this room may need help in this area?"

### Practice Your Pitch

Armed with an elevator pitch that you have practiced until it sounds and feels natural, you can practice on friends, family, colleagues and acquaintances. Ask for honest feedback. Pay attention to their suggestions and make any changes necessary to create a more effective pitch.

## 7.3 Marketing Techniques

In this section we'll look at various marketing techniques, including advertising, networking, cold calling, mailing, speaking and writing. Consider as many of these techniques as possible to help you get the word out about who you are and what you do. Generating clients from a marketing campaign is not formulaic and not every strategy works for every consultant with the same success. The key is to determine what combination works best for you.

> *"You need to be a strong self-promoter, but do it in a way that benefits your clients and potential clients and contributes positively to your profession."*
>
> — John Baldoni
> Baldoni Consulting, LLC

### 7.3.1 Advertising

Advertising is normally part of an overall marketing strategy for consultants. The key to effective advertising for a consultant is to ensure that the right sector is receiving your message. To do this, focus on the media used most by those who need your services.

### Trade Publications

Many consultants and other professionals advertise in trade publications. Trade publications are those produced for individuals working in a specific industry. Virtually industry has at least one publication dedicated to it. Trade publications that cater to the businesses that you're targeting offers an audience that may be looking for your specific consulting skills. Gebbie Press offers a directory with links to trade magazines at **www.gebbieinc.com/magurl.htm**.

## Yellow Pages

Look under "Business Consultants," "Consultants," or "Management Consultants" in any city's Yellow Pages and you'll discover that many in the business value this form of advertising. They choose the Yellow Pages for its ubiquity and visibility.

On the other hand, a Yellow Pages ad is expensive, and many new business owners find a Yellow Pages ad does not make the phone ring off the hook with buyers. If someone does respond to your ad, they may be "shopping around," so you must be prepared to invest time as well as advertising dollars if you use this method of advertising.

If you decide to try an ad in the Yellow Pages, you may want to consider something business card-sized. Also, look around for a Yellow Pages alternative, since many areas have competing telephone directories and these can offer similar ad space for less money. Be sure to check into the alternative's circulation or you might waste money on an ad that doesn't reach very many people.

You can either design the ad yourself, have the Yellow Pages design it for you or simply have them print the contents of your business card. Take a look at the ads in the "Business Consultants" or "Management Consultants" category in the Yellow Pages to get ideas for your own ad. If you are interested in advertising, contact your local Yellow Pages to speak with a sales rep. Check your phone book or online for contact information.

There are also companies that specialize in online listings. One such service is Superpages.com. They offer a free business listing service as well as an enhanced version for a fee. Check their website at **www.superpages.com** for details.

### Newspapers and Magazines

Magazine and newspaper advertising can be expensive, and may not create enough business to cover the cost. You could spend thousands of dollars on an "advertorial" (an advertisement written as an article) and not get a single new client as a result.

If you choose to buy advertising, it will likely be most cost-effective to place ads in local business magazines, the business section of local newspapers, or business classifieds. Some prospects need to see an ad seven times before they act. If you decide to advertise, plan to run ads repeatedly in the same publication for best results.

The publications you advertise in will usually design your ad for an additional cost, and give you a copy of the ad to run in other publications. Here are a few tips for effective advertising:

- Rather than just listing your services, explain how clients can benefit from your services. Use your unique selling proposition.
- Have a call to action (e.g. "Call now for a free initial consultation")
- Make sure you're available for people who respond to your ad. If someone keeps getting your voice mail, they may give up.

A more effective and much less expensive marketing option is to write columns or articles. See the sidebar on the next page for some useful tips on that subject.

## 7.3.2 Cold Calling

Cold calling is a form of marketing in which you phone a company or individual without having been first contacted by them. Cold contacts are people you've never met or talked to before.

Although it can be intimidating to make cold calls, this marketing technique can be effective. Even well-established independent consultants, like Martin Wilkins of Calgary, swear by the cold call. He says, "I make 200 phone calls a week. It's the best way to get your name and business into the minds of the president or CEO of that company. And it's the only way to get an interview."

**Write a Column or Article**

One of the best ways to establish yourself as an expert is to write articles or a column for a newspaper, magazine, or newsletter. While it can be tough to break into large daily newspapers, there may be an opportunity to write for smaller newspapers or local magazines.

You could write on any topic related to business consulting, or propose an "Ask the Consultant" column where you would answer questions from readers. The length and frequency of your column will depend on the publication. You might produce a weekly 500-word column for a local newspaper, or a monthly 1,000-word column for a newsletter or magazine.

Make sure your article or column provides valuable information to the publication's readers. Articles that sound like an ad for your services are not likely to get published. Write about something in your area of expertise; for example, if you're a consultant to small business, you could write about how to write a good business start-up plan or create a bookkeeping system.

Once you have written your first column or article, phone or email the editor to ask if he or she would be interested in reading it. If so, you will probably be asked to email it. If your article is worth publishing, the newspaper may offer to pay you for it. However, even if they don't pay, you should consider letting them publish it in return for including a brief bio and your contact information at the end of the article or column.

Here are some tips to make your cold calling more successful.

## Make a List

Do some research and come up with a list of prospective clients. Section 7.1 offers advice on finding prospects in your target market. If you're considering pitching to a particular company or individual, find out as much as you can about the company or individual, what they do, and how they can benefit from your services.

## Talk to the Decision-maker

When you make your cold call to a prospective client be sure to talk with the executive or manager who will make the decision about whether or not to use your services. (Unless you are a human resources consultant, the decision-maker will not be in the HR department.)

Most busy executives have administrative assistants who field calls for them so they don't have to talk with everyone who calls. A friendly attitude can help you get past these gatekeepers. If you must leave a voice-mail message for the decision-maker, consider leaving it after hours so it will be among the first messages the person hears in the morning.

## Be Persistent

You may not get through to your target client on the first call. Even after you do get through to a decision-maker, you may not make the sale on the first try. Try again. Unless a prospect gives you a definite "yes" or "no," be prepared to call five or more times before you are able to set up a meeting with your prospect.

## Have a Script

Having a script to follow when you make a cold call can make the difference between failure and success. A script shouldn't be followed verbatim, because you'll sound stilted and rehearsed. Instead, use your script to organize your thoughts and to provide you with a guideline so that you don't leave out any vital information. Practice the script several times before making your first call. It will become easier the more you do it, and eventually you won't need the script right in front of you.

Here is a sample script compiled from suggestions from several independent consultants.

> "Good morning (afternoon) Mr. /Ms. Decision-maker,
>
> My name is ______. I'm an independent business consultant located in ______. I specialize in ______.
>
> I've been conducting research on local businesses, and see that your company specializes in ______ and I think my services can benefit your business by ______.

I'd like set up a meeting with you at your firm to discuss how my skills can contribute to the success of your business. I have a couple of openings this week. Would Tuesday afternoon or Wednesday morning be better for you?

Thank you and I look forward to our meeting."

As you can see, there is plenty of room to adjust your dialogue according to how the conversation evolves. But having a script will help you to sound professional and keep the conversation on track.

**TIP:** You are much more likely to get your call returned if you say you were referred by someone the decision-maker knows and respects. Ask for referrals and, wherever possible, slip "_____ suggested I call you" into the script after your name.

## Stay Organized

An important part of cold calling, once you've decided whom to call, is to keep track of everyone you've called. When gathering information for cold calls, the amount of information can be overwhelming. To keep yourself organized and help ensure success, use a detailed contact spreadsheet like the one below:

**Sample Contact Sheet**

| Company Name/ Address | First Call | Second Call | Contact Name | Meeting Date |
|---|---|---|---|---|
| | | | | |
| | | | | |
| | | | | |
| | | | | |
| | | | | |

You can also use software like Microsoft Outlook or FileMaker Pro (**www.filemaker.com**) to create a client contact database, track meeting dates and make notes about your meetings. Or you could use a website such as FreeCRM (**www.freecrm.com**), which allows you to set up a free account to track detailed client contact information, create company notes, calendars, task lists, and more.

## 7.3.3 Mail Campaigns

There are three types of mail campaigns you might consider using to market your consulting business:

- **Broadcast Mailing:** This is a mailing without a personal name, sent to addresses in a geographic area, or to a specific industry
- **Targeted Mailing:** Mail is personally addressed to individuals that you have not met
- **Courtship Mailing:** This is an ongoing mail campaign to people you have met and are actively "courting"

The first two types of campaigns are used to prepare the recipient for a phone call from you. Don't make the mistake of using a mail campaign to avoid direct sales. If you do not follow up mailings with a phone call you have probably thrown your money away. A letter or anything else in the mail rarely results in the recipient calling you. Always follow up.

### What to Say in Your Mailing and Call

If you are using targeted broadcast mail, be sure that you know something about the target industry that is relevant to the recipient and will make it more likely they will want to talk with you when you call them.

For example, you could target the printing industry by starting your letter like this:

> The Department of Labor warns that 30% of the printers in the country will experience significant challenges before 2013. They attribute this problem to massive retirement of experienced staff.
>
> Is [company name] workforce approaching retirement?

> Our consultants have created long-term, staffing programs for many clients and saved them money at the same time! They can do the same for you.

The trick here is to make your promise easy for them to digest quickly. Then, in the rest of the letter, provide reasons why they will be satisfied if they act on this offer. Close with your commitment to call within a week and pace sending out your mailing so that you can do that.

Your mail then becomes a support to your telephone sales. In targeting a specific recipient, you already have the personal name of the individual you want to contact. In the first case, you may have to do some fishing on your first call. Either way, you can open your sales pitch with: "We sent you some information about the challenges printers will face in the next decade. Did that make its way into your hands?"

## Courtship Mailing

With people you have already met, you will take a different approach. A flexible, monthly mailing schedule can keep you in mind and remembered between mailings. You can send your prospects friendly, personalized notes in your handwriting, with helpful information relevant to their industry. Both parts are important: helpful information and a handwritten note.

What will you send this circle of prospects that you are actively courting? Again, think of their issues, problems, and areas of concern. You want to get helpful information into their hands without overloading them with information. Sometimes you can produce your own items; other times you can send copies of existing material such as:

- How-to instructions
- Samples and examples
- Research results
- Articles
- Diagrams
- Statistics

- Relevant cards for holidays, seasons, events
- Invitations

In your handwritten note with your signature, let them know the information is specifically for them and motivate them to read it. Include personal comments such as:

- "Great to see you last week."
- "Here's the info I promised you."
- "I thought of you when I saw this article."
- "I'm fascinated by these statistics. Want to talk about them?"
- "Are you going to be at the next Chamber meeting?"

Good note-keeping is essential to maintain accurate mailing lists. Stay current with the information for people on your mailing list and record updates in your client contact file. As a business consultant, it is unlikely that you will have an onerous mailing volume. When it gets to be more than 100 names, start to weed out the low return prospects. You want to massage your mailing list regularly so that it is performing optimally for you. Remember that closing a sale takes time. This is the courtship phase and you are keeping it moving along by staying in touch in a helpful, friendly way.

## Mailing Labels

Your office suite software probably will include a spreadsheet that converts easily into mailing labels. It will probably even list the sizes of major brand labels for label setup. You can maintain a spreadsheet to which you add names as you get them and then generate fresh labels from that updated list each time you do a mailing. Inserting them in alphabetical order by first or last name or company will help you manage the list and find gaps and repetition.

## Tracking

One of the best features of a mailing campaign is the ease of tracking. Keep a file of what you sent out with each mailing. Keep a copy of the mailing list on your hard drive. Record any responses you receive. This will help you detect which kinds of mailing are best received.

## 7.3.4 Networking

There are different definitions of networking, but a particularly useful definition is the one given in the American Heritage Dictionary of the English Language: "To interact or engage in informal communication with others for mutual assistance or support."

As you can see from this definition, two keys to networking are that it is "informal" and it is "mutual." This type of networking includes meeting and interacting with people informally at social and business events. Most consultants agree that networking is one of their most powerful tools for generating new business and making the contacts they need to do business more effectively. Linda Popky is the President of L2M Associates, a Redwood City, California-based strategic marketing company that helps organizations improve the return they get on their marketing program, processes and people. She says:

> *"I've found that networking with friends, colleagues and acquaintance is the most effective way to generate new business. Be sure to let these people know what you offer and who can benefit from your services. Then don't be afraid to promote what you've done and ask for leads and referrals.*
>
> — Linda Popky
> L2M Associates

**TIP:** In addition to helping connect you with people and businesses in your target market, you will also find networking indispensable for finding other businesses and services you may need yourself when working on projects for clients. Having a wide variety of resources at your disposal can increase your ability to take on projects for which you might need additional expertise.

### Your Warm Market

Unlike prospects that you cold call, your "warm market" are people who know you. Your warm market includes friends, family members, neighbors, former co-workers, and anyone else you know. These are people that you already have a relationship with. If you phone them, you know they will return the call.

Chances are, your warm market includes a number of people who are "decision-makers" in an organization that could use your services. In other words, they are in a position where they could hire your company. If not, they may be able to recommend your services to the decision-maker. So get the word out to friends, family, colleagues and acquaintances that you have started a consulting business. Tell them what your skills are and how you might be able to help them, and show them the areas in which you can help enhance their business.

> *"When you approach people say that you have a number of years experience at whatever your expertise is, and that you're building a consulting practice and are seeking clients who could benefit from your expertise. Let them know that instead of hiring you full-time and incurring many costs, that you could be available for a smaller fee on a part-time basis."*
>
> — Nido Qubein, Business Consultant,
> Speaker, Author, President
> High Point University

## Meeting New People

There are many different events you can attend that will greatly increase your network of contacts, including professional associations, networking clubs, trade shows, and more. This is where it really pays to have clearly defined your target markets, because when you're networking you are laying the groundwork for future business.

### Professional Associations

If you have a professional designation like CPA or CFA or something similar, you may already be a member of a professional organization. Often, professional associations have seminars and industry events to address issues of importance both to their own industry and those of related industries. For example, the various branches of the Society of Financial Analysts across North America regularly host luncheons and multi-day events with guest speakers and presenters from a variety of industries speaking on many different topics.

Attending events like these can expose you to industries you may not have thought about working with but may very well have a need for your specific expertise. You'll also meet other professionals working in a variety of industries, which may generate additional ideas and leads. So if you're not already a member of a professional organization you should consider joining one. See section 8.3 for a list of professional associations for consultants.

### Trade Shows and Conferences

There are many trade shows and conferences you can attend in virtually any industry or discipline. Attending trade shows and conferences will help you to meet potential clients in your industry or help you to connect with other businesses whose assistance you might need. These events can be important networking opportunities for you.

You can find out about upcoming events through your local Convention & Visitors Bureau, at professional association websites or by typing "Trade Shows" into a search engine such as Google. You can also search for upcoming events at the TSNN Trade Show Directory at **www.tsnn.com**.

### Networking Clubs

Networking clubs typically include one member each from a variety of industries (e.g. insurance, financial planning, law, real estate, etc.). Meetings may include a meal, an opportunity to network, and presentations by speakers. In some clubs, each member is expected to bring a certain number of leads to the group each week or month.

To become a member you are either recommended to the group by an existing member or you might approach the group and ask to sit in as an observer for a couple of meetings then apply for membership if you find the group is a good fit for you. You may be asked to give a short presentation about your own business and what you can bring to the group. The types of activities will vary with different groups, so don't settle on the first one you visit if they don't seem to offer what you're looking for. Make sure the members represent the kind of people you're trying to connect with for clients, or who might know others who would benefit from your consulting services.

One way to find a networking club is through word of mouth. Ask people you know who are in sales such as financial planners. You can also look for networking groups online. Business Network International (**www.bni.com**) has more than 2,300 chapters around the world.

### Connecting at a Networking Event

To help you strike up a conversation at a networking event, use an elevator pitch and develop a tag line that you can use to quickly identify yourself and what you do. If your tag line is interesting or intriguing people will naturally ask you to elaborate on what it is you do.

You could try something like:

> "I'm Jane Tax Consultant and I save companies millions of dollars in taxes each year."

Once you start talking about your business, ask others about theirs and show an honest interest in what they do; don't start scanning the room for your next prospect. For the next few minutes at least, the person in front of you is the most important person in the room. Meeting people and getting to know them a little better is the first step toward effective networking.

### Charitable Organizations

Many professional people attend charitable fundraising events such as luncheons, dinners, museum openings, etc., and many large corporations sponsor these events. Attending these events yourself is one way to connect with potential clients, but it can be expensive. Since they are fundraisers getting into an event could cost you $100 or more. Plus, there may not be much time to meet and mingle with other attendees.

You will have a much greater opportunity to connect with people and support a good cause by volunteering to help with an event. As a volunteer you may work closely with the type of people you want to attract as clients. Or you might meet representatives of corporations who can introduce you to the decision-makers in their company who hire consultants.

Volunteer for activities that will bring you into contact with these people. In other words, leave the envelope stuffing to other volunteers and focus on activities such as fundraising. In addition to serving on committees, see if you can volunteer the services of your consulting business. To volunteer, simply phone up the organizations in your community that interest you. You can find more information on volunteering in section 4.4.1.

### Membership Organizations

Another excellent way to network is by joining associations that prospective clients may belong to. Some examples include:

- Civic and service clubs such as Rotary Club or Kiwanis Club
- Business organizations such as your Chamber of Commerce
- Clubs that attract the wealthy, for example, golf, polo, yachting, and country clubs

Membership fees may vary from $20 to hundreds or even thousands of dollars (the latter if you want to join an exclusive country club or private golf club). The more expensive clubs usually require current members to introduce you and put you up for membership, so you may have to join some less exclusive clubs in order to meet people who might also belong to the more expensive clubs. Many less exclusive clubs will let you attend a few times for a nominal fee so you can decide if you really want to join.

If you simply attend club functions without getting involved, the value of the membership will not be as great as if you pitch in. What sorts of things can you do to help out and gain the attention of others whose good will can help your business grow?

Here are some suggestions:

- Serve on a committee
- Write articles for the newsletter
- Volunteer to help out with the organization's events
- Run for election to the Executive Committee

### Speaking Engagements

Speaking engagements at luncheons, conventions, industry meetings, etc. are an excellent way to gain exposure and get established as an expert in the business world.

Many consultants find speaking engagements to be one of their most effective marketing tools. Jill Lublin, CEO of Promising Promotion and author of the bestselling book *Guerilla Publicity*, says "speaking at industry events fills my clientele pipeline." ArLyne Diamond, Ph.D., owner of Diamond Associates and author of *Training Your Board of Directors*, says "free samples, e.g. a one hour talk, often helps get the larger contract."

Opportunities for speaking engagements are numerous, a local Chamber of Commerce lunch, a luncheon at your alma mater, lunch or dinner party for any local organization that might want to include a guest speaker.

Try to find an organization or group such as a service club that you might have an affinity with in terms of your services or area of expertise. For example, if you're a consultant who specializes in helping companies integrate eco-friendly businesses practices into their business operating models, you might offer your services as a speaker to a group such as the Lions Club, which has a well-developed environment service program, to talk about the relationship between business and the environment.

On the day that you deliver your speech, be sure you bring plenty of business cards and brochures so you can hand them out to members of the audience. You'll want people to remember you and have your contact information if they decide they might be able to use your services.

## 7.4 Creating Proposals

### 7.4.1 Requests for Proposal (RFP)

Clients may first issue a Request for Proposal (RFP) when choosing an outside consultant, particularly for large corporation or government contracts. An RFP is a written statement of the client's specific needs and information about the client's organization. The RFP outlines in detail what the client's project entails and why they want to hire a consultant; what they expect in the project proposals received from consultants; and the kinds of expertise required.

The RFP typically will offer an overview of the company and its business structure, some background on the planned project, how and where to submit your proposal, how the proposal should be formatted, and what specific papers, documents and other submissions need to be included. It will also include the project's proposed budget, time frame, and any other conditions the project is subject to, as well as eligibility requirements for those wishing to submit a proposal, including the client's selection process and hiring criteria. Typically, RFPs will include the following sections:

## Introduction

The introduction often includes an overview of the organization and its organizational structure, a brief summary of the project and how it fits into the client's overall business objectives, a summary of the specific objectives for the project being considered, details of the project budget, and an explanation of why the client believes the services of an outside consultant are required.

## Scope of Work/Services

This section details the work the client needs the consultant to perform. The scope of work or services obviously will vary from project to project and will be within your own area(s) of expertise for the most part or you wouldn't be considering responding to it. The client will outline exactly what services or work you are expected to provide for the project and may specify in this section any reports on performance and progress (i.e. how you are meeting the objectives) required during and at the end of the project.

The client may also request from you in this section any specific background documentation regarding your qualifications for performing the work or services required by the project.

## Contract Deliverables

During the course of the work being performed you may be required to submit certain plans, reports and other documents analyzing and detailing project planning, implementation, identification of any issues affecting the services provided and a detailed outline of cost allocations for the project as each stage is implemented. This section will detail what those requirements are.

## Proposal Instructions

This section details the format for your proposal submission and what you must include in your proposal package. The client will specify where and to whom you will submit your proposal, and the format of any documents you provide. This may include seemingly trivial things like the maximum length of documents and line spacing (e.g. 15 single-spaced pages).

The instructions may include other specifics about various forms, reports and other documents to be provided, such as any documents requiring signatures. Some examples of what may be required are:

### Technical

Detailing methodologies, evaluation of objectives and identification of issues, draft work plans, etc.

### Management

Including who will do the work, how the work will be organized and managed, and the relevant experience of participants.

### Budget/Cost

How will the budget be allocated including labor and other expenses, identification of staff and the work they will do including their rates of pay, a breakdown of costs per project objective, etc.

### Human Resources

Labor and related issues such as time and costs, expertise specifics, details about any partner(s) and ancillary staff you will be bringing with you, etc.

To see some examples of RFPs you can check out the American Planning Association's website at **www.planning.org/consultants/request search.htm**, which maintains a list of RFPs for government and other contracts.

## 7.4.2 Responding to RFPs

If the client has a formal request for proposal process you will use that as the guideline in preparing your proposal. When you submit your proposal, you are making a "bid" to do the work.

The bid process may also require you to make an oral presentation. The organization requesting the RFP will usually hold a session (sometimes called a bidding meeting) for interested parties to attend in order to learn more about the project before submitting their response to the RFP. This is the time to ask questions and elicit clear answers. The more clearly you understand the goals and purpose of the project, the better your chances of being the successful bidder.

When responding to an RFP, make sure your response is submitted before the stated deadline and answers all of the questions accurately. Keep a current personal or company resume on file for these occasions, and don't overstate your qualifications to win a bid. Include written references from past consulting projects—even where you provided a service for free—and include a list of qualifications. Advise them of your availability and make certain you point out exactly how you will meet their objectives and what services are not within the scope of your contract.

### How Clients Choose

The client may not be obligated to award the contract to the lowest cost bidder. Instead, they may make their decision based on a number of factors, including the company's previous experience with similar projects.

Following is a list of criteria that clients use for choosing a business consultant. Closely examine these criteria and try to incorporate these ideas into your proposals.

#### Credentials

Clients want to know what credentials a potential consultant brings to the job, including education and affiliation with an accredited association.

#### Experience

Clients are looking for consultants with demonstrated experience in the field they require help with and the ability to get the job done on time and within the budget.

#### Fit

Clients want someone who is a good fit with their organization and who will work well with members of their team. This includes making sure the consultant's objectives and methods fit with those of the client.

#### Cost-Effectiveness

Clients want the best value for their money, so even though they may not choose a business consultant based solely on fee, they choose a consultant based on a combination of factors that includes price.

## 7.4.3 Why Organizations Ask for Proposals

Sometimes the request for a proposal may come "out of the blue" from a company you haven't approached. The beginning business consultant typically thinks this is great news. After all, why would they ask for a proposal if they were not interested? Actually, there are a number of reasons companies ask for proposals:

### It May Be Necessary for the Job

In some cases, a proposal is necessary for the job. As mentioned, many government departments require the decision-maker to review written proposals from several different prospects before a contract is awarded. They will often have formal RFP guidelines such as those discussed above for you to follow. Likewise, some large companies require written proposals following strict submission guidelines.

If you pay attention to how they communicate with you, you should get a sense of how your proposal will be treated when it is received. Are they encouraging? Do they return your calls promptly? Do they sound positive about your chances? If the answer is "yes" and you want the job, then submitting a proposal is probably worth your time and energy.

## It May Be a "Brush Off"

Some clients find it difficult to say "no" and want to avoid a confrontation. They can delay saying no by having you submit a proposal. The client can then say it is "under review" until you either give up or they finally work up the courage to tell you they are not interested.

## It May Be Used to Confirm a Hiring Decision

Some clients ask for proposals because they want to have written comparisons of several consultants. Often, they have a "preferred" consultant they want to hire, and the purpose of the written proposal is to help them confirm their decision, or show their manager or a committee that they have "shopped around."

> **TIP:** If you are the preferred consultant you will know it. The client will have discussed the project with you in detail, and you will have reached a tentative agreement to do the work. They will explain that their regulations require them to review written proposals and may even assure you that it will be "just a formality."

If you are the preferred consultant and you want the job, then it is worth your time to put together a proposal confirming the details you have discussed with the clients. Otherwise, your time might be better spent focusing on clients who are seriously interested in you.

A prospect who approaches you will not generally start off by asking for a proposal if they are seriously interested in working with you. If they do need more information, they will usually want to discuss it first. If you suspect that a prospective client is not serious, but don't want to miss out on what could potentially be a good opportunity, you might try what a few consultants do when asked for a proposal. They charge a nominal "proposal preparation fee" which is deductible from their fee if they get the engagement. Here is an example of what you can say about a proposal preparation fee:

> "If you are currently exploring several options and would like a written proposal from us, the fee is $250 which is deductible from the project cost."

### Bidding for Projects Online

If you don't mind competing with lots of other consultants for a project, you can find opportunities advertised online. There are a number of websites that offer a marketplace for connecting businesses with professionals in a variety of categories, including business consulting. Companies and individuals post projects for professionals to bid on. You can also post your resume and qualifications for potential clients to browse.

Most websites that offer these kinds of services have a similar membership structure. A subscriber membership allows you access to more information or benefits, such as more bidding opportunities.

- *Guru*
  **www.guru.com/pro**
- *Elance*
  **www.elance.com**
- *Sologig*
  **www.sologig.com**

## 7.4.4 Creating a Winning Proposal

### What to Include in Your Proposal

If the client has not given you any formal guidelines you can still put together a winning proposal following the outline of RFP components listed in section 7.4.1.

Be sure to include:

- A description of your company
- A detailed description of the qualifications you will bring to the project and how those fit into the client's objectives
- A description of the methodologies you will use to meet the needs of the project and how those will benefit the client
- A detailed budget of cost and expense allocations and specific resources you will use in completing the objectives on time and within the budget
- References from other organizations for which you have done similar projects

An excellent resource is the ProposalWriter.com website with links to proposal writing and government contracting. Visit **www.proposalwriter.com/links.html**. Canadian consultants should also check the advice offered on bidding on the Canadian government's Buy and Sell website at **https://buyandsell.gc.ca/for-businesses**.

## 7.4.5 Sample Letter of Proposal

Providing clients with a thorough, insightful and professional letter of proposal, solicited or not, will give you the edge over consultants who don't follow up with a proposal, either because they are not familiar with the process or simply don't recognize its value.

This section includes a sample letter that you might submit to a client after an initial meeting. It is similar in structure to a response to a request for proposal. However, a letter of proposal differs from a proposal written in response to an RFP in that it is not necessarily solicited by the client, and that there are no direct questions to be answered.

A letter of proposal is a formal document, although presented in a letter-style format, which demonstrates your understanding of the client's issues and objectives. It should also include a description of your approach as a consultant. Use headings that suit your personality and business philosophy. The letter of proposal below has sample headings you might include, as well as guidelines for the information you would provide under each heading.

**TIP:** It's important to keep in mind that you should be as prompt as possible with providing a letter of proposal following an initial meeting; within five business days is a good rule of thumb.

In the samples that follow, information shown in *italics* is advice. Information that is not italicized is an example of what you might write.

## Sample Cover Letter

*The cover letter of your proposal should reacquaint the client with your discussion about their needs and introduce the letter of proposal. It should be on your company letterhead and can be formatted as shown below:*

Mr. John Q. Client
Operations Vice-President
XYZ Industries, Inc.
99 Corporate Drive
Successville, NY 12345

July 2, 2012

Dear John:
*(This should be directly addressed to the person(s) you had the initial meeting with)*

As a follow-up to our recent meeting, in which we discussed issues surrounding inefficiencies in your workplace, I have crafted a formal letter of proposal that outlines our discussion about the issues at hand and my strategies for resolving those issues.

As I think you'll see, I have a clear understanding of your company and the specific issues for which you seek a consultant's help. What's more, my solution is practical, efficient and cost-effective.

I will call you next week to discuss a timeline for moving forward with this project.

Regards,
Chris Consultant

## Sample Letter of Proposal

### Personal/Business Overview

*This section is an opportunity to remind the client who you are, but it's also a further chance to market yourself. Be sure to include your background and information about your company, including any relevant education, how long you've been in the business, any directly related jobs that you've held outside of consulting and any recent consulting experience. This section should be no longer than a page or two at most.*

### Issue Interpretation

*This section should reiterate the issue(s) addressed at the meeting, in order to demonstrate a clear and focused understanding of the problem. It is also an opportunity to illustrate your critical-thinking skills by offering further insight. This section might read something like this:*

During our meeting, you identified three primary areas as direct causes of inefficiency in your organization. These included:

1)...

2)...

3)...

In addition to these, my preliminary research has identified other areas that may be at the root of inefficiency in your organization. These include:

1)...

2)...

3)...

### Resolution Proposal

*This section explains to the client how you will approach bringing their issue to resolution, which is at the heart of why one hires a consultant and could be a deciding factor for the client in choosing one consultant over another.*

*The key to success in this area is to provide a clear and systematic approach that is easy to read and understand. For a client looking to reduce inefficiencies, this section might be approached as follows:*

The first step in resolving this issue is to identify how long each employee spends on assembling each widget, and how this can be improved, i.e. through the introduction of new tools, better training for employees, or an increase of staff.

A second procedure will be to identify redundant tasks being performed throughout the organization. This will be achieved through job evaluations and job shadowing in order to create updated job descriptions.

## Implementation Strategies

*Although you likely won't be in a position to offer a precise implementation strategy at this point, you can still offer the client a window into how your professional approach will provide results. This might include items such as:*

- Graded implementation of new procedures, such as one department at a time
- Provide training first, then institute changes
- Half-day implementation that utilizes slow periods to evaluate effectiveness of changes
- Introduce new technology in a cycle to allow employees to train each other

## Scope of Services

*This section defines your roles and responsibilities for the project. This is an important section and is subject to negotiation once the contract is awarded. With this said, however, attempt to be as definitive as possible when drafting this section. Some of your responsibilities that fall under scope of services may include:*

- Data collection, management and analyses
- Survey creation, implementation and results postings

- Weekly reports and status meetings
- Employee interviews
- Final presentation
- Implementation

*Also, it's important to include in this section not only what you will do, but how you will do it, including a timeline. This can be presented in the following way:*

**Data collection, management and analyses** – Data will be collected from pertinent areas using an electronic monitoring system over a week's period, in order to provide an accurate sampling.

**Employee interviews** – Employee interviews will be conducted using an in-house survey and will be done in a single day to reduce disruption of services.

## Consulting Fees and Invoicing

*This section informs the client of your fee structure and overall charges, which allows them to compare your costs with those of other consultants' fees. It also defines your personal invoicing procedures and timelines. A typical Fee and Invoicing section might read:*

My preferred method of payment is a flat fee, based on overall scope of services and length of engagement. As it has been determined that this project will be over a four week period, the total for this project is estimated at $16,000 plus expenses.

This price projection is based on 8 weeks @ $2,000 per week = $16,000. Over these 8 weeks, the following tasks will be performed:

| | |
|---|---|
| Weeks 1-2: | Data collection, interviews and surveying |
| Weeks 3-4: | Survey delivery, feedback and finalize processes |
| Weeks 5-6: | Training and implementation |
| Weeks 7-8: | Finalize procedures and review |

*Note: If you're not charging a flat fee for your services, this section will contain an itemized list of charges, such as:*

**Survey Development**
7 hours interviewing, 4 hours designing @ $100/hr $1,100

**Training**
10 hours of Employee Training @ $100/hr $1,000

**Total** $2,100

*Also to be included in this section is how and when you would like to be paid. This might read:*

An invoice will be delivered at the end of the second week and again on the conclusion of the project for the final two weeks.

**Contract Agreement**

*In this section, let the client know that this letter of proposal can form the basis of a formal contract. This assures them that there won't be any surprises upon creating a formal contract, and that much of the work on the contract has already been done.*

*Another option is to include in your letter of proposal the elements you would include in a letter of engagement or services agreement (see section 6.3 for samples).*

**Summary**

*This section summarizes, in brief, the letter of proposal, including a recap of the issues and your proposed solutions. It should also thank the client for the opportunity.*

*Another item to include in the summary is a statement that the letter of proposal is proprietary information and should not be shared outside of the client's business. This statement may read:*

Please note that this letter of proposal is the intellectual property of *[insert your name]* and is not to be shared with any third-party vendors.

# 7.5 Your Sales Presentation

A good proposal may be what gets your foot in the door, but it's the presentation following it that makes or breaks your chance of signing a contract. Even if you gain access to a potential client through some means other than the RFP process chances are strong that you will still be asked to deliver a formal presentation before they give you the go-ahead.

Remember that a presentation is a sales pitch. You want to make a client feel confident that choosing your services was the right move.

## Before the Presentation

Before you can make an effective presentation that addresses the client's needs, you will need to have an initial meeting with the client. During the initial meeting you will be defining the scope of the work, timelines, and so on. All of this information will eventually be recorded in the services agreement or letter of engagement. See section 2.2.1 for information on how to conduct a needs analysis, including questions to ask the client.

When setting up the initial meeting, try to arrange a block of time that is at least one hour and no more than two hours long. Also, try to ensure that all the key players will attend. This will eliminate repeat meetings. At this stage, it is important to find out what length of presentation the client would prefer. Ask the most senior person who will attend or other reliable contact what the group might prefer and time your presentation accordingly. The meeting will probably be an hour long unless the project is huge.

> **TIP:** Another important aspect of the initial meeting is the opportunity to begin building a relationship with your prospective client. Ruth Ann Karty of Taking Care of Business Consulting Services, offers this advice about initial meetings with clients: "Let them know that you're vitally interested in seeing them succeed, and present to them some of your ideas. What you're doing is building a level of trust with your client, so impart to them that your business is their business."

## Presentation Format

Presentations should be structured and easy to follow, much like written documents. Remember that you only get one chance to present, whereas a written document can be reread so make your presentation engaging and informative.

Although the details of your presentation may be complex, you should follow a simple structure when presenting:

### Introduction

The introduction should outline what you will talk about and introduce yourself and any other speakers from your consulting firm.

### Details

This is the body of your presentation, divided into subsections such as:

- How you interpret the project
- Your approach to implementing the goals of the project
- Project details including timeline
- Costs
- Expertise to be provided

### Closing

In closing your presentation, hit your high points again, and reiterate your enthusiasm and commitment. Leave enough time for a question and answer period.

If possible, encourage questions throughout your presentation as long as doing so doesn't make you lose track of your presentation or interrupt its flow. You can start your presentation by suggesting that questions are best asked when they first come to mind and that the audience is welcome to ask questions at any time. This encourages interaction and takes the pressure off you by moving the meeting from a presentation to a discussion. It tells your audience that you are confident in your material and open to their questions and comments; an important part of building teamwork.

Your presentation is the time to demonstrate excellent listening skills and calm body language. This will take practice. For a big, important project, the giant consulting firms will stage repeated dress-rehearsals of their whole team until they achieve this effect. And just like your proposal, infuse it with your enthusiasm and commitment.

## Presentation Equipment and Materials

Microsoft PowerPoint continues to be the most widely used presentation tool for business. Keep your visuals lively, interactive, and relevant. Don't let the special effects take over the meeting.

There is always the risk of technical problems when you're incorporating technology into your presentation. Be prepared for this: give yourself plenty of time beforehand to ensure that any technology you'll be using is working and don't assume that the client has the necessary technology on hand, such as projectors and laptop. Be sure to ask ahead of time or better yet, take your own and leave yourself plenty of setup time and a quick dry-run if possible.

Handouts can be an excellent addition to a presentation. Many people hand out their entire PowerPoint presentations in hard copy. A condensed version that hits the high points would work for people who were there to use as a refresher or for people who weren't there a full copy of the PowerPoint presentation would be better.

For more information about making presentations see section 2.2.6 .

## Letter of Engagement or Services Agreement

If you already have enough information prior to the initial meeting to put together a draft letter of engagement or services agreement, then the initial meeting is the perfect opportunity to present this document. To advance the process as efficiently as possible, bring your working copy of the letter or agreement to the meeting. With this, you'll be able to iron out any issues and finalize the section that details the scope of work for the project. This way you'll have the necessary information to craft a final contract in order to have it read and signed at a later date.

## Following Up

After this initial meeting, make sure you follow up with the client. Decisions can take time, especially when a committee is involved, but keeping in touch ensures the client keeps you in mind. Sending the client a summary of points you addressed in your meeting is a nice touch.

When you get the good news that a client wants to work with you, you'll be putting other parts of this guide to use. You'll need to send out a letter of engagement or services agreement (see section 6.3) and carry out the steps of the project as described in section 2.2.

After these initial stages, be sure to concentrate continually on making your clients happy with your work. The next chapter offers tips and advice on how to keep clients satisfied.

# 8. Succeeding as a Consultant

Throughout this book you have been given many ideas to achieve success in your new career. In this chapter we offer some bonus ideas to help you ensure client satisfaction, followed by expert career advice from successful consultants, and finally a list of consulting organizations to assist you in moving forward with your career.

## 8.1 Ensuring Client Satisfaction

While the best way to ensure client satisfaction is to solve your clients' problems, there are a number of things you can do to ensure that the project proceeds smoothly, on time and on budget.

### Make Realistic Promises

When discussing the scope of the engagement with your client, evaluate the challenges involved and make realistic, sound decisions about what you will be able to change or fix. Point out barriers to successful completion based on your specialty and experience.

Clients don't like to hear that something can't be achieved, or that a certain approach is a bad idea, particularly if it is their idea. But what they like to hear even less is that you won't be following through on something that you assured them would be completed by the end of the engagement. Therefore, it's imperative that you not over-promise. Don't say "I can do that" unless you know that you can.

## Meet Commitments and Deadlines

Possibly the only thing a client likes to hear less than "I can't" are excuses as to why something did not get done. When you have signed a contract and promised to fulfill it, you are obligated to meet your commitments.

Excuses such as "I lost my file on the computer" and "I thought my partner sent it" just won't cut it. This does not mean, however, that unforeseen circumstances won't and don't arise or that you won't ever be put in a position where you'll have to inform your client of a delay in some aspect of the engagement. Such things happen in daily life and they happen in business. You, as a professional, must be proactive about doing the best job you can and try to be prepared for any foreseeable problems. Excellent organization, time management and due diligence are all important factors in trying to meet your commitments.

A big part of your responsibility is sticking to your price and time estimates for the job. Clients won't be happy if the project stalls or is delayed because of something you were responsible for and even less happy if you present them with a bill that exceeds what they originally agreed to pay.

A crucial aspect of completing the engagement within the time frame agreed upon is meeting deadlines as the project progresses. Of course, unforeseen circumstances do arrive and there may be legitimate reasons that a deadline must be pushed back. If this is the case, inform the client well ahead of time and set a new and reasonable date of completion.

> **TIP:** One way to avoid missing deadlines is to keep a submission or completion schedule of all the tasks involved in the engagement, and set these dates a few days or a week in advance of the actual deadline.

On the other hand, clients may be the cause of missed deadlines. In that case, keep your cool and try to be flexible. Your clients will be impressed with your professionalism and your creativity in resolving unexpected delays.

## Be Available

When you're self-employed and free to come and go as you please, one of your responsibilities to clients is to be accessible to them when they need to contact you. Being accessible does not mean that you must be available for the client 24/7, but it does mean that you provide the client with several different ways to contact you.

Below is a list to consider of ways for clients to contact you.

- **Phone Number:** You should definitely provide the client with your business phone number. It's up to you whether or not to also provide your home phone number. For any numbers you provide, be sure to have voicemail and check messages frequently.

- **Cell Phone Number:** A cell phone is an essential part of doing business today; it is also a good idea to have voicemail on your cell phone, primarily so that you won't have to take calls at inconvenient times.

- **Pager/Paging Service:** Pagers allow clients to send a message to you. However, because communication is only one way (you'll need to use another device to reply to your client), this form of communication is not widely used in most businesses.

- **Email Address:** An email address is another essential in today's business world. Not only is it an excellent mode of communication, but it provides fast delivery of documents between the consultant and the client.

**TIP:** To ensure you present a professional image, avoid using free email addresses such as Hotmail or Yahoo. If possible, use an email address containing your company domain name. If that's not possible, use an email address consisting of your name or your company name at your internet service provider (e.g. chrisconsultant@comcast.com).

- **Fax Number:** This can be particularly useful when dealing with clients still uncomfortable with the computer age. Even clients that are comfortable with computers may occasionally need to send the occasional document by fax.

**TIP:** Consider getting a wireless handheld device such as a BlackBerry, which you can use for phone calls, emails, and other functions (Internet faxing, text messaging, web browsing).

## Be Visible

Being visible means people want to see you during your engagements. Clients like to see the person hard at work that they are paying the high consulting fees to, preferably at their place of business.

Some of the business consultants interviewed for this guide said that during engagements they like to work either a 50/50 or 70/30 on-site to off-site work ratio. Choosing to be on-site at least half the time has to do with being visible and available as needed, but it also depends on the available workspace at your client's offices. Try to make arrangements with the client before you start the engagement to ensure that you have a suitable workspace, especially if they expect to see you every day until it concludes.

## Be Professional

That you need to be professional at all times during an engagement should not come as a surprise. Being professional extends beyond formalities and should pervade your work habits. Here are a few reminders about keeping a professional edge at all times, and keeping a happy client as result of that behavior.

### Handshakes and Eye Contact

Be sure to formally introduce yourself in a professional manner to everyone you meet, even those that may be considered your subordinates or with whom you won't be working. You don't want anyone to feel "snubbed" or that you are dismissive of them.

### Professional Dress

Even if you're working on a Saturday, wear at least business casual attire because you never know who's going to drop by. Your client has built a certain, professional image of you and you don't want to replace that one with the image of you in sweat pants and sneakers.

### Keep a Cool Head

Stress affects everyone, but you'll only add stress to your life and damage your reputation by taking it out on colleagues and clients. Take a time out and always use a professional tone when dealing with clients and their staff.

## Dealing with Scope Creep

Scope creep is when clients try to extend your functions as a consultant beyond the terms agreed upon in the letter of engagement. This can mean anything from the client asking for free advice, extra accounting duties, training of staff, or any other free service.

There is no hard and fast rule on how business consultants should deal with this, but probably the best way to deal with a client whom you feel should not be given "the extras," or one who is continually pushing the boundaries of your scope of services, is to treat your letter of engagement as a flexible document that changes with the needs of the client.

In other words, if a client is adding extras to the project that you believe should be billable, discuss with your client adding these extras to the letter of engagement and that they will have to sign-off on them before completion. Be tactful and flexible when negotiating extras. You may have to try to reach a compromise if the client balks at the notion of adding more costs to the project.

However, where possible, be prepared to step beyond the contract requirements and do a bit more for your clients when you must. Not only will this keep them happy, it may increase your chances of being recommended to others or hired back for future projects.

## 8.2 Advice from the Experts

Throughout this guide we have included much helpful advice from industry insiders – successful consultants who have "been there, done that" and are willing to share their expertise.

In addition to that excellent advice, we asked successful consultants to share with us their best tips for beginning consultants, including what they wish they had known before they started, and how to avoid common mistakes made by new consultants. The consultants who have generously shared their advice include marketing and small business experts as well as consultants to Fortune 500 companies and best-selling authors. Below is a selection of their valuable advice.

**TIP:** The Acknowledgements section at the start of this book includes some more information about the consultants quoted below and throughout this book, but you should visit their websites for more detailed information.

### Provide Value

*"Think of yourself in terms of the clients you will work with: how you can add value to what they do, improve their situation, solve their problems. What you know and what you can do is only important to a client if it is relevant to how you can help them improve their business."*

— Linda Popky, L2M Associates, Inc.
**www.L2Massociates.com**

*"You must have a high level of knowledge in the field you wish to consult in, but it does not stop there, because you have to continually research and have more knowledge than your client."*

— Diane Lewis,
Executive Dimensions, LLC

*"You must be exceptionally good at what you do – because mediocrity doesn't get invited back, nor do existing clients refer you to others."*

— ArLyne Diamond, Ph.D., Diamond Associates
**www.DiamondAssociates.net**

*"Get a deep understanding of what your client struggles with day in and day out and make it your personal mission to solve his or her problem. When you*

*demonstrate deep understanding and focus on the client's problem and help them with the solution you create value for your client."*

— Lonnie Pacelli,
Leading on the Edge International
**www.leadingonedge.com**

## Plan for Success

*"Set goals: You are in the first days of an entirely new career (and life). Do you know EXACTLY what you want from it? If you are like many independent consultants, you may have arrived in this position due to an outside influence, such as downsizing, frustration with the bureaucracy of corporate America, etc. Take the time to create written goals for your new business. Be sure to make them specific, and give yourself a deadline, for example: 'By December 31st, 2012, I will have 5 new clients, generating $45,000 per month in revenue.'"*

— Marty M. Fahncke, FawnKey & Associates
**www.fawnkey.com**

*"It takes a plan to be successful. Without a plan people get discouraged and often give up. With enough time, planning and effort one can succeed."*

— Seth Hishmeh, USAS Technologies, LLC
**www.usastechnologies.com**

*"To stay competitive, business consultants need to keep up with new trends, embrace them, and use them for their business. Always take time for research. If you can't do this yourself, hire a part timer to help you."*

— Harry Husted, Creating Words
**www.creatingwords.com**

## Specialize

*What is the most important piece of advice you can give to someone who is considering a career as a business consultant? "I suggest finding what it is that is going to make you different. Find your expertise."*

— Jill Lublin, Promising Promotion
**www.jilllublin.com**

*"Be yourself: Many consultants I've seen starting out try to be all things to all people. Just to generate revenue, they often take projects they shouldn't take, in areas in which they have no expertise. Don't be tempted into doing*

*this. Clients are hiring you for your knowledge and skill. If you try to sell them on knowledge or skill you don't have, sooner or later it will come back to bite you. Furthermore, while you're struggling to manage a project outside of your comfort zone, you never even notice the perfect project for you passing by."*

— Marty M. Fahncke, FawnKey & Associates
**www.fawnkey.com**

## Avoid Costly Mistakes

Here's what successful consultants answered in response to the question *"What is the biggest mistake you see new consultants make, and how can someone avoid making that mistake?"*

*"Seeing themselves as vendors and not partners. You have to look and act the part. Develop a strong vocabulary, pay attention to your dress and grooming, and do not talk to human resources people. Find the line executives."*

— Alan Weiss, Ph.D., Summit Consulting Group
**www.summitconsulting.com**

*"New consultants often think much too small. They limit themselves in terms of the services they offer, the work they do, the markets they serve and the fees they charge. Remember that there is no longer a 'boss' or an organization to put you in a pre-defined box and limit your scope of activities. You have a wealth of experience and expertise from your previous employment and life experiences. Learn how to draw on this to provide value to your clients across a broad area of capabilities."*

— Linda Popky, Leverage 2 Market Associates
**www.leverage2market.com**

*"Not understanding sales enough. Not realizing how difficult sales is, getting proper training in sales and understanding lead times to close deals they need in order to keep cash coming in."*

— Seth Hishmeh, USAS Technologies, LLC
**www.usastechnologies.com**

*"Giving work away for free. When you start out, you may believe that you are not "good enough" to charge for your time. Nonsense. You are a professional; act like it and that includes billing for services rendered. That said, one way to improve your consulting skills is to offer your services pro bono to non-profit organizations. That is a reputable way to build your resume as well as build*

*your reputation. But avoid at all costs giving work away to for profit businesses. They are in business to make money and so are you."*

— John Baldoni, Baldoni Consulting, LLC
**www.johnbaldoni.com**

*"The one thing I wish I'd known before I started is how important it is to retain every name you come across."*

— Alan Weiss, Ph.D., Summit Consulting Group
**www.summitconsulting.com**

## 8.3 Professional Associations

Although some fields that consultants work in (such as accounting, engineering, and financial planning) require licensing, certification, or membership in a professional association, there are no such requirements for general business consultants. You nevertheless should consider joining one or more professional organizations.

Professional associations provide consultants with a variety of benefits ranging from networking opportunities to continuing education. Membership in these organizations can also enhance your professional image. Simply joining a professional association may demonstrate to clients and prospective employers that you are serious about your career.

Check out the following organizations, listed alphabetically, to learn more about what they have to offer. Some may be right for you at this stage of your career, while others may be right for you after you've been in business for a while. While some organizations have membership requirements such as a minimum period of employment as a consultant, you can join the International Association of Professional Business Consultants (**www.iapo.net/consultants.html**) immediately.

- *Academy of Management*
  **www.aomonline.org**

- *Association of Internal Management Consultants*
  **www.aimc.org**

- *Association of Management Consulting Firms*
  **www.amcf.org**

- *Canadian Association of Management Consultants*
  **www.cmc-canada.ca**

- *Institute of Management Consultants (IMC-USA)*
  **www.imcusa.org**

TIP: If you want to be certified as a professional consultant, IMC-USA awards the Certified Management Consultant (CMC) designation to consultants who meet the requirements. For details visit **www.imcusa.org/certification**.

- *International Association of Professional Business Consultants*
  **www.iapo.net/consultants.html**

- *Management Consultancies Association (U.K.)*
  **www.mca.org.uk**

- *Society for Advancement of Consulting*
  **www.consultingsociety.com/benefits.html**

## Consulting Specializations

The following are just a few of the many associations of interest to consultants who specialize in these areas.

- *Association for Financial Professionals*
  **www.afponline.org**

- *American Marketing Association*
  **www.marketingpower.com**

- *Association of Professional Communication Consultants*
  **www.consultingsuccess.org**

- *International Association of Business Communicators*
  **www.iabc.com**

- *International Council of E-Commerce Consultants*
  **www.eccouncil.org/benefits.htm**

- *American Tech Association*
  **www.americantechassociation.com**

- *Society For Human Resource Management*
  **www.shrm.org/consultants**

## Save 50% on Your Next Purchase

Please visit **www.FabJob.com/feedback.asp** to tell us how this guide has helped prepare you for your dream career. If we publish your comments, we will send you a gift certificate for 50% off your next purchase of a FabJob guide.

## Get Free Career Advice

Get valuable career advice for free by subscribing to the FabJob newsletter. You'll receive insightful tips on: how to break into the job of your dreams or start the business of your dreams. You'll also receive discounts on FabJob guides. Subscribe to the FabJob newsletter at **www.FabJob.com/newsletter.asp**.

## Join FabJob on Facebook

Go to **www.facebook.com/FabJob** and click the "Like" button to be among the first to get FabJob news and special offers.

## Does Someone You Love Deserve a Dream Career?

Giving a FabJob® guide is a fabulous way to show someone you believe in them and support their dreams. Help them break into the career of their dreams with more than 75 career guides to choose from.

**Visit www.FabJob.com to order guides today!**

# More Guides to Build Your Business

Increase your income by offering additional services. Here are some recommended FabJob guides to help you build your business:

## Get Paid to Coach Executives

Imagine having a fulfilling career coaching people how to achieve success in their careers, relationships, and life. In the **FabJob Guide to Become a Life Coach** you will discover:

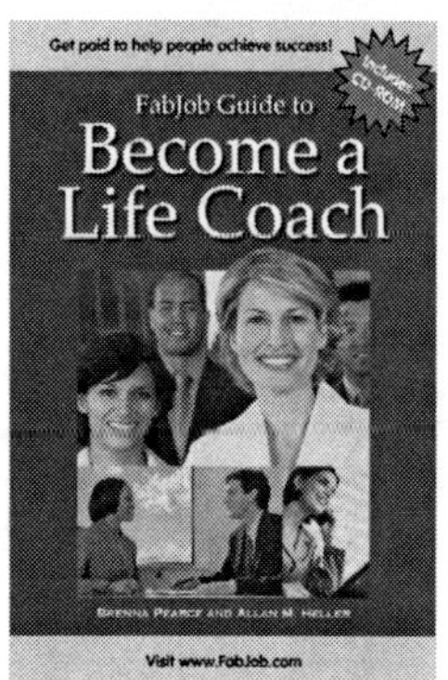


- How to choose a coaching specialization
- How to conduct a coaching session in person, by phone, or online (includes sample exercises and questions to ask clients)
- How to present a group coaching session (how to lead a support group, conduct corporate training sessions, or present workshops and retreats)
- How to start your own part-time or full-time coaching business, set your prices, and get clients

## Get Paid to Consult on Business Etiquette

Imagine having a rewarding career teaching people essential skills they need to succeed in business and in life. In the **FabJob Guide to Become an Etiquette Consultant** you will learn how to:

- Become an expert in business, dining, social, children's or international etiquette
- Coach individuals on proper etiquette
- Create a part-time or full-time job as an etiquette consultant
- Start an etiquette consulting business, price your services, and find clients
- Present etiquette seminars or workshops and corporate training programs

**Visit www.FabJob.com to order guides today!**

# How to Install the CD-ROM

The bonus CD-ROM found at the end of this book contains helpful forms and checklists you can revise and use in your own business. It also includes an electronic version of this book, which you can use to quickly connect to the websites we've mentioned (as long as you have access to the Internet and the Acrobat Reader program on your computer).

To install the CD-ROM, these simple steps will work with most computers:

1. Insert the CD-ROM into your computer CD drive.
2. Double click on the "My Computer" icon (PC) or the "Finder" icon (Mac) on your desktop.
3. Double click on the icon for your CD-ROM drive.
4. Read the "Read Me" file on the CD-ROM for more information.

CPSIA information can be obtained at www.ICGtesting.com
Printed in the USA
BVOW070626260912

301393BV00005B/6/P